Easy Spanish
STEP-BY-STEP

Master High-Frequency Grammar for Spanish Proficiency—FAST!

Barbara Bregstein

McGraw·Hill

New York   Chicago   San Francisco   Lisbon   London   Madrid   Mexico City
Milan   New Delhi   San Juan   Seoul   Singapore   Sydney   Toronto

Library of Congress Cataloging-in-Publication Data

Bregstein, Barbara.
    Easy Spanish step-by-step : mastering high-frequency grammar for Spanish
proficiency—fast! / Barbara Bregstein.
        p.   cm.
    Includes index.
    ISBN 0-07-146338-0

    1. Spanish language—Grammar. 2. Spanish language—Self-instruction.
3. Spanish language—Textbooks for foreign speakers—English.

PC4112.5 .B75 2005
468.2'421—dc22   2005049557

39 LCR 23

ISBN: 978-0-07-146338-6
MHID: 0-07-146338-0

McGraw-Hill books are available at special quantity discounts to use as premiums and
sales promotions, or for use in corporate training programs. For more information, please
write to the Director of Special Sales, Professional Publishing, McGraw-Hill, Two Penn
Plaza, New York, NY 10121-2298. Or contact your local bookstore.

This book is printed on acid-free paper.

Contents

I   Elements of a Sentence

1   Nouns, Articles, and Adjectives   3

2   *Estar, Ser,* and Subject Pronouns   14

12 Reflexive Verbs 193

13 The Present Subjunctive 206

Preface

Easy Spanish Step-by-Step will help you learn Spanish—talking, reading, and writing—as quickly and as thoroughly as possible. Written for beginner and advanced-beginner learners, it teaches grammar and conversation in the most logical order to enable you to develop your language skills naturally.

To take full advantage of the unique grammatical progression of the book, you should study each chapter, or step, one after another. Do not skip around. Each step you take will lead you to the next. Each chapter contains clear grammar explanations; be sure to understand every concept before moving on to the next. Notice that there are few exceptions to rules, so once you have learned a concept, it is yours.

Try to learn the vocabulary and verbs provided; they have been carefully selected on the basis of usefulness and frequency. The vocabulary lists will help enhance your communication, while complete verb conjugations are given so that you can practice pronunciation as you learn verbs. Over 300 of the most common verbs in Spanish are presented.

Varied written and oral exercises are included to check your understanding and progress. (The book has a complete answer key in the back.) It is also a good idea to write your own questions and sentences and practice them aloud. Sometimes, your own creations are more interesting and aid in learning.

Original readings are included in every chapter; they become progressively more challenging in form and content throughout the book. Use these reading comprehension sections to learn new vocabulary and to practice reading aloud.

Easy Spanish Step-by-Step is divided into three parts. The first gives you all the fundamentals of the language in the present tense. You will notice that the word order of English and Spanish in this part is essentially the same. This makes learning in the early stages very quick. The second part explains indirect objects, direct objects, direct object pronouns, reflexive verbs, and the present subjunctive. The third part presents the two most used tenses in the past, the preterit and the imperfect.

A student once asked me if Spanish is truly easy. It is, in comparison to any of the other languages of the world. To start with, the pronunciation is easy. Spanish is a phonetically perfect language, which means that once you learn to pronounce each vowel and consonant, you will be able to pronounce all words correctly. Before you begin, practice all the sounds outlined in the Guide to Pronunciation in the following pages. If possible, try to practice with a native speaker. Then, remember to read and answer questions aloud as much as you can to develop your pronunciation.

This book is written with a logical approach that makes it accessible, whether you are a self-study learner or a student in an organized teaching program. With *Easy Spanish Step-by-Step*, you will see that everything falls quickly into place. In a few weeks, you will be able to read and write Spanish quite easily. And once you learn the Spanish in this book, you will be able to get along in any Spanish-speaking country. The grammar is standard in all parts of the Spanish-speaking world, and although accents change from place to place, you will get accustomed to the sounds very quickly. Have fun and enjoy using Spanish everywhere you need it.

Acknowledgments

I would like to thank Nestor Rodriguez, teacher of English and Spanish at City College of New York, for his invaluable contribution to the editing and structure of *Fundamental Spanish,* upon which *Easy Spanish Step-by-Step* is based, and for his language insights and expertise. I gratefully acknowledge his assistance throughout the development of this book.

I would also like to thank Silvia Ballinas, teacher and director of Escuela Experiencia in Tepoztlán, Mexico, Antonio Zea, linguist and professor at Escuela Acacias in Málaga, Spain, Alonia King, Janet Odums, and Lois Shearer. I would also like to thank all my students from District Council 37 in New York City.

Guide to Pronunciation

Spanish spelling is an exact reflection of the pronunciation of the language. The pronunciation of each letter is subject to precise and consistent rules, and words are pronounced by adding together the sounds of each individual letter.

Vowels

The sounds of the vowels are clear and short. Pronounce the examples.

Letter	Pronounced like	Examples
a	the *a* in *father*	la casa, la tapa, Panamá, Canadá
e	two sounds:	
	the *e* in *café* when final	elefante, come, vive, verde, que
	the *e* in *set* elsewhere	pero, es, hotel
i	the *i* in *machine*	sí, cine, comida
o	two sounds:	
	the *o* in *hope*	oso, otro, hospital
	the *o* in *for* if followed by **r**	doctor, profesor
u	the *u* in *rule*	uno, tú, puro
	written as **ü** when pronounced in **güe** and **güi**	agüero, güira
	silent in **gue** and **gui** elsewhere	guerra, guitarra
y	Spanish **i**	y, soy, hay

Consonants

b/v	the *b* in *boat* when they occur at the beginning of a breath group, or following **l**, **m**, or **n**	baño, burro, embargo, alba, el vino, el voto, invierno, vamos
	softer elsewhere, produced through slightly opened lips	Cuba, la boca, Havana, la vaca

In Spanish, the *b* and *v* have the same sound. The sound of English *v* does not exist in Spanish.

c	the *c* in *cat* before **a**, **o**, **u**, or before a consonant	camisa, color, concreto
	the *s* in *sail* before **e** or **i**	centavo, cita, cinco
ch	the *ch* in *chum*	chocolate, chorizo

Letter	Pronounced like	Examples
d	two sounds:	
	the *d* in *dog* when it occurs at the beginning of a breath group, or following **l** or **n**	donde, falda, conde
	the *th* in *other* elsewhere	boda, poder, verdad, nada, cada, estudio
f	English *f*	futuro, fila, oficina
g	the *g* in *game* before **a**, **o**, **u**, or before a consonant	gato, gusto, grande
	the *h* in *hat* before **e** or **i**	genio, generoso, gitano
h	silent	hombre, hasta, hablar
j	English *h* (It can also be given a slightly guttural sound.)	Juan, ojo, mujer
k	English *k*	kayak, kilómetro, kiwi
l	English *l*, but with the tip of the tongue touching the roof of the mouth	el, hotel, mil, palo
ll	the *y* in *beyond,* or in some countries, the *s* in *pleasure*	caballo, bello, llave
m	English *m*	menos, cama, marrón
n	English *n*	nota, nación, nariz
ñ	the *ny* in *canyon* or the *ni* in *onion*	mañana, España, señor
p	English *p*, but not explosive (without the puff of air in the English sound)	papel, persona, pobre
q	the *k* in *key* (found only in the combinations **que** and **qui**)	Quito, queso, equipo
r	the *dd* in *ladder* (a single tongue flap)	caro, barato, para, hablar
	The **r** at the beginning of a word or after **l**, **n**, or **s** is trilled like **rr**.	rosa, el río, Enrique, las rosas
rr	a trill or tongue roll (There is no equivalent sound in English.)	perro, horrible, carro

Letter	Pronounced like	Examples
s	English *s*	sopa, sala, blusa
t	English *t*, but not explosive (with the tip of the tongue against the back of the upper front teeth)	torta, talento, tesoro
v	Spanish **b** (There is no *v* sound in Spanish.)	
w	The letter **w** exists in Spanish only in words of foreign origin and is not considered part of the Spanish alphabet.	
x	English *x*	experto, examen
y	Spanish **ll** (the *y* in *beyond* or, in some countries, the *s* in *pleasure*)	papaya, papagayo, ayer
z	the *s* in *sail*	azul, brazo, luz

Stress, Written Accentuation, and Spelling

Natural Stress

Words that end in a vowel (**a**, **e**, **i**, **o**, **u**) or the consonants **n** or **s** have their natural stress on the next to last syllable.

cucaracha	volumen
mañana	examen
triste	tomates
hablo	

Words that end in any consonant other than **n** or **s** have their natural stress on the final syllable.

salud	mujer
amistad	cantar
papel	doctor
vegetal	nariz
azul	

Written Accents

When a word does not follow one of these two rules, it will have a written accent on the syllable that is stressed.

tel<u>é</u>fono	can<u>ció</u>n
<u>lá</u>mpara	le<u>cció</u>n
<u>mú</u>sica	di<u>fí</u>cil
caf<u>é</u>	<u>fá</u>cil

If a one-syllable word has a written accent, it means that there is another word in the language that has the same spelling, but another meaning.

el	*the*	él	*he*
si	*if*	sí	*yes*
tu	*your*	tú	*you*
se	*oneself*	sé	*I know*

If a two-syllable word has a written accent that does not affect the pronunciation, it means that there is another word that has the same spelling, but a different meaning.

este	*this*	éste	*this one*
ese	*that*	ése	*that one*

Interrogative words have an accent mark that does not affect pronunciation.

¿qué?	*what?*	¿cómo?	*how?*
¿quién?	*who?*	¿por qué?	*why?*
¿dónde?	*where?*	¿cuál?	*which?*

Spelling Changes

- **z** to **c**

  Nouns and adjectives that end in **z** change to **c** to form the plural.

el lápiz	los lápices
la nariz	las narices
feliz	felices

  Z followed by **a** or **o** changes to **c** before an **e** or **i**. The sound of **z** and **c** are the same.

comienza	comience
empiezo	empiece

- **Other spelling changes**

  All other spelling changes occur in order to maintain a required sound.

  Tocar, for example, has a hard *c* sound that must be preserved in other forms of the verb. If you see **toque**, with **qu** replacing the **c**, it is to maintain the *k* sound.

  Llegar, for example, has a hard *g* sound, which must be preserved. If you see **llegue**, with **gu** replacing the **g**, it is to maintain the hard *g* sound.

Castilian Spanish

There are only a few differences in pronunciation between the Spanish spoken in Latin America and that spoken in Spain.

- Both the **c** that precedes **e** or **i** and the **z** have the *th* sound heard in English *thought* and *thing*.

- When **j** or **g** precedes **e** or **i**, it has a slightly more guttural sound.

Tips for Pronunciation

- While practicing, remember to keep the vowel sounds short and clear.

- Always use the Spanish **r** sound. Resist the use of the English *r*.

- Implode the sounds of **p** and **t**. Make sure there is no puff of air.

- Always pronounce **z** like the letter **s**.

- Give the syllables an almost equal emphasis, a sort of staccato sound. Pronounce every syllable clearly and precisely in order to develop an even speech pattern.

The Alphabet

El alfabeto o abecedario

Letter(s)	Name	Letter(s)	Name
A	a	N	ene
B	be larga / be grande	Ñ	eñe
C	ce	O	o
CH	che	P	pe
D	de	Q	cu
E	e	R	ere
F	efe	RR	erre
G	ge	S	ese
H (always silent)	hache	T	te
I	i	U	u
J	jota	V	ve corta
K	ka	W	doble ve / doble u
L	ele	X	equis
LL	elle	Y	i griega / ye
M	eme	Z	zeta

Greetings and Salutations

Hola.	*Hello.*
Buenos días.	*Good morning.*
Buenas tardes.	*Good afternoon.*
Buenas noches.	*Good evening.*
Me llamo Susana.	*My name is Susan.*
¿Cómo se llama usted?	*What's your name?*
Me llamo David.	*My name is David.*
Mucho gusto.	*Pleased to meet you.*
¿Cómo está usted?	*How are you?*
Bien, gracias, ¿y usted?	*Fine, thanks. And you?*
Regular. Más o menos.	*So-so. More or less.*
Hasta luego.	*So long.*
Hasta mañana.	*Until tomorrow.*
Hasta pronto.	*See you soon.*
Adiós.	*Good-bye.*

I

Elements of a Sentence

1

Nouns, Articles, and Adjectives

The Gender of Nouns and the Definite Article

A noun is a person, place, or thing.

In Spanish, all nouns are either *masculine* or *feminine*.

In Spanish, the definite article (English *the*) agrees with the noun in gender (masculine or feminine) and number (singular or plural): **el**, **la**, **los**, **las**.

Singular Nouns

Masculine

The masculine singular noun takes the definite article **el**.

Most nouns that end in **-o** are masculine. Pronounce the following words aloud.

el amigo	*the friend*	el libro	*the book*
el banco	*the bank*	el muchacho	*the boy*
el baño	*the bathroom*	el niño	*the little boy, the child*
el carro	*the car*	el perro	*the dog*
el gato	*the cat*	el teléfono	*the telephone*
el hermano	*the brother*	el vino	*the wine*

Many masculine nouns do not end in **-o**; therefore, it is necessary to learn each noun with its article.

el animal	*the animal*	el hospital	*the hospital*
el café	*the coffee*	el hotel	*the hotel*
el doctor	*the doctor*	el tomate	*the tomato*
el hombre	*the man*	el tren	*the train*

3

Some masculine nouns end in **-a** or **-ma**.

el clima	*the climate*	el planeta	*the planet*
el día	*the day*	el poema	*the poem*
el drama	*the drama*	el problema	*the problem*
el idioma	*the language*	el programa	*the program*
el mapa	*the map*	el sistema	*the system*

Feminine

The feminine singular noun takes the definite article **la**.

Most nouns that end in **-a** are feminine. Pronounce the following words aloud.

la amiga	*the friend*	la lámpara	*the lamp*
la blusa	*the blouse*	la mesa	*the table*
la bolsa	*the bag*	la muchacha	*the girl*
la cama	*the bed*	la niña	*the little girl*
la casa	*the house*	la persona	*the person*
la cerveza	*the beer*	la planta	*the plant*
la comida	*the meal*	la silla	*the chair*
la hermana	*the sister*	la tienda	*the store*
la iglesia	*the church*	la ventana	*the window*

Nouns that end in **-ción**, **-sión**, **-dad**, **-tad**, or **-tud** are feminine.

la canción	*the song*	la televisión	*the television*
la conversación	*the conversation*	la ciudad	*the city*
la invitación	*the invitation*	la verdad	*the truth*
la lección	*the lesson*	la amistad	*the friendship*
la ilusión	*the illusion*	la actitud	*the attitude*

A few nouns that end in **-o** are feminine.

la foto	*the photograph*
la mano	*the hand*
la radio	*the radio*

Many feminine nouns do not follow these patterns; therefore, it is important to learn each noun with its article.

la clase	*the class*	la mujer	*the woman*
la flor	*the flower*	la piel	*the skin*
la luz	*the light*	la suerte	*the luck*

Exercise 1.1

Write the appropriate masculine or feminine form of the definite article for each of the following nouns. As you write the answer, make sure you know the meaning of the word.

1. _____ amigo
2. _____ hombre
3. _____ casa
4. _____ luz
5. _____ hotel
6. _____ hermano
7. _____ ciudad
8. _____ carro
9. _____ tomate
10. _____ cerveza

11. _____ persona
12. _____ canción
13. _____ teléfono
14. _____ muchacho
15. _____ flor
16. _____ mujer
17. _____ baño
18. _____ vino
19. _____ comida
20. _____ conversación

A noun ending in **-ista** can be masculine or feminine, depending on whether it refers to a male or a female. The article indicates the gender of the noun.

el artista	*the (male) artist*	el pianista	*the (male) pianist*
la artista	*the (female) artist*	la pianista	*the (female) pianist*
el dentista	*the (male) dentist*	el taxista	*the (male) cabdriver*
la dentista	*the (female) dentist*	la taxista	*the (female) cabdriver*

A noun ending in **-nte** can be masculine or feminine, depending on whether it refers to a male or a female. The article indicates the gender of the noun.

el cantante	*the (male) singer*
la cantante	*the (female) singer*
el estudiante	*the (male) student*
la estudiante	*the (female) student*
el gerente	*the (male) manager*
la gerente '	*the (female) manager*
el presidente	*the (male) president*
la presidente	*the (female) president*

Plural Nouns

Masculine

A masculine noun that ends in a vowel adds **-s** to form the plural; it takes the definite article **los**.

Singular	Plural
el día	los días
el hermano	los hermanos
el libro	los libros
el muchacho	los muchachos
el perro	los perros
el problema	los problemas

If the noun ends in a consonant, **el** changes to **los** and the noun adds **-es**.

el animal	los animales
el doctor	los doctores
el hospital	los hospitales
el hotel	los hoteles
el tren	los trenes

Feminine

A feminine noun that ends in a vowel adds **-s** to form the plural; it takes the definite article **las**.

la bolsa	las bolsas
la lámpara	las lámparas
la niña	las niñas
la persona	las personas
la tienda	las tiendas
la ventana	las ventanas

If the noun ends in a consonant, **la** changes to **las** and the noun adds **-es**.

la canción	las canciones
la ciudad	las ciudades
la flor	las flores
la invitación	las invitaciones
la lección	las lecciones
la mujer	las mujeres

Exercise 1.2

Write the plural form of each of the following singular nouns.

EXAMPLE   el hotel   *los hoteles*

1. el animal _____
2. la amistad _____
3. el teléfono _____
4. el tren _____
5. la ventana _____
6. el doctor _____
7. la ciudad _____
8. la bolsa _____
9. la mesa _____
10. el idioma _____

11. la planta _____
12. la flor _____
13. el perro _____
14. la ilusión _____
15. la clase _____
16. la lección _____
17. el taxista _____
18. la lámpara _____
19. la silla _____
20. la luz _____

The Indefinite Article

The Spanish singular indefinite article (English *a, an*) is **un** before a masculine noun and **una** before a feminine noun. Pronounce the words in the following lists aloud. By learning these nouns, you are building your vocabulary.

Singular Indefinite Articles

Masculine

un amigo	*a (male) friend*	un jardín	*a garden*
un baño	*a bathroom*	un museo	*a museum*
un carro	*a car*	un pianista	*a (male) pianist*
un espejo	*a mirror*	un sillón	*an armchair*
un gato	*a cat*	un tiquete	*a ticket*

Feminine

una amiga	*a (female) friend*	una mujer	*a woman*
una biblioteca	*a library*	una página	*a page*
una ciudad	*a city*	una persona	*a person (male or female)*
una idea	*an idea*		
una librería	*a bookstore*	una pluma	*a pen*
una maleta	*a suitcase*		

Plural Indefinite Articles

The Spanish plural indefinite article (English *some*) is **unos** before a masculine plural noun and **unas** before a feminine plural noun.

Masculine

unos barcos	*some boats*	unos idiomas	*some languages*
unos gatos	*some cats*	unos libros	*some books*

Feminine

unas artistas	*some (female) artists*
unas casas	*some houses*
unas conversaciones	*some conversations*
unas flores	*some flowers*

Exercise 1.3

Translate the following nouns into English. Remember to practice pronouncing the words.

1. el libro _____
2. la página _____
3. la casa _____
4. las flores _____
5. el baño _____
6. el vino _____
7. el muchacho _____
8. el hermano _____
9. la biblioteca _____
10. el café _____
11. el tren _____
12. el planeta _____
13. el dentista _____
14. el jardín _____
15. la flor _____

16. la cerveza   _____

17. la planta   _____

18. la amistad   _____

19. la verdad   _____

20. la suerte   _____

21. la gerente   _____

22. la tienda   _____

23. la ventana   _____

24. un museo   _____

25. un espejo   _____

26. una librería   _____

27. una pluma   _____

28. una lección   _____

29. una idea   _____

30. una maleta   _____

31. el sillón   _____

32. los amigos   _____

Adjectives

An adjective is a word that describes a noun.

A Spanish adjective agrees in gender and number with the noun it modifies. In Spanish, an adjective almost always follows the noun it describes.

Singular Form of Adjectives

Adjectives that end in **-o** are *masculine* in form and agree with a masculine noun. As you pronounce the following examples aloud, note that the *adjective follows the noun* it describes.

el libro blanco	*the white book*
el gato negro	*the black cat*
el carro rojo	*the red car*
el muchacho simpático	*the nice boy*
el hombre hermoso	*the handsome man*

Adjectives that end in **-o** change the **-o** to **-a** when describing a feminine noun.

la casa blanca	*the white house*
la chaqueta negra	*the black jacket*
la lámpara roja	*the red lamp*
la muchacha simpática	*the nice girl*
la mujer hermosa	*the beautiful woman*

Adjectives that do not end in **-o** have the same form for describing both masculine and feminine nouns. It doesn't matter what letter ends the adjective, as long as it is not **-o**.

Masculine	Feminine
el libro excelente	la comida excelente
el perro horrible	la cucaracha horrible
el poema difícil	la lección difícil
el barco azul	la pluma azul
el baño verde	la cama verde
el tren gris	la mesa gris
el tema interesante	la idea interesante
el hombre fuerte	la mujer fuerte

 **Key Vocabulary**

Los colores (The colors)

amarillo	*yellow*	morado	*purple*
anaranjado	*orange*	moreno	*brown-skinned*
azul	*blue*	negro	*black*
blanco	*white*	rojo	*red*
gris	*gray*	rosado	*pink*
marrón, pardo	*brown*	verde	*green*

Other Adjectives

agradable	*agreeable, pleasant*	delgado	*slender*
alegre	*happy*	difícil	*difficult*
barato	*inexpensive*	estupendo	*great, terrific*
caro	*expensive*	excelente	*excellent*
débil	*weak*	fácil	*easy*

fantástico	*fantastic*	interesante	*interesting*
feliz	*happy*	joven	*young*
feo	*ugly*	maravilloso	*marvelous, wonderful*
flaco	*thin*	pequeño	*little, small*
frágil	*fragile*	pobre	*poor*
fuerte	*strong*	rico	*rich*
gordo	*fat*	simpático	*nice*
grande	*big*	sincero	*sincere*
guapo	*handsome,*	tacaño	*stingy*
	beautiful	típico	*typical*
hermoso	*beautiful*	triste	*sad*
horrible	*horrible*	viejo	*old*
inteligente	*intelligent*		

Exercise 1.4

Complete the following phrases with the following Spanish adjective.

1. el hombre _____ (*old*)

2. la situación _____ (*difficult*)

3. el idioma _____ (*marvelous*)

4. la persona _____ (*nice*)

5. la flor _____ (*yellow*)

6. el jardín _____ (*beautiful*)

7. la muchacha _____ (*slender*)

8. el vino _____ (*white*)

9. el apartamento _____ (*expensive*)

10. el carro _____ (*inexpensive*)

11. el hotel _____ (*small*)

12. el clima _____ (*fantastic*)

13. la hermana _____ (*intelligent*)

14. el libro _____ (*interesting*)

15. la cíudad _____ (*big*)

16. el hombre _____ (*rich*)

17. el dentista _____ (*young*)

18. la bolsa _____ (*red*)

19. la ventana _____ (*blue*)

20. la planta _____ (*green*)

Plural Form of Adjectives

Adjectives that end in a vowel add **-s** to form the plural.

Singular	Plural
blanco	blancos
roja	rojas
verde	verdes
excelente	excelentes

Adjectives that end in a consonant add **-es** to form the plural.

gris	grises
fácil	fáciles
joven	jóvenes
marrón	marrones

Adjectives agree in gender and number with the noun they modify. Review each singular and plural form as you pronounce the following nouns and the adjectives that describe them.

Masculine

Singular	Plural
el libro blanco	los libros blancos
el tomate rojo	los tomates rojos
el hombre hermoso	los hombres hermosos
el baño verde	los baños verdes
el barco marrón	los barcos marrones
el tren gris	los trenes grises
el tiquete caro	los tiquetes caros

Feminine

la casa blanca	las casas blancas
la persona simpática	las personas simpáticas
la mujer hermosa	las mujeres hermosas

la comida excelente   las comidas excelentes
la lección fácil   las lecciones fáciles
la muchacha fuerte   las muchachas fuertes
la tienda vieja   las tiendas viejas

Exercise 1.5

Write the plural form of each of the following noun and adjective phrases.

1. la lámpara azul   _____

2. el amigo fantástico   _____

3. el perro gris   _____

4. la cerveza negra   _____

5. el vino rosado   _____

6. la persona fuerte   _____

7. el día maravilloso   _____

8. la luz verde   _____

9. la ciudad pequeña   _____

10. el muchacho joven   _____

Exercise 1.6

Translate the following phrases into Spanish.

1. *the red tomatoes*   _____

2. *the strong men*   _____

3. *the thin women*   _____

4. *the yellow blouses*   _____

5. *the interesting songs* _____

6. *the green planets*   _____

7. *the blue windows*   _____

8. *the old hotels*   _____

2

Estar, Ser, and Subject Pronouns

Subject Pronouns

Singular		Plural	
yo	*I*	**nosotros**	*we*
tú	*you*	**vosotros**	*you*

The familiar singular form **tú** is used with friends and family; its usage varies from country to country.	The familiar plural form **vosotros** is used only in Spain.

él	*he*	**ellos**	*they*

	The masculine plural form **ellos** refers to a group of males or to a group that includes both males and females.

ella	*she*	**ellas**	*they*

	The feminine plural form **ellas** refers to a group that includes only females.

usted	*you*	**ustedes**	*you*

Usted is more formal than **tú**. It is used when meeting people for the first time, in business situations, and with a person you might not know well. Its abbreviation is **Ud.**	The plural form **ustedes** is used to address more than one person. Latin Americans use **ustedes** for the plural of both **tú** and **Ud.** (since **vosotros** is used only in Spain). Its abbreviation is **Uds.**

There is no subject pronoun *it* in Spanish. **Él** and **ella** refer to people and sometimes to animals, but not to things.

Estar (to be)

Spanish has two verbs that are equivalent to English *to be.* Begin with the conjugation of the verb **estar**.

yo **estoy**	*I am*	nosotros **estamos**	*we are*
tú **estás**	*you are*	vosotros **estáis**	*you are*
él **está**	*he is*	ellos **están**	*they are*
ella **está**	*she is*	ellas **están**	*they are*
Ud. **está**	*you are*	Uds. **están**	*you are*

Practice the conjugations of the verb aloud. Notice that **él**, **ella**, and **Ud.** have the same form of the verb (the third-person singular). Notice also that **ellos**, **ellas**, and **Uds.** have the same form of the verb (the third-person plural).

Estar is used to express four basic concepts: location, health, changing mood or condition, and personal opinion in terms of taste or appearance.

- **Location**

    Estar is used to describe where something or someone is physically located.

Yo estoy en la clase.	*I am in the class.*
Nosotros estamos en el carro.	*We are in the car.*
El restaurante está en la ciudad.	*The restaurant is in the city.*
Ellas están en el baño.	*They are in the bathroom.*
¿Estás tú en el hospital?	*Are you in the hospital?*

The verb, which carries the action of the phrase, is the essential element of the Spanish sentence or question because of the amount of information it contains.

Verb Definitions

The **infinitive** is the unconjugated form of the verb. For example, *to be* is an infinitive in English. The **conjugations** are the forms of the verb that belong to a particular pronoun or noun subject. *I am* and *he is* are examples of conjugations of the infinitive *to be.*

- **Health**

Yo estoy bien, gracias.	*I am fine, thanks.*
Ella está enferma.	*She is sick.*
Los doctores están enfermos.	*The doctors are sick.*
¿Cómo están Uds.?	*How are you?*
Estamos bien.	*We are well.*

- **Changing Mood or Condition**

La muchacha está contenta.	*The girl is happy.*
Estoy feliz.	*I am happy.*
Los hombres están cansados.	*The men are tired.*
Estamos alegres.	*We are happy.*
¿Estás enojado?	*Are you angry?*

Often the pronouns **yo**, **tú**, and **nosotros** are omitted. This is possible because **estoy** can only mean *I am*, **estás** means *you are* whether **tú** is included or not, and **estamos** carries the meaning *we are*.

- **Personal opinion in terms of taste or appearance**

When **estar** is used with food, the English equivalent is *taste* or *tastes*. When **estar** is used with appearance, the English equivalent is *look* or *looks*.

La comida está buena.	*The meal is (tastes) good.*
El pescado está delicioso.	*The fish is (tastes) delicious.*
La sopa está sabrosa.	*The soup is (tastes) delicious.*
Ella está hermosa hoy.	*She is (looks) pretty today.*
Él está guapo.	*He is (looks) handsome.*

A Word About Word Order
As you begin learning the basic structure of the Spanish language, you will discover that the word order of English and Spanish is essentially the same for the material covered in Part I, which includes the basic elements of a sentence.

Key Vocabulary

These words will help enhance your ability to communicate. As you learn them, remember to practice them aloud.

Interrogative Words

¿cómo?	*how?*
¿dónde?	*where?*
¿quién?	*who?*

Adverbs of Location

aquí, acá	*here*
allí, allá	*there*

Adjectives

alegre	*happy (merry)*	enojado	*angry*
bonito	*pretty*	feliz	*happy*
bueno	*good*	guapo	*beautiful, handsome*
cansado	*tired*	hermoso	*beautiful, handsome*
contento	*happy (contented)*	lindo	*pretty*
delicioso	*delicious*	sabroso	*delicious*
enfermo	*sick*		

NOTE: **Guapo** describes people only; **bonito**, **hermoso**, and **lindo** are used to describe both people and things.

Exercise 2.1

Complete the following sentences with the correct form of **estar**. *Pay attention to the meaning of each sentence. Then indicate whether the sentence expresses health, location, changing mood, or changing condition.*

EXAMPLES   Nosotros __*estamos*__ en la clase. (__*location*__)

La profesora __*está*__ enferma. (__*health*__)

1. Daniel _____ muy cansado hoy. (_____)

2. El teléfono y el libro _____ en la mesa. (_____)

3. La mujer _____ bien; el hombre _____

   enfermo. (_____)

4. ¿Cómo _____ Uds.? (_____)

5. ¿Dónde _____ _____ ellos? (_____)

6. ¿Dónde _____ el baño, por favor? (_____)

7. El niño _____ enojado y la niña _____ triste.

   (_____)

8. Los muchachos _____ alegres. (_____)

9. Yo _____ contento. (_____)

10. ¿Quién _____ aquí? (_____)

Exercise 2.2

Translate the following sentences into Spanish.

1. *I am in the yellow house. Where are you?*

   _____

2. *The red blouses are in the big store.*

   _____

3. *The white flower is in the window.*

   _____

4. *We are in the train.*

   _____

5. *How are you? I am fine, thanks.*

   _____

6. *We are tired, and we are happy.*

   _____

Ser (to be)

The Spanish verb **ser** is also equivalent to English *to be*.

In English, there is a single verb that means *to be*. We say, for example:

*The dog **is** here.* (location)
*The dog **is** brown.* (description)

The verb is the same in both cases. But in Spanish, there is a difference, and you have to choose the correct verb.

yo **soy**	*I am*	nosotros **somos**	*we are*
tú **eres**	*you are*	vosotros **sois**	*you are*
él **es**	*he is*	ellos **son**	*they are*
ella **es**	*she is*	ellas **son**	*they are*
Ud. **es**	*you are*	Uds. **son**	*you are*

Ser is used to express seven basic concepts: description, profession, point of origin, identification, material, possession or ownership, and where an event takes place.

- **Description**

La casa es roja.	*The house is red.*
El libro es azul.	*The book is blue.*
Los carros son viejos.	*The cars are old.*
Somos simpáticos.	*We are nice.*
¿Es la flor amarilla?	*Is the flower yellow?*

- **Profession**

Yo soy estudiante.	*I am a student.*
Él es arquitecto.	*He is an architect.*
Ellas son maestras excelentes.	*They are excellent teachers.*
Somos doctores.	*We are doctors.*
Roberto es abogado.	*Robert is a lawyer.*
¿Eres tú ingeniero?	*Are you an engineer?*

  Spanish does not translate *a/an* when stating an unmodified profession.

Unmodified	José es estudiante.
Modified	José es un estudiante fantástico.

- **Point of origin**

  De here means *from*.

¿De dónde es Ud.?	*Where are you from?* (sing.)
¿De dónde son Uds.?	*Where are you from?* (pl.)
Yo soy de Nueva York.	*I am from New York.*
¿De dónde es ella?	*Where is she from?*
Somos de Italia.	*We are from Italy.*
Ellos son de los Estados Unidos.	*They are from the United States.*

El vino es de Portugal.
La cerveza es de México.
El café es de Brazil.

The wine is from Portugal.
The beer is from Mexico.
The coffee is from Brazil.

In common English usage, we often end a sentence with a preposition, for example, *Where are you from?* This never occurs in Spanish; the preposition cannot ever end a sentence, so the preposition, in this case **de**, is placed in front of the interrogative word **dónde**.

- ### Identification

  Identification specifies characteristics such as relationship, nationality, race, or religion.

  Somos amigos.
  José y Eduardo son hermanos.
  Pablo es español.
  ¿Eres tú cubano?
  Ella es católica.

  We are friends.
  Joe and Ed are brothers.
  Paul is Spanish.
  Are you Cuban?
  She is Catholic.

- ### Material

  De here means *of.*

  La mesa es de madera.
  La bolsa es de plástico.
  Los zapatos son de cuero.
  Las ventanas son de vidrio.
  La casa es de piedra.

  The table is of wood.
  The bag is of plastic.
  The shoes are of leather.
  The windows are of glass.
  The house is of stone.

- ### Possession or ownership

  De here means *of.*

  La muñeca es de la niña.

  It's the child's doll.
  (The doll is of the child.)

  Los amigos son de María.

  They are María's friends.
  (The friends are of María.)

  La idea es de Pedro.

  The idea is Pedro's.
  (The idea is of Pedro.)

  El barco es del hombre rico.

  The boat belongs to the rich man.
  (The boat is of the rich man.)

  Los perros son del muchacho.

  The dogs belong to the boy.
  (The dogs are of the boy.)

Los gatos son del niño.	*The cats belong to the child.*
	(The cats are of the child.)
El carro es de los amigos.	*The car belongs to the friends.*
	(The car is of the friends.)

NOTE: The contraction: **de** + **el** (*of* + *the*) = **del**. There are only two contractions in the Spanish language; **del** is one of them. Use **de** (English *of*) to express possession or ownership. When **de** (English *of*) is followed by the masculine **el** (English *the*), the words contract to **del**, meaning *of the*.

A Word About Possessives

You can see that the translations above are not exact. There is no apostrophe in Spanish, so when you think of *Peter's car*, for example, the Spanish structure is **el carro de Pedro** (*the car of Peter*). Make sure you understand this concept and use whichever English translation seems clearest to you.

- **Where an event takes place**

La fiesta es en la casa de José.	*The party is (takes place) in Joe's house.*
El concierto es en el club.	*The concert is (takes place) in the club.*
La protesta es en la capital.	*The protest is (takes place) in the capital.*

The equivalent English translation is *take* or *takes place.*

The party takes place at Joe's house.
The concert takes place at the club.
The protest takes place in the capital.

Exercise 2.3

*Complete the following sentences with the appropriate form of **ser** in each blank. Indicate whether the sentence expresses description, profession, point of origin, identification, material, or possession in parentheses.*

EXAMPLE   El hombre __es__ guapo. La mujer __es__ guapa también.
(__description__)

  1. El café _____ de Colombia. (_____)

2. Ellos _____ doctores. Ella _____ profesora.

   (_____)

3. ¿De dónde _____ los turistas? (_____)

4. Los hermanos de Pablo _____ simpáticos.

   (_____)

5. El hotel viejo _____ excelente. (_____)

6. Nosotros _____ amigos de Raúl. (_____)

7. Los zapatos _____ de cuero. (_____)

8. La mujer y el hombre _____ de Ecuador. (_____)

9. Yo _____ de Puerto Rico. ¿De dónde _____ Ud.?

   (_____)

10. El apartamento _____ de los estudiantes jóvenes.

    (_____)

11. ¿_____ tú una estudiante maravillosa? (_____)

12. Los tomates _____ verdes y rojos. (_____)

13. ¿Quién _____ el presidente de los Estados Unidos?

    (_____)

Exercise 2.4

A. *Complete the following sentences with the appropriate form of* **ser**. *Indicate the reason for your choice in parentheses.*

1. Helena _____ de Colombia. (_____)

2. El hermano de ella _____ católico. (_____)

3. Ellos _____ profesores excelentes. (_____)

4. Los carros _____ grises. (_____)

5. Nosotros _____ estudiantes. (_____)

B. *Complete the following sentences with the appropriate form of* **estar**. *Indicate the reason for your choice in parentheses.*

1. San Francisco _____ en California. (_____)

2. ¿Cómo _____ Ud.? Yo _____ bien.

   (_____)

3. El profesor _____ enfermo. (_____)

4. Nosotros _____ en la clase. (_____)

5. ¿_____ tú triste? (_____)

6. Los perros _____ en el carro. (_____)

C. *Complete the following sentences with the appropriate form of either* **ser** *or* **estar***. Indicate the reason for each choice in parentheses.*

EXAMPLES   Yo __soy__ español. (__identification__)

   Ellos __están__ aquí. (__location__)

1. José y Juan _____ enfermos. (_____)

2. Tú _____ abogado. (_____)

3. La lección _____ fácil. (_____)

4. Los estudiantes _____ en la ciudad. (_____)

5. ¿Cómo _____ Uds.? Nosotros _____ bien,

   gracias. (_____, _____)

6. Ellas _____ inteligentes. (_____)

7. ¿Dónde _____ los doctores? (_____)

8. El profesor _____ contento. (_____)

9. Los espejos en el baño _____ grandes. (_____)

10. La mesa, las sillas blancas y la lámpara _____ en la casa,

    pero la casa _____ pequeña. (_____,

    _____)

11. La amiga de Sara _____ enferma y Sara _____

    triste. (_____, _____)

12. Las puertas de la casa _____ fuertes. (_____)

13. Los tomates _____ en la tienda. Los tomates verdes

    _____ de California; los tomates rojos _____

    de Guatemala. (_____, _____,

    _____)

14. ¿De dónde _____ el vino blanco? (_____)

15. Los muchachos y las muchachas _____ en el tren.

    Ellos _____ contentos porque _____ amigos.

    (_____, _____, _____)

16. ¿Quién _____ en el baño? (_____)

17. ¿Dónde _____ la familia de Fernando? (_____)

18. Nosotros _____ contentos porque nosotros

    _____ estudiantes excelentes. (_____,

    _____)

19. ¿_____ Ud. de Suramérica? Ellos _____

    de España. (_____, _____)

20. Julia _____ alegre porque la fiesta _____

    fantástica. (_____, _____)

 ## Exercise 2.5

*Answer the following questions aloud using the appropriate form of **ser** or **estar**.*

1. ¿Cómo estás?

2. ¿Dónde está la hermana de Teresa?

3. ¿De dónde es Ud.?

4. ¿Quién está en el carro caro?

5. ¿Dónde es el concierto?

6. ¿Está Ud. alegre?

7. ¿Es fácil la lección?

8. ¿Dónde están las flores hermosas? ¿De dónde son?

9. ¿Es grande el apartamento de Tomás?

10. ¿Estás cansado?

11. ¿Están los periódicos en la casa de Alicia?

12. ¿Dónde está el restaurante barato de la ciudad?

13. ¿Es Ud. de Europa?

14. ¿Eres estudiante o profesor?

Exercise 2.6

Complete the following letter with the appropriate form of **ser** *or* **estar.**

Queridos amigos,

¿Cómo _____ (1.) Uds.? Yo _____ (2.) aquí

en Madrid. La ciudad _____ (3.) hermosa. El museo del Prado

_____ (4.) en el centro de la ciudad y _____ (5.)

muy interesante. La gente _____ (6.) simpática y la comida

_____ (7.) deliciosa. Hasta luego.

 ## Reading Comprehension

La casa

Mi casa es vieja y grande, con muchas ventanas. Las cortinas en toda la casa son gruesas. Las paredes del interior de la casa son blancas; el exterior es gris. El patio es bonito, con flores todavía. Un espejo antiguo y una mesa de madera fina están en el vestíbulo. El comedor es sencillo, con una mesa y seis sillas; la alfombra es roja y azul marino. La cocina es amplia, con paredes amarillas y gabinetes blancos.

La nevera es bastante grande, y la estufa y el horno están limpios. Dos sillones cómodos y un piano están en la sala. Mi alcoba con un baño privado es azul y blanca. Mis libros, mis cuadernos, mis lápices y bolígrafos, mi colección de discos compactos, y mis videos están en el estudio. Hoy es un día hermoso.

Nombres (Nouns)

la alcoba	*the bedroom*	el gabinete	*the cabinet*
la alfombra	*the rug*	el horno	*the oven*
el bolígrafo	*the ballpoint pen*	el lápiz	*the pencil*
la cocina	*the kitchen*	la madera	*the wood*
la colección	*the collection*	la nevera	*the refrigerator*
el comedor	*the dining room*	la pared	*the wall*
la cortina	*the curtain*	el patio	*the yard*
el cuaderno	*the notebook*	la sala	*the living room*
el espejo	*the mirror*	el sillón	*the easy chair*
el estudio	*the study*	el vestíbulo	*the entryway*
la estufa	*the stove*	el video	*the video*

Adjetivos (Adjectives)

amplio	*ample*	limpio	*clean*
antiguo	*old*	mi, mis	*my* (sing., pl.)
azul marino	*navy blue*	privado	*private*
cómodo	*comfortable*	sencillo	*simple*
fino	*fine, delicate*	todo	*all*
grueso	*thick*		

Adverbios (Adverbs)

bastante	*enough*
todavía	*still*

Preguntas (Questions)

After you have read the selection, answer the following questions in Spanish.

1. ¿Es nueva la casa? _____

2. ¿Es bonito el día? _____

3. ¿Es grande la cocina? _____

4. ¿Dónde está el piano? _____

3

Hay, Interrogative Words, Days, and Months

Hay

The single Spanish word **hay** (pronounced like English *eye*) means *there is, there are, is there?,* and *are there?* in English.

Spanish sentences with **hay** and English sentences with *there is, there are* follow the same pattern with regard to the inclusion or omission of definite and indefinite articles. The Spanish definite articles **el, la, los,** and **las** (English *the*) never follow **hay**.

Hay una alfombra en la casa.	*There is a rug in the house.*
Hay un árbol en el jardín.	*There is a tree in the garden.*
Hay dos vasos en la mesa.	*There are two glasses on the table.*
Hay tres libros en el piso.	*There are three books on the floor.*

A question formed with **hay** uses the same word order as a statement. When written, it carries a question mark at the beginning and end, as all Spanish interrogative sentences do. When spoken, it should be pronounced with a rising intonation.

¿Hay una lámpara azul en la casa?	*Is there a blue lamp in the house?*
¿Hay un libro en el baño?	*Is there a book in the bathroom?*
¿Hay un hotel en la ciudad?	*Is there a hotel in the city?*
¿Hay una mesa marrón en el cuarto?	*Is there a brown table in the room?*

When **hay** is followed by a plural noun, the article is omitted.

Hay tigres en el zoológico.	*There are tigers in the zoo.*
Hay estrellas en el cielo.	*There are stars in the sky.*

¿Hay periódicos en esta tienda?   *Are there newspapers in this store?*
¿Hay tomates rojos en este   *Are there red tomatoes in this*
   mercado?   *market?*

To make a sentence negative, place **no** before **hay**.

No hay luz en el baño.   *There is no light in the bathroom.*
No hay teléfonos aquí.   *There are no telephones here.*
No hay revistas en el hotel.   *There are no magazines in the hotel.*

 Exercise 3.1

A. *Translate the following Spanish sentences into English.*

1. ¿Hay una lección fácil en el libro?

   _____

2. No hay cucarachas en el restaurante.

   _____

3. ¿Hay blusas rojas en la tienda?

   _____

4. Hay flores en el balcón del apartamento.

   _____

5. ¿Hay clase hoy?

   _____

6. ¿Hay más preguntas de los estudiantes?

   _____

B. *Translate the following English sentences into Spanish.*

1. *There are many pens on the teacher's desk.*

   _____

2. *Is there a doctor in the hospital?*

   _____

3. *There are two women in the class.*

   _____

4. *There is no beer in Lisa's house.*

_____

Interrogative Words

All interrogative words carry written accents; the accent marks do not affect the pronunciation of the word.

¿Cómo? *How?*

¿Cómo estás tú?   *How are you?*
¿Cómo están los muchachos?   *How are the boys?*

¿Dónde? *Where?*

¿Dónde está la casa del alcalde?   *Where is the mayor's house?*
¿Dónde estamos?   *Where are we?*

¿Quién? (sing.), **¿Quiénes?** (pl.) *Who?*

¿Quién está aquí?   *Who is here?*
¿Quién es la persona con José?   *Who is the person with Joe?*
¿Quiénes están en el carro?   *Who is in the car?*
¿Quiénes son ellos?   *Who are they?*

¿Qué? *What?*

¿Qué día es hoy?   *What day is today?*
¿Qué libro está en la mesa?   *What book is on the table?*
¿Qué hay en el menú?   *What is there on the menu?*

¿Qué? used before **ser** asks for a definition.

¿Qué es comunicación?   *What is communication?*
¿Qué es esto?   *What is this?*
¿Qué es filosofía?   *What is philosophy?*

¿Cuál? (sing.), **¿Cuáles?** (pl.) *Which, which one? Which ones?*

¿Cuál? used immediately before **ser** asks for a selection or choice from among various possibilities.

¿Cuál es la capital de Perú?   *What (which city) is the capital of Peru?*

¿Cuál es el problema?	*What (which problem) is the problem?*
¿Cuál es el nombre de la niña?	*What (which name) is the girl's name?*
¿Cuáles son los días de la semana?	*What (which days) are the days of the week?*

¿Por qué? *Why?*

¿Por qué estamos alegres?	*Why are we happy?*
¿Por qué es azul el cielo?	*Why is the sky blue?*

¿Cuánto? *How much?*

¿Cuánto es?	*How much is it?*
¿Cuánto cuesta?	*How much does it cost?*
¿Cuánto vale?	*How much is it worth?*

¿Cuántos?, **¿Cuántas?** *How many?*

¿Cuántos gatos hay en la ciudad?	*How many cats are there in the city?*
¿Cuántas estrellas hay en el cielo?	*How many stars are there in the sky?*

Cuántos and **cuántas** are adjectives and must agree in gender with the plural nouns they describe.

¿Cuándo? *When?*

¿Cuándo es la fiesta?	*When is the party?*
¿Cuándo es el concierto?	*When is the concert?*

Exercise 3.2

Complete the following questions with the appropriate interrogative word. As you do this exercise, review **ser**, **estar**, *and* **hay**.

1. ¿_____ es la bolsa de María, la bolsa roja o la bolsa azul?

2. ¿_____ día es hoy?

3. ¿_____ están los estudiantes?

4. ¿_____ hay muchas personas en el parque hoy?

5. ¿_____ es la mujer con el perro marrón?

6. ¿_____ no hay espejos en el baño de los hombres?

7. ¿_____ libros hay en la librería?

8. ¿_____ están Uds.?

Prepositions

You have already learned three of the most common prepositions in Spanish.

en   *in, on*
de   *from, of*
con   *with*

You can combine these prepositions with an interrogative word to further your ability to ask questions.

¿En qué tienda hay muchos libros?	*In what store are there many books?*
¿En cuál parque hay animales exóticos?	*In which park are there exotic animals?*
¿De dónde es el hombre?	*Where is the man from?*
¿De qué color es la mesa?	*(Of) what color is the table?*
¿De quién es la idea fantástica?	*Whose fantastic idea is it? (Of whom is the fantastic idea?)*
¿Con quién estás?	*Whom are you with?*

Exercise 3.3

Complete the following questions with the appropriate preposition.

1. ¿_____ qué ciudad está la estatua de la libertad?

2. ¿_____ qué color es la casa grande?

3. ¿_____ qué material es la ventana?

4. ¿_____ quiénes están Uds.?

5. ¿_____ cuáles países hay plazas hermosas?

6. ¿_____ quién es el carro caro?

Days of the Week, Months, and Seasons

Los días de la semana (The days of the week)

To refer to a day of the week in English, we say *Monday* or *on Monday*. In Spanish, the article **el** is used with the name of the day to express this idea. Days of the week are not capitalized in Spanish.

el lunes	*Monday, on Monday*
el martes	*Tuesday, on Tuesday*
el miércoles	*Wednesday, on Wednesday*
el jueves	*Thursday, on Thursday*
el viernes	*Friday, on Friday*
el sábado	*Saturday, on Saturday*
el domingo	*Sunday, on Sunday*

To form the plural of the days of the week, **el** changes to **los** and **-s** is added only to **el sábado** and **el domingo**. The names of the days of the week from **el lunes** to **el viernes** already end in **-s**.

los lunes	*Mondays, on Mondays*
los martes	*Tuesdays, on Tuesdays*
los miércoles	*Wednesdays, on Wednesdays*
los jueves	*Thursdays, on Thursdays*
los viernes	*Fridays, on Fridays*
los sábados	*Saturdays, on Saturdays*
los domingos	*Sundays, on Sundays*

Hay clase los lunes.	*There is class on Mondays.*
¿Hay fiestas los sábados?	*Are there parties on Saturdays?*
¿Dónde está Tomás los domingos?	*Where is Thomas on Sundays?*
El jueves es el día de acción de gracias.	*Thursday is Thanksgiving Day.*
El martes es el día del amor y la amistad.	*Tuesday is St. Valentine's Day.*
Estamos en clase los miércoles.	*We are in class on Wednesdays.*
¿Dónde estás los viernes?	*Where are you on Fridays?*

Los meses (The months)

enero	*January*	abril	*April*
febrero	*February*	mayo	*May*
marzo	*March*	junio	*June*

julio	*July*	octubre	*October*
agosto	*August*	noviembre	*November*
septiembre	*September*	diciembre	*December*

Las estaciones (The seasons)

el verano	*the summer*
el otoño	*the autumn, the fall*
el invierno	*the winter*
la primavera	*the spring(time)*

Partes del día (Parts of the day)

la mañana	*the morning*
la tarde	*the afternoon*
la noche	*the night, the evening*

 # Reading Comprehension

Un pueblo colonial

Estoy, con unos amigos, en Guanajuato, un pueblo° colonial y antiguo°
en el centro de México. Estamos aquí con los padres de Laura. Laura y yo
somos estudiantes de español; la madre de ella es arqueóloga° y el padre
es político.° Hay una escuela con clases de música, de guitarra, de baile
y de historia. Es el verano, el clima es maravilloso y los mexicanos son muy
simpáticos. Hay fiestas los viernes y los sábados. Hay muchas clases de
lunes a viernes° también y somos estudiantes serios.° La madre de Laura
está contenta porque hay unas ruinas de los Olmecas° en el campo. El padre
de ella está contento también porque el viaje es tranquilo y relajante.°
Estoy feliz en la casa de piedra en las montañas. Hay música en la mañana,
una comida en la tarde y conversación durante° el día. Todo está bien.

°el pueblo *town*
°antiguo *old, ancient*
°la arqueóloga *archeologist*
°el político *politician*
°de lunes a viernes *from Monday through
   Friday*

°serio *serious*
°los Olmecas *an ancient people of Mexico
   who disappeared around 600 A.D.*
°relajante *relaxing*
°durante *during*

Nombres masculinos

el año	*the year*	el lápiz	*the pencil*
el árbol	*the tree*	el mensaje	*the message*
el ascensor	*the elevator*	el mes	*the month*
el avión	*the airplane*	el niño	*the child*
el bolígrafo	*the ballpoint pen*	el país	*the country*
el bus	*the bus*	el papel	*the paper*
el campo	*the countryside*	el parque	*the park*
el coche	*the car*	el periódico	*the newspaper*
el cuarto	*the room*	el piso	*the floor*
el cumpleaños	*the birthday*	el precio	*the price*
el día	*the day*	el ruido	*the noise*
el dinero	*the money*	el salón	*the classroom*
el edificio	*the building*	el sitio	*the place*
el equipaje	*the baggage*	el sueño	*the dream*
el hogar	*the home*	el teatro	*the theater*
el jardín	*the garden*	el tema	*the theme*
el lapicero	*the ballpoint pen*	el viaje	*the trip*

Nombres femeninos

la avenida	*the avenue*	la hoja	*the leaf*
la biblioteca	*the library*	la librería	*the bookstore*
la calle	*the street*	la llave	*the key*
la camisa	*the shirt*	la medicina	*the medicine*
la carta	*the letter*	la música	*the music*
la ciudad	*the city*	la obra	*the play*
la cocina	*the kitchen*	la página	*the page*
la cuenta	*the check, the bill*	la palabra	*the word*
la ducha	*the shower*	la pared	*the wall*
la entrada	*the entrance*	la playa	*the beach*
la escalera	*the stairs*	la pregunta	*the question*
la escuela	*the school*	la puerta	*the door*
la fiesta	*the party*	la salida	*the exit*
la frase	*the sentence*	la salud	*the health*
la gente	*the people*	la semana	*the week*
la guerra	*the war*	la tarea	*the homework*
la habitación	*the room*	la tarjeta	*the postcard*

Adjetivos

alto	*tall*	flojo	*lax*
amable	*kind*	gracioso	*amusing*
amistoso	*friendly*	hondo	*deep*
ancho	*wide*	largo	*long*
bajo	*low, short* (in height)	lento	*slow*
bello	*beautiful*	libre	*free*
cariñoso	*affectionate*	nuevo	*new*
ciego	*blind*	orgulloso	*proud*
corto	*short* (in length)	peligroso	*dangerous*
dulce	*sweet*	pesado	*heavy, dull*
duro	*hard*	rápido	*rapid, fast*
elegante	*elegant*	raro	*strange*
emocionante	*exciting*	sencillo	*simple*
especial	*special*	sordo	*deaf*
estrecho	*narrow*	suave	*soft*
fiel	*faithful*	tranquilo	*tranquil*

Conjunciones (Conjunctions)

Conjunctions are words that connect words, phrases, or clauses.

mientras	*while*	porque	*because*
o	*or*	si	*if*
pero	*but*	y	*and*

 # Exercise 3.4

You now have a new vocabulary of nouns and adjectives; test how many you recall in the following exercises.

A. *Translate the following Spanish phrases into English.*

1. el cuarto bello _____

2. la persona agradable _____

3. la amistad dulce _____

4. la obra emocionante _____

5. el día lindo _____

6. el edificio bajo   _____

7. el sueño raro   _____

8. la guerra larga   _____

9. la avenida ancha   _____

10. el año nuevo   _____

B. *Translate the following English phrases into Spanish. Make sure the adjective agrees with the noun.*

1. *the affectionate child*   _____

2. *the simple homework*   _____

3. *the dangerous city*   _____

4. *the short person*   _____

5. *the short month*   _____

6. *the beautiful beach*   _____

7. *the friendly woman*   _____

8. *the kind man*   _____

9. *the narrow avenue*   _____

10. *the proud people*   _____

 # Exercise 3.5

Answer the following questions aloud using **hay**, **ser**, *or* **estar**.

1. ¿Hay hojas en los árboles en el verano?

2. ¿Con quiénes estás tú en la escuela?

3. ¿De qué color es la habitación de Julia?

4. ¿De quién es el jardín?

5. ¿En qué tienda hay tomates?

6. ¿Dónde están las playas bonitas de la ciudad?

7. ¿Hay perros en el campo?

8. ¿Qué hay en el agua?

9. ¿Cuál es la idea del estudiante inteligente?

10. ¿Dónde está Ud.?

11. ¿Cuál es bella, la paz o la guerra?

12. ¿Quién está aquí con Ud.?

13. ¿Dónde está el baño, por favor?

14. ¿Hay preguntas?

 ## Exercise 3.6

Complete the following sentences with the appropriate form of **ser**, **estar**, *or* **hay**. *Be sure to include accent marks when they are needed.*

EXAMPLE   Si hoy __es__ sábado, ¿por qué __están__ enojados los hombres?

1. ¿Cuál _____ la escuela de los niños?

2. ¿Quién _____ aquí?

3. ¿De qué color _____ la puerta?

4. ¿Por qué _____ cariñosa la amiga de Laura?

5. ¿_____ mucha gente en el hotel hoy?

6. La palabra _____ en la frase; la frase _____ en la página; la página _____ en el libro.

7. ¿_____ edificios altos en Madrid?

8. Las playas y las piscinas _____ en el campo.

   ¿Qué _____ en la ciudad?

9. _____ muchos lápices y bolígrafos en la mesa de la mujer.

   ¿_____ ella la profesora de la clase?

10. En el verano, _____ plantas verdes y flores hermosas en los parques.

11. Los hombres _____ altos. Los niños _____ bajos.

12. Nosotros _____ estudiantes excelentes porque las lecciones no _____ difíciles.

13. ¿_____ ella flaca porque ella _____ enferma?

14. Yo _____ en la clase pero el maestro no _____ aquí.

15. ¿_____ peligrosa la ciudad en la noche?

16. _____ luces en las avenidas porque es Navidad.

17. El carro negro _____ barato; el coche verde es caro.

    ¿Cuál _____ el carro del hombre rico?

18. Si Manuel y Jorge _____ estudiantes excelentes,

    ¿por qué _____ tristes en la clase?

19. ¿Quiénes _____ en la casa los miércoles en la mañana?

    ¿Dónde _____ Ud. en la noche?

20. ¿Cuál _____ la bolsa de Sara, la bolsa roja o la bolsa gris?

21. El tren gris _____ pequeño; los buses _____
    grandes.

Exercise 3.7

Translate the following Spanish sentences into English.

1. ¿Dónde están los estudiantes los domingos?

   _____

2. El sábado y el domingo son días de fiesta.

   _____

3. En la primavera, hay flores bellas en los parques.

   _____

4. En el otoño, hay hojas amarillas y rojas en los árboles.

   _____

5. ¿Qué día es hoy? Hoy es miércoles. ¿Qué mes es? Es septiembre.

   _____

6. ¿Cuántos días hay en junio? ¿Cuántos días hay en un año?

   _____

7. Las calles de México son estrechas. Las casas son bajas y bonitas.

   _____

8. ¿Por qué están los periódicos y las revistas en el piso?

   _____

9. Hay clase, pero los estudiantes están en la playa donde hay una piscina también. El profesor está enojado pero los estudiantes están alegres.

_____

10. Los edificios de las ciudades grandes son altos.

_____

11. Los niños están en la playa porque es el verano.

_____

12. Mucha gente está en los restaurantes porque es el invierno.

_____

 # Reading Comprehension

El cine

Roberto Vélez es director de cine.° Él es de España y las películas°
de él son cómicas.° Rosa Morales es argentina y es directora también.
Las películas de ella son más tristes porque en la Argentina hay mucha
pobreza.° Hoy, ellos están contentos porque están en Cannes, el festival
de la Palma de Oro. Hay actores, directores, jurados° y gente importante
en la ciudad. Roberto y Rosa están emocionados.° La presentación de
los premios° es esta noche. Muchas películas son interesantes este año,
¿pero cuál es la película favorita de los jurados?

Preguntas
After you have read the selection, answer the following questions in Spanish.

1. ¿De dónde es Roberto Vélez? ¿De dónde es Rosa Morales?

_____

2. ¿Dónde están? _____

3. ¿Son ellos amigos? _____

————

°el cine *the movies (in general)*
°la película *the film*
°cómico(a) *funny*
°la pobreza *poverty*

°el jurado *judge*
°emocionado *excited*
°el premio *award, prize*

4

Numbers, Dates, and Time

Cardinal Numbers

A cardinal number is any number that expresses an amount, such as *one, two, three.* Here are the Spanish cardinal numbers up to 100.

0	cero				
1	uno	21	veintiuno	50	cincuenta
2	dos	22	veintidós	60	sesenta
3	tres	23	veintitrés	70	setenta
4	cuatro	24	veinticuatro	80	ochenta
5	cinco	25	veinticinco	90	noventa
6	seis	26	veintiséis		
7	siete	27	veintisiete		
8	ocho	28	veintiocho		
9	nueve	29	veintinueve		
10	diez	30	treinta		
11	once	31	treinta y uno		
12	doce	32	treinta y dos		
13	trece	33	treinta y tres		
14	catorce	34	treinta y cuatro		
15	quince	35	treinta y cinco		
16	dieciséis	36	treinta y seis		
17	diecisiete	37	treinta y siete		
18	dieciocho	38	treinta y ocho		
19	diecinueve	39	treinta y nueve		
20	veinte	40	cuarenta		

Note the following rules for the use of cardinal numbers in Spanish.

- Numbers after 15, **quince**, are formed by combining numbers: 10 + 6 = 16, **diez y seis son dieciséis**.

- The numbers from 16 to 19 and from 21 to 29 are expressed as one word: 22, **veinte y dos** → **veintidós**.

- Numbers after 30, **treinta**, end in **-a** and do not combine with the next number. They are expressed as individual words: 34, **treinta y cuatro**, for example. This is true for the numbers 31 to 99, **treinta y uno** to **noventa y nueve**.

- In English we say *one hundred and ten*. Spanish does not use **y** to connect hundreds and the following number: 110, **ciento diez**; 220, **doscientos veinte**; 315, **trescientos quince**.

- When a masculine noun follows the number 21, 31, 41, 51, 61, 71, 81, or 91, the **-o** is dropped from **uno**.

veintiún años	*21 years*
treinta y un libros	*31 books*
cincuenta y un gatos	*51 cats*
sesenta y un hombres	*61 men*
noventa y un amigos	*91 friends*

- When a feminine noun follows a number ending in **uno** (English *one*), the feminine form is **una**.

cuarenta y una mujeres	*41 women*
setenta y una muchachas	*71 girls*
ochenta y una amigas	*81 friends*

- The number 100 in Spanish uses the following pattern.

cien	*100*
ciento uno	*101*
ciento cincuenta	*150*
ciento noventa y nueve	*199*

Cien becomes **ciento** if it is followed by any number less than itself. Before all nouns, masculine or feminine, it remains **cien**.

cien libros	*100 books*	cien hombres	*100 men*
cien casas	*100 houses*	cien mujeres	*100 women*

- The numbers 200 to 900 agree with the noun they modify.

200	doscientos	
	doscientos hoteles	*200 hotels*
	doscientas puertas	*200 doors*
300	trescientos	
	trescientos gatos	*300 cats*
	trescientas tiendas	*300 stores*
400	cuatrocientos	
	cuatrocientos trenes	*400 trains*
	cuatrocientas luces	*400 lights*
500	quinientos	
	quinientos animales	*500 animals*
	quinientas flores	*500 flowers*
600	seiscientos	
	seiscientos árboles	*600 trees*
	seiscientas fiestas	*600 parties*
700	setecientos	
	setecientos barcos	*700 boats*
	setecientas plantas	*700 plants*
800	ochocientos	
	ochocientos sueños	*800 dreams*
	ochocientas mesas	*800 tables*
900	novecientos	
	novecientos espejos	*900 mirrors*
	novecientas siestas	*900 naps*

- Spanish numbers beginning with 1000, **mil**, are not counted in hundreds.

1.000	mil	
	mil años	*1000 years*
	dos mil años	*2000 years*
1.000.000	un millón (de)	
	un millón de dólares	*a million dollars*
2.000.000	dos millones (de)	
	dos millones de preguntas	*two million questions*

Mil does not change (**dos mil**, **tres mil**, **cinco mil**), nor does it need the article **un** (English *a*) in front of it.

Spanish does not count in hundreds after 1,000. The number 1992 is formed by combining 1000 + 900 + 92: **mil novecientos noventa y dos**. The number 2006 is **dos mil seis**.

The plural **miles** is used only to refer to a large but inexact amount, the way English uses *tons*: **Hay miles de personas en el restaurante.** *There are tons of people in the restaurant.*

• Note that Spanish uses the period to separate thousands; the comma is used to indicate decimals: $90,25 is **noventa dólares y veinticinco centavos**.

A Word About Numbers

Numbers are an important part of everyday life. People tell you their telephone numbers or ask you to meet them at a specific address. Try to practice numbers with a partner, perhaps a native speaker.

Exercise 4.1

Complete the following sentences by writing in the Spanish numbers (in words).

1. En febrero, hay _____ (28) días; cada

   _____ (4) años, hay _____ (29) días.

2. ¿En qué meses hay _____ (31) días?

3. Hay _____ (7) días en una semana;

   _____ (52) semanas en un año.

4. Hay _____ (76) lápices en la tienda y

   _____ (67) plumas.

5. Hay _____ (21) muchachas en el baño, pero hay

   solamente _____ (1) espejo.

6. Hay _____ (135) libros de español en
   la librería.

7. En la biblioteca, hay _____ (2,456) libros.

8. _____ (91) y _____ (542)

   son _____ (633).

9. _____ (860) menos _____ (50)

   son _____ (810).

10. Hay _____ (100) camisas rojas en la tienda y hay

    _____ (100) pantalones.

11. Hay _____ (15) capítulos en el libro; hay

    _____ (254) páginas.

12. Hay _____ (235) restaurantes en la ciudad.

Ordinal Numbers

Ordinal numbers express position in a series, such as *first, second, third*.

primero	*first*	sexto	*sixth*
segundo	*second*	séptimo	*seventh*
tercero	*third*	octavo	*eighth*
cuarto	*fourth*	noveno	*ninth*
quinto	*fifth*	décimo	*tenth*

Note the following rules for the use of ordinal numbers in Spanish.

• Ordinal numbers in Spanish precede the noun and agree in gender with the noun they describe.

• **Primero** and **tercero** drop the **-o** before a masculine noun: **el primer piso**, **el tercer piso**.

primero *first*
    el primer hombre   *the first man*
    la primera mujer   *the first woman*

segundo *second*
    el segundo mes   *the second month*
    la segunda parte   *the second part*

tercero *third*
    el tercer día   *the third day*
    la tercera semana   *the third week*

cuarto *fourth*

    el cuarto piso   *the fourth floor*

    la cuarta lección   *the fourth lesson*

quinto *fifth*

    el quinto mes   *the fifth month*

    la quinta avenida   *Fifth Avenue (the fifth avenue)*

sexto *sixth*

    el sexto tren   *the sixth train*

    la sexta calle   *Sixth Street (the sixth street)*

séptimo *seventh*

    el séptimo capítulo   *the seventh chapter*

    la séptima página   *the seventh page*

octavo *eighth*

    el octavo libro   *the eighth book*

    la octava pregunta   *the eighth question*

noveno *ninth*

    el noveno presidente   *the ninth president*

    la novena fiesta   *the ninth party*

décimo *tenth*

    el décimo sueño   *the tenth dream*

    la décima razón   *the tenth reason*

¿Dónde está la quinta avenida?   *Where is Fifth Avenue?*

Hay una librería en la sexta calle.   *There is a bookstore on Sixth Street.*

El tercer capítulo es interesante.   *The third chapter is interesting.*

La oficina del doctor está en el sexto piso.   *The doctor's office is on the sixth floor.*

Ana y María son las primeras estudiantes en la clase.   *Ana and María are the first students in the class.*

- Ordinal numbers are used for kings, queens, popes, and centuries; in this case, they follow the noun they describe.

    el siglo segundo   *the second century*

    Carlos Quinto   *Charles the Fifth*

- Beginning with the ordinal number *eleventh*, state the noun first, then the cardinal number. Thus *Eleventh Street* is expressed as **la calle once** (English *the street eleven*).

el piso catorce	*the fourteenth floor* *(the floor fourteen)*
la calle once	*Eleventh Street* *(the street eleven)*
la lección veintitrés	*the twenty-third lesson* *(the lesson twenty-three)*
el piso ciento tres	*the one hundred and third floor* *(the floor one hundred and three)*

Exercise 4.2

Complete the following sentences with the Spanish equivalent (in words) of each phrase.

EXAMPLE   Hay una feria en ___*la tercera avenida*___ (Third Avenue).

1. Hay una biblioteca en _____ (72nd Street).

2. El trabajo de Lola está en _____ (the 40th floor).

3. Hay un restaurante en _____ (135th Street).

4. _____ (The third chapter) es interesante.

5. _____ (The fourth lesson) es horrible.

6. Mayo es _____ (the fifth month) del año.

The Date

Spanish uses the cardinal numbers 2 to 31 to indicate all days of the month except the first.

¿Cuál es la fecha de hoy?	*What is today's date?*
Hoy es el cinco de mayo.	*Today is May 5.*
Mañana es el seis de mayo.	*Tomorrow is May 6.*
Es el veintiocho de febrero.	*It is February 28.*
Es el treinta y uno de octubre.	*It is October 31.*

Spanish uses an ordinal number only to indicate the *first of the month,* **el primero del mes**.

> Hoy es el primero de junio.   *Today is June 1.*
> Mañana es el primero de octubre.   *Tomorrow is October 1.*

 ## Exercise 4.3

Complete the following sentences with the Spanish term or number. Always write numbers as words.

1. Hoy es _____ (*Thursday*), el _____ (*11th*) de mayo.

2. ¿Por qué estamos en clase _____ (*on Saturdays*)?

3. Hay _____ (*100*) personas en el restaurante nuevo.

4. La fecha del nacimiento de Sandra es _____

   _____ (*Oct. 18, 1973*).

5. Es el _____ (*14th*) de diciembre del

   _____ (*2006*).

6. ¿Quién es el _____ (*first*) hombre y la

   _____ (*first*) mujer?

Telling Time

To express *time* in the sense of *telling time,* Spanish uses **la hora**.

¿Qué hora es?   { *What hour is it?*
                                 { *What time is it?*

In order to tell time, Spanish always uses the third-person singular or plural of **ser**. Start by learning the expressions for telling exact time on the hour, from one o'clock to twelve o'clock. **La** represents **la hora**, and **las** represents **las horas**.

> Es la una.   *It is one o'clock.*
> Son las dos.   *It is two o'clock.*
> Son las tres.   *It is three o'clock.*
> Son las cuatro.   *It is four o'clock.*

Son las cinco.	*It is five o'clock.*
Son las seis.	*It is six o'clock.*
Son las siete.	*It is seven o'clock.*
Son las ocho.	*It is eight o'clock.*
Son las nueve.	*It is nine o'clock.*
Son las diez.	*It is ten o'clock.*
Son las once.	*It is eleven o'clock.*
Son las doce.	*It is twelve o'clock.*

The part of day is specified as follows.

de la mañana	*(of the) morning,* A.M.
de la tarde	*(of the) afternoon,* P.M.
de la noche	*(of the) night,* P.M.
Son las dos de la mañana.	*It is two o'clock in the morning.*
Es la una de la tarde.	*It is one o'clock in the afternoon.*
Son las ocho de la noche.	*It is eight o'clock at night.*

To indicate the exact hour or "sharp," Spanish uses **exactamente** or **en punto**.

Son las cinco exactamente.	*It's exactly five o'clock.*
Son las diez en punto.	*It's ten o'clock sharp.*

To indicate an approximate time, Spanish uses **a eso de** + the hour or the hour + **más o menos**.

Es a eso de la una.	*It's about one o'clock.*
Es la una, más o menos.	*It's one o'clock, more or less.*

To express a time *after* the hour, state the hour + **y** (English *and, plus*) + the number of minutes. This adds the minutes to the hour.

Es la una y veinte.	*It is 1:20.*
	(It is one o'clock plus twenty minutes.)
Son las cinco y diez.	*It is 5:10.*
	(It is five o'clock plus ten minutes.)
Son las dos y cinco.	*It is 2:05.*
	(It is two o'clock plus five minutes.)

When it is a *quarter* after the hour, Spanish uses **quince** (English *fifteen*) or **cuarto** (English *quarter*).

Son las tres y quince.	*It is 3:15.*
	(It is three o'clock plus fifteen minutes.)
Son las seis y cuarto.	*It is 6:15.*
	(It is six o'clock plus a quarter hour.)

When it is *half* past the hour, Spanish uses **treinta** (English *thirty*) or **media** (English *half*).

Son las nueve y treinta.	*It is 9:30.*
	(It is nine o'clock plus thirty minutes.)
Son las ocho y media.	*It is 8:30.*
	(It is eight o'clock plus a half hour.)

To express a time *before* the hour, state the hour + **menos** (English *minus*) + the number of minutes. This subtracts the minutes from the hour.

Son las tres menos diez.	*It is 2:50.*
	(It is three o'clock minus ten minutes.)
Son las once menos cinco.	*It is 10:55.*
	(It is eleven o'clock minus five minutes.)
Son las nueve menos cuarto.	*It is 8:45.*
	(It is nine o'clock minus a quarter hour.)
Son las doce menos quince.	*It is 11:45.*
	(It is twelve o'clock minus fifteen minutes.)

An alternate way to express time *before* the hour is to state the number of minutes + **para** + the hour. This expression, which closely follows English syntax, is not a full sentence.

Cinco para las tres.	*Five (minutes) to three (o'clock).*
Veinticinco para las dos.	*Twenty-five (minutes) to two (o'clock).*
Quince para las seis.	*Fifteen (minutes) to six (o'clock).*

To indicate that something is happening *at* a certain time, Spanish uses an expression with the preposition **a** (English *at*).

¿A qué hora?
{ *At what hour?*
  At what time?

A la una.   *At one o'clock.*
A las dos.   *At two o'clock.*
A las tres.   *At three o'clock.*

The expressions for *after* the hour (the hour + **y** + the number of minutes) and *before* the hour (the hour + **menos** + the number of minutes) remain the same after **a**.

A las cuatro y diez.   *At 4:10.*
A las cinco y cuarto.   *At 5:15.*
A las seis y cinco.   *At 6:05.*
A las siete y tres.   *At 7:03.*
A las ocho y media.   *At 8:30.*
A las nueve menos quince.   *At 8:45.*
A las diez menos veinte.   *At 9:40.*
A las once menos veinticinco.   *At 10:35.*
A la una menos diez.   *At 12:50.*

Exercise 4.4

A. *Complete the following sentences with the appropriate Spanish time. Include* **de la mañana**, **de la tarde**, *or* **de la noche**, *and always write numbers as words.*

1. El programa es _____ (*at 6 P.M.*).

2. _____ (*At 8 A.M.*) estoy en casa.

3. _____ (*At 1 P.M.*) estamos en la oficina.

4. _____ (*At 7:15 P.M.*) estamos en un restaurante.

5. _____ (*It is 10 P.M.*) ¿Dónde están los niños?

B. *Translate the following time expressions into Spanish. Include the appropriate expression to indicate morning, afternoon, or evening, and always write numbers as words.*

1. *It is 2:20 P.M.* _____

2. *It is 4:30 A.M.* _____

3. *It is 9:15 P.M.* _____

4. *It is 6:00 P.M. sharp.* _____

5. *It is 3:35 P.M.* _____

6. *It is 7:10 A.M.* _____

7. *At about 2:00 P.M.* _____

8. *At 9 A.M. exactly.* _____

 # Reading Comprehension

El restaurante

Es la una de la tarde y el restaurante español está lleno.° Es un restaurante popular y económico. Hay dieciocho mesas y cinco camareros excelentes. En cada mesa hay cuatro o cinco personas. El ambiente° es espectacular. La gente está alegre porque es un día de fiesta° y no hay trabajo. Hay dos pisos; en el primer piso, hay bebidas° y tapas;° en el segundo piso, hay bebidas también y el plato del día. En el menú, hay pollo, carne y mucho pescado.° En el especial del día, hay sopa, papas, vegetales, ensalada, postre,° y café o té. Todo° está sabroso hoy.

°lleno *full*
°el ambiente *the atmosphere*
°un día de fiesta *holiday*
°una bebida *a drink*
°tapas *small appetizers, Spanish style*

°pollo, carne, pescado *chicken, meat, fish*
°sopa, papas, vegetales, ensalada, postre
   soup, potatoes, vegetables, salad, dessert
°todo *everything*

Preguntas

After you have read the selection, answer the following questions in Spanish.

1. ¿Por qué está lleno el restaurante?

   _____

2. ¿Cuántos pisos hay?

   _____

3. ¿En que país está este restaurante?

   _____

4. ¿Cuántas personas hay en el restaurante?

   _____

Nombres

el agua	*the water*	el desayuno	*the breakfast*
el almuerzo	*the lunch*	el impuesto	*the tax*
el camarero	*the waiter*	el mantel	*the tablecloth*
la carta	*the menu*	el menú	*the menu*
la cena	*the supper*	el mozo	*the waiter*
el cheque	*the check*	el plato	*the plate*
la cocina	*the kitchen*	la propina	*the tip*
el comedor	*the dining room*	la servilleta	*the napkin*
la comida	*the meal*	la tarjeta de	*the credit card*
la cuchara	*the spoon*	crédito	
el cuchillo	*the knife*	el tenedor	*the fork*
la cuenta	*the check, the bill*	el vaso	*the glass*

Spanish nouns ending in **-a** that begin with a stressed **a** or **ha** are feminine, but they take the masculine article **el** in the singular and the feminine article **las** in the plural. **El agua** is the most common of these nouns: **el agua fría**, **las aguas frías**.

el águila, las águilas	*the eagle, the eagles*
el alma, las almas	*the soul, the souls*
el arma, las armas	*the weapon, the weapons*
el hacha, las hachas	*the axe, the axes*

Adjetivos

caliente	*warm, hot*	picante	*spicy*
delicioso	*delicious*	sabroso	*delicious*
fresco	*fresh*	sano	*healthy*
frío	*cold*	seco	*dry*
limpio	*clean*	sucio	*dirty*
lleno	*full*	vacío	*empty*

Expresiones de la hora en general (Expressions of time in general)

Es mediodía.	*It is midday. / It is noon.*
Es medianoche.	*It is midnight.*
Es temprano.	*It is early.*
Es tarde.	*It is late.*

Expresiones cuantitativas (Quantitative expressions)

una vez	*one time, once*
doble	*double*
dos veces	*two times, twice*
triple	*triple*
tres veces	*three times*
la mitad	*(a) half*

Exercise 4.5

Translate the following Spanish sentences into English.

1. Son las dos de la tarde y los estudiantes están en clase.

   _____

2. La cocina está sucia pero el baño está limpio.

   _____

3. ¿Dónde están los trece camareros del restaurante?

   _____

4. Hay clase los lunes y los jueves.

   _____

5. A las ocho y media, la sopa está fría y los platos están sucios.

   _____

6. ¿Cuántos vasos hay en la mesa a las siete de la mañana en la casa de Ricardo?

 Exercise 4.6

Answer the following questions aloud.

1. ¿Cuántas semanas hay en un año?

2. ¿Cuántos días hay en un año?

3. ¿Cuánto es ochenta y dos menos veintiséis?

4. ¿Cuánto es sesenta y siete y ciento treinta?

5. En la casa hay cuatro comedores y dos cocinas. ¿Es grande la casa o es pequeña?

6. ¿Por qué están Uds. contentos los miércoles en la primavera?

7. ¿Es deliciosa la comida italiana?

8. ¿A qué hora es el desayuno?

 Reading Comprehension

El oficio de la casa

Es el otoño y el aire está fresco. Son las once de la mañana y es un buen día para el oficio de la casa. Hoy, todo es un desorden.

En el dormitorio, la ropa está en el piso; las sábanas y las almohadas están sucias. La cocina es otro cuento. Hay polvo encima de la nevera y la estufa; las cucharas, los cuchillos, los tenedores y los platos están en el lavaplatos. Hay manchas feas en el piso de la cocina. El baño del primer piso está sucio pero por lo menos, es pequeño. ¿Dónde está mi esponja para la cocina y el baño? Siempre están en el gabinete. También, hay una escoba para la sala y una aspiradora para la alfombra roja del comedor.

¿Qué hora es? Son las dos ya. Es la hora del almuerzo. En la nevera, hay sopa sabrosa de pescado y vegetales, pollo y papas fritas, y hay una torta y helado para el postre. Es el veintiuno de septiembre, el día de mi cumpleaños, un día agradable para estar en la casa.

Nombres

la almohada	*the pillow*
la aspiradora	*the vacuum cleaner*
el cumpleaños	*the birthday*
un desorden	*a mess*
el dormitorio	*the bedroom*
la escoba	*the broom*
la esponja	*the sponge*
el helado	*the ice cream*
el lavaplatos	*the dishwasher*
la mancha	*the stain*
el oficio	*the work, the job*
el polvo	*the dust*
la ropa	*the clothes*
la sábana	*the sheet*

Expresiones

al principio	*at the beginning*
es otro cuento	*it's another story*
por lo menos	*at least*

Preguntas

After you have read the selection, answer the following questions in Spanish.

1. ¿Qué estación es?

   _____

2. ¿Qué hora es al principio del cuento?

   _____

3. ¿Dónde están las cucharas, los cuchillos y los tenedores?

   _____

4. ¿Está sucia o limpia la casa?

   _____

5. ¿Es hoy el día de cumpleaños?

   _____

5

Regular Verbs

All Spanish verbs belong to one of three classifications, called conjugations, depending on the ending of the infinitive.

All infinitives end in **-ar**, **-er**, or **-ir**.

Each conjugation has its own set of endings that are added to the stem of the verb.

verb stem + infinitive ending = infinitive

cant + **ar** = **cantar**
com + **er** = **comer**
viv + **ir** = **vivir**

Verbs are considered *regular* if there is *no change in the stem* when it is conjugated.

Uses of the Present Tense

The present tense is used to express the English simple present (*I sing*) and the English present progressive tense (*I am singing*).

Ella canta una canción triste. $\left\{ \begin{array}{l} \textit{She sings a sad song.} \\ \textit{She is singing a sad song.} \end{array} \right.$

Questions are formed by inverting the subject and the verb. In this case, the translation of the Spanish present tense includes the English helping verb *do*. Questions can also be indicated by rising intonation, without a change in word order.

¿Cantas tú los domingos?   *Do you sing on Sundays?*
¿Tú cantas los domingos?   *You sing on Sundays?*

The present tense can be used to express a future event if an adverbial expression of future time is included.

Ella canta con Ud. mañana.   *She'll sing with you tomorrow.*

To make a sentence negative, place **no** directly before the verb.

Yo canto en el baño.   *I sing in the bathroom.*
No canto en el tren.   *I don't sing in the train.*

-Ar Verbs

To conjugate a regular **-ar** verb in the present tense, drop the infinitive ending and add **-o**, **-as**, **-a**, **-amos**, **-áis**, **-an** to the stem.

cantar *to sing*

cantar	Infinitive
cant-	Stem
-ar	Ending

yo **canto**	*I sing*	nosotros **cantamos**	*we sing*
tú **cantas**	*you sing*	vosotros **cantáis**	*you* (pl.) *sing*
él **canta**	*he sings*	ellos **cantan**	*they sing*
ella **canta**	*she sings*	ellas **cantan**	*they* (f.) *sing*
Ud. **canta**	*you sing*	Uds. **cantan**	*you* (pl.) *sing*

A Word About Pronunciation

It is important to pronounce Spanish precisely and correctly. All words that end in the vowels **a**, **e**, **i**, **o**, **u**, or the consonants **n** or **s** have their natural stress on the second-to-last, or penultimate, syllable. Make sure you pronounce the verbs this way: **yo canto, tú cantas, él canta, nosotros cantamos, ellos cantan**. If a word carries an accent mark, you will stress that syllable: **vosotros cantáis**, for example.

Frequently Used *-ar* Verbs

bailar *to dance*

yo bailo	nosotros bailamos
tú bailas	vosotros bailáis
él baila	ellos bailan
ella baila	ellas bailan
Ud. baila	Uds. bailan

bajar *to go down, to descend*

yo bajo	nosotros bajamos
tú bajas	vosotros bajáis
él baja	ellos bajan
ella baja	ellas bajan
Ud. baja	Uds. bajan

caminar *to walk*

yo camino	nosotros caminamos
tú caminas	vosotros camináis
él camina	ellos caminan
ella camina	ellas caminan
Ud. camina	Uds. caminan

cocinar *to cook*

yo cocino	nosotros cocinamos
tú cocinas	vosotros cocináis
él cocina	ellos cocinan
ella cocina	ellas cocinan
Ud. cocina	Uds. cocinan

comprar *to buy*

yo compro	nosotros compramos
tú compras	vosotros compráis
él compra	ellos compran
ella compra	ellas compran
Ud. compra	Uds. compran

contestar *to answer*

yo contesto	nosotros contestamos
tú contestas	vosotros contestáis
él contesta	ellos contestan
ella contesta	ellas contestan
Ud. contesta	Uds. contestan

A Word About Verbs

The verbs above are presented with full conjugations so that you can practice and learn them one by one. These verbs form an essential base for all future studies. All three forms of both the third-person singular and the third-person plural conjugations have the same endings. From this point forward, only one pronoun will be used for each singular or plural third-person conjugation.

descansar *to rest*

yo descanso	nosotros descansamos
tú descansas	vosotros descansáis
ella descansa	ellas descansan

entrar (en) *to enter (in)*

yo entro	nosotros entramos
tú entras	vosotros entráis
Ud. entra	Uds. entran

escuchar *to listen to*

yo escucho	nosotros escuchamos
tú escuchas	vosotros escucháis
él escucha	ellos escuchan

estudiar *to study*

yo estudio	nosotros estudiamos
tú estudias	vosotros estudiáis
ella estudia	ellas estudian

Pronunciation Reminder
The Spanish **d** is pronounced like the **d** in English *dog* when it appears at the beginning of a breath group or follows an **l** or **n**: **donde, la falda, el conde**. In all other cases, the Spanish **d** is pronounced like the soft **th** sound in English *other*. Practice **estudiar** with a **th** sound.

hablar *to speak*

yo hablo	nosotros hablamos
tú hablas	vosotros habláis
Ud. habla	Uds. hablan

limpiar *to clean*

yo limpio	nosotros limpiamos
tú limpias	vosotros limpiáis
ella limpia	ellas limpian

llegar *to arrive*

yo llego	nosotros llegamos
tú llegas	vosotros llegáis
él llega	ellos llegan

Pronunciation Reminder
The **ll** in Spanish is pronounced like the **y** in English *beyond,* or the **s** in English *pleasure.*

mirar *to look at*

yo miro	nosotros miramos
tú miras	vosotros miráis
Ud. mira	Uds. miran

nadar *to swim*

yo nado	nosotros nadamos
tú nadas	vosotros nadáis
él nada	ellos nadan

practicar *to practice*

yo practico	nosotros practicamos
tú practicas	vosotros practicáis
ella practica	ellas practican

regresar *to return*

yo regreso	nosotros regresamos
tú regresas	vosotros regresáis
Ud. regresa	Uds. regresan

trabajar *to work*

yo trabajo	nosotros trabajamos
tú trabajas	vosotros trabajáis
él trabaja	ellos trabajan

Pronunciation Reminder
Stress the penultimate syllable of the conjugated verb: **trabajo**, **trabajas**, **trabaja**, **trabajamos**, **trabajan**.

viajar *to travel*

yo viajo	nosotros viajamos
tú viajas	vosotros viajáis
ella viaja	ellas viajan

Pronunciation Reminder
The **v** in Spanish is pronounced like the **b** in English *boy*.

The Preposition *a*

The preposition **a** means *to* in English.

When **a** is followed by the masculine **el** (meaning *the*), the words contract to **al** (meaning *to the*). This is one of only two contractions in Spanish.

Caminamos **al** hotel.	*We walk **to the** hotel.*
Yo camino **al** restaurante.	*I walk **to the** restaurant.*

A contraction is *not* formed when **a** is followed by the feminine **la** or by the plural articles **los** or **las**.

Caminamos a la tienda.	*We walk to the store.*
Ellos viajan a los estados del sur.	*They travel to the Southern states.*
Ella viaja a las ciudades grandes.	*She travels to the large cities.*

Exercise 5.1

Complete the following sentences with the correct form of the appropriate verb. Choose from the verbs listed below, but don't use any verb more than once.

bailar, bajar, caminar, cantar, cocinar, comprar, contestar, descansar, entrar, escuchar, estudiar, hablar, limpiar, llegar, mirar, nadar, practicar, regresar, trabajar, viajar

EXAMPLE   Las estudiantes __*caminan*__ a la escuela. Ellos __*regresan*__ en bus.

1. Ricardo _____ en la piscina.

2. Ella _____ mucho porque las lecciones son difíciles.

3. En la noche, si estamos cansados, _____ en la cama.

4. María siempre _____ a casa a las seis de la noche.

5. Los niños _____ y _____ en la fiesta.

6. En conversaciones, ¿quiénes _____ más, los hombres o las mujeres?

7. ¿Por qué _____ la mujer la blusa si es cara?

8. Enrique _____ en un restaurante. Él es cocinero y _____ en la cocina.

9. Los estudiantes _____ en el salón a las ocho de la mañana.

10. Yo _____ la música a las ocho de la noche los martes.

11. Ella _____ la televisión los domingos a las nueve.

12. Los músicos están contentos porque los estudiantes _____ mucho el piano.

13. Las dos amigas _____ el apartamento cuando está sucio.

14. Yo _____ en carro a la oficina. Trabajo en el piso cuarenta. A las cinco de la tarde _____ al primer piso.

15. Roberto _____ las preguntas en la clase.

Exercise 5.2

Answer the following questions aloud.

1. ¿Canta Ud. en la ducha?

2. ¿A qué hora escucha Ud. la música?

3. ¿Viajas tú mucho?

4. ¿Quiénes estudian más, los muchachos o las muchachas?

5. ¿Quién cocina bien en la familia de Ud.?

6. ¿Si estás en un baile, bailas mucho?

-Er Verbs

To conjugate a regular **-er** verb in the present tense, drop the infinitive ending and add **-o**, **-es**, **-e**, **-emos**, **-éis**, **-en** to the stem.

comer *to eat*	
comer	Infinitive
com-	Stem
-er	Ending

yo **como**	nosotros **comemos**
tú **comes**	vosotros **coméis**
él **come**	ellos **comen**
ella **come**	ellas **comen**
Ud. **come**	Uds. **comen**

Frequently Used *-er* Verbs

aprender *to learn*	
yo aprendo	nosotros aprendemos
tú aprendes	vosotros aprendéis
él aprende	ellos aprenden

beber *to drink*	
yo bebo	nosotros bebemos
tú bebes	vosotros bebéis
ella bebe	ellas beben

comprender *to understand*

yo comprendo	nosotros comprendemos
tú comprendes	vosotros comprendéis
Ud. comprende	Uds. comprenden

correr *to run*

yo corro	nosotros corremos
tú corres	vosotros corréis
él corre	ellos corren

leer *to read*

yo leo	nosotros leemos
tú lees	vosotros leéis
ella lee	ellas leen

meter *to put in*

yo meto	nosotros metemos
tú metes	vosotros metéis
Ud. mete	Uds. meten

prender *to turn on*

yo prendo	nosotros prendemos
tú prendes	vosotros prendéis
él prende	ellos prenden

romper *to break*

yo rompo	nosotros rompemos
tú rompes	vosotros rompéis
ella rompe	ellas rompen

vender *to sell*

yo vendo	nosotros vendemos
tú vendes	vosotros vendéis
Ud. vende	Uds. venden

 ## Exercise 5.3

Complete the following sentences with the correct form of the appropriate verb. Choose from the verbs listed below, but don't use any verb more than once.

aprender, beber, comer, comprender, correr, leer, romper, vender

1. Si ella camina, y él _____, ¿quién llega primero?

2. Mariana _____ ocho vasos de agua cada día.

3. Nosotros _____ en los restaurantes excelentes todos los jueves.

4. Las muchachas estudian bien las lecciones de violín y _____ mucho.

5. Yo _____ un libro cada semana. ¿Cuántos libros _____ Uds. cada año?

6. Somos buenos estudiantes y _____ las ideas difíciles.

7. El hombre y la mujer _____ el apartamento y compran una casa.

8. Los niños _____ los platos y los vasos.

-*Ir* Verbs

To conjugate a regular **-ir** verb in the present tense, drop the infinitive ending and add **-o**, **-es**, **-e**, **-imos**, **-ís**, **-en** to the stem.

vivir *to live*

vivir	Infinitive
viv-	Stem
-ir	Ending

yo **vivo**	nosotros **vivimos**
tú **vives**	vosotros **vivís**
el **vive**	ellos **viven**
ella **vive**	ellas **viven**
Ud. **vive**	Uds. **viven**

Frequently Used -*ir* Verbs

abrir *to open*

yo abro	nosotros abrimos
tú abres	vosotros abrís
él abre	ellos abren

compartir *to share*

yo comparto	nosotros compartimos
tú compartes	vosotros compartís
ella comparte	ellas comparten

decidir *to decide*

yo decido	nosotros decidimos
tú decides	vosotros decidís
Ud. decide	Uds. deciden

describir *to describe*

yo describo	nosotros describimos
tú describes	vosotros describís
él describe	ellos describen

discutir *to discuss*

yo discuto	nosotros discutimos
tú discutes	vosotros discutís
ella discute	ellas discuten

escribir *to write*

yo escribo	nosotros escribimos
tú escribes	vosotros escribís
Ud. escribe	Uds. escriben

recibir *to receive*

yo recibo	nosotros recibimos
tú recibes	vosotros recibís
él recibe	ellos reciben

subir *to go up, to ascend*

yo subo	nosotros subimos
tú subes	vosotros subís
ella sube	ellas suben

sufrir *to suffer*

yo sufro	nosotros sufrimos
tú sufres	vosotros sufrís
Ud. sufre	Uds. sufren

Exercise 5.4

Complete the following sentences with the correct form of the appropriate verb. Choose from the verbs listed below.

abrir, compartir, decidir, discutir, escribir, recibir, subir, vivir

1. Hay mucha comida en la mesa pero el muchacho no come mucho.

   Él _____ la porción con Elena.

2. ¿Por qué _____ Ud. la puerta si hay mucho ruido afuera?

3. Ella trabaja en la ciudad, pero _____ en el campo.

4. Hablamos y _____ las noticias del día. La conversación es interesante.

5. ¿_____ tú frases y preguntas con una pluma o usas una computadora?

6. ¿Por qué _____ Uds. estudiar el español?

7. Cecilia siempre _____ muchas cartas de la familia los lunes.

8. Todos los estudiantes _____ al noveno piso para la clase de química.

-Ar and *-er* Verbs with More than One Meaning

deber *should, ought to, must* (plus infinitive), *to owe*

yo debo	nosotros debemos
tú debes	vosotros debéis
él debe	ellos deben

Ella debe comer mejor.	*She ought to eat better.*
Él debe mucho dinero.	*He owes a lot of money.*

ganar *to win, to earn*

yo gano	nosotros ganamos
tú ganas	vosotros ganáis
ella gana	ellas ganan

Cecilia siempre gana el primer premio.	*Cecilia always wins first prize.*
Raúl gana quinientos dólares cada semana.	*Ralph earns 500 dollars each week.*

llevar *to carry, to wear*

yo llevo	nosotros llevamos
tú llevas	vosotros lleváis
Ud. lleva	Uds. llevan

Llevo una bolsa de plástico a la tienda.	*I carry a plastic bag to the store.*
Ella no lleva un abrigo hoy.	*She isn't wearing a coat today.*

pasar *to pass (by), to happen, to spend* (time)

yo paso	nosotros pasamos
tú pasas	vosotros pasáis
él pasa	ellos pasan

El tiempo pasa.	*Time passes.*
¿Qué pasa?	*What's happening?*
Ella pasa mucho tiempo con los turistas.	*She spends a lot of time with the tourists.*

tocar *to touch, to play* (an instrument)

yo toco	nosotros tocamos
tú tocas	vosotros tocáis
él toca	ellos tocan

El experto toca la mesa antigua.   *The expert touches the antique table.*
María toca bien el piano.   *Maria plays the piano well.*

tomar *to take, to have* (something to drink), *to have* (breakfast, lunch, dinner)

yo tomo	nosotros tomamos
tú tomas	vosotros tomáis
ella toma	ellas toman

Tomamos el tren al trabajo.   *We take the train to work.*
Tomo café negro cada mañana.   *I drink black coffee every morning.*
Ella toma el desayuno a las ocho.   *She has breakfast at eight o'clock.*
Toma el almuerzo a la una y   *She has lunch at one o'clock and*
    la cena a las siete.   *dinner at seven o'clock.*

Exercise 5.5

Complete the following sentences with the correct form of the appropriate verb. Choose from the verbs listed below; this time you can use the verbs more than once!

    deber, ganar, llevar, pasar, tocar, tomar

1. ¿A qué hora _____ Uds. el almuerzo?

2. La niña está enferma porque no _____ una chaqueta en el invierno.

3. Ella _____ caminar treinta minutos cada día.

4. Victoria _____ bien el violín.

5. Nosotros _____ compartir la torta de chocolate con Jorge y con Guillermo.

6. Yo _____ dos bolígrafos y tres lápices a la clase de matemáticas.

7. El profesor _____ mucho tiempo en las montañas en el verano.

8. El muchacho _____ la mesa antigua con las manos sucias.

9. Ricardo es maestro; no _____ mucho dinero, pero está feliz.

10. ¿_____ Ud. café con leche en la mañana?

Reading Comprehension

Una escuela en México

Es el año mil novecientos sesenta y tres. Es una época° de paz en los
Estados Unidos. En la ciudad donde vivimos este verano, hay paz también
pero no estoy segura° si hay paz en el resto de México.

   La ciudad es muy linda, con calles estrechas y casas del estilo español.
Hay unas plazas hermosas y muchas iglesias. Vivimos en las montañas y
estamos a tres millas de° la ciudad. Laura y yo caminamos treinta minutos
y llegamos a la escuela a las diez de la mañana; la madre de Laura pasa
el día en el campo porque estudia las civilizaciones antiguas. El padre
de Laura descansa en la casa hasta las diez. Después,° él baja a la ciudad
y pasa la mañana en un restaurante bonito donde él toma uno o dos cafés
más; lee un periódico y habla con la gente. Ellos hablan bien el español,
pero Laura y yo no hablamos mucho; estudiamos en la escuela secundaria
porque necesitamos practicar más.

   Laura y yo decidimos tomar un curso de historia de México, una clase
de baile, una clase donde los estudiantes aprenden canciones mexicanas
y aprenden a tocar la guitarra. Guanajuato está ubicada° en las montañas
y la clase de baile es difícil porque es trabajoso° respirar° en las montañas.
Las clases de música son fantásticas porque hablamos y practicamos la
pronunciación.

   En la noche, regresamos a la casa y discutimos las experiencias del día.
La madre cocina bien y comemos una comida saludable.° Laura y yo
lavamos° los platos y el padre escucha la conversación y descansa.

°la época *period of time*
°estar seguro(a) *to be sure*
°estar a tres millas de *to be three miles from*
°después *afterward*
°estar ubicado(a) *to be located*

°trabajoso *difficult*
°respirar *to breathe*
°saludable *healthy, healthful*
°lavar *to wash*

Preguntas

After you have read the selection, answer the following questions in Spanish.

1. ¿Cómo es Guanajuato?

_____

2. ¿Qué estación del año es?

_____

3. ¿Cómo pasa el día el padre de ella?

_____

4. ¿Qué estudian Laura y la amiga de ella?

_____

5. En la noche, ¿de qué hablan?

_____

6

Irregular Verbs

Spanish verbs are considered *irregular* if there is a *change in the stem* when they are conjugated.

Each verb conjugation has its own set of endings that are added to the verb stem.

The **nosotros** and **vosotros** forms are *unaffected by the stem change* in the present tense.

-Ar Verbs

Irregular verbs that end in **-ar** have two possible changes in their stem. The endings are the same as those you have learned for the regular verbs: add **-o**, **-as**, **-a**, **-amos**, **-áis**, **-an** to the stem.

Stem Change e > ie

cerrar *to close*

yo c**ie**rro	nosotros cerramos
tú c**ie**rras	vosotros cerráis
él c**ie**rra	ellos c**ie**rran

empezar *to begin*

yo emp**ie**zo	nosotros empezamos
tú emp**ie**zas	vosotros empezáis
ella emp**ie**za	ellas emp**ie**zan

pensar *to think*

yo p**ie**nso	nosotros pensamos
tú p**ie**nsas	vosotros pensáis
Ud. p**ie**nsa	Uds. p**ie**nsan

A Word About Irregular Verbs
It is a good idea to learn these verbs one by one. Make sure you read them aloud. Practice as much as you can.

Stem Change o > ue

almorzar *to lunch*

yo alm**ue**rzo	nosotros almorzamos
tú alm**ue**rzas	vosotros almorzáis
él alm**ue**rza	ellos alm**ue**rzan

encontrar *to find*

yo enc**ue**ntro	nosotros encontramos
tú enc**ue**ntras	vosotros encontráis
ella enc**ue**ntra	ellas enc**ue**ntran

recordar *to remember*

yo rec**ue**rdo	nosotros recordamos
tú rec**ue**rdas	vosotros recordáis
ella rec**ue**rda	ellas rec**ue**rdan

jugar *to play, to play* (a sport)

yo j**ue**go	nosotros jugamos
tú j**ue**gas	vosotros jugáis
Ud. j**ue**ga	Uds. j**ue**gan

NOTE: The stem change for **jugar** is **u > ue**.

Exercise 6.1

Complete the following sentences with the correct form of the appropriate verb. Choose from the verbs listed below; use each verb only once.

almorzar, cerrar, empezar, jugar, pensar, recordar

1. Yo _____ la ventana del salón porque hay mucho ruido afuera.

2. ¿Qué _____ Ud. de la situación del mundo?

3. Los muchachos y las muchachas _____ al béisbol todas las tardes a las cinco.

4. Al mediodía, nosotros _____ en un restaurante económico con los colegas del trabajo.

5. ¿_____ tú toda la letra de las canciones?

6. La maestra _____ la clase a las seis en punto.

-Er Verbs

Irregular verbs that end in **-er** have two possible changes in their stem. The endings are the same as those you have learned for the regular verbs: add **-o**, **-es**, **-e**, **-emos**, **-éis**, **-en** to the stem.

Stem Change e > ie

entender *to understand*	
yo ent**ie**ndo	nosotros entendemos
tú ent**ie**ndes	vosotros entendéis
ella ent**ie**nde	ellas ent**ie**nden

perder *to lose*	
yo p**ie**rdo	nosotros perdemos
tú p**ie**rdes	vosotros perdéis
Ud. p**ie**rde	Uds. p**ie**rden

querer *to want*	
yo qu**ie**ro	nosotros queremos
tú qu**ie**res	vosotros queréis
él qu**ie**re	ellos qu**ie**ren

tener *to have*	
yo **tengo**	nosotros tenemos
tú t**ie**nes	vosotros tenéis
ella t**ie**ne	ellas t**ie**nen

NOTE: **Tener** also has an irregular **yo** form.

Stem Change o > ue

devolver *to return* (something), *to give back*	
yo dev**ue**lvo	nosotros devolvemos
tú dev**ue**lves	vosotros devolvéis
ella dev**ue**lve	ellas dev**ue**lven

poder *to be able, can, may*	
yo p**ue**do	nosotros podemos
tú p**ue**des	vosotros podéis
él p**ue**de	ellos p**ue**den

volver *to return*	
yo v**ue**lvo	nosotros volvemos
tú v**ue**lves	vosotros volvéis
Ud. v**ue**lve	Uds. v**ue**lven

Verbs Irregular in the *yo* Form Only

hacer *to do, to make*	
yo **hago**	nosotros hacemos
tú haces	vosotros hacéis
él hace	ellos hacen

poner *to put*	
yo **pongo**	nosotros ponemos
tú pones	vosotros ponéis
ella pone	ellas ponen

saber *to know* (a fact), *to know how*		**ver** *to see*	
yo **sé**	nosotros sabemos	yo **veo**	nosotros vemos
tú sabes	vosotros sabéis	tú ves	vosotros veis
Ud. sabe	Uds. saben	él ve	ellos ven

Sentence Formation

You have learned to form sentences and questions with one verb.

| Ella tiene un gato. | *She has a cat.* |
| ¿Tiene ella un perro? | *Does she have a dog?* |

The word order in English and Spanish is basically the same. This allows you to put two verbs together in a similar sequence. Note that the negative word **no** comes directly before the first verb.

Yo no quiero cantar.	*I don't want to sing.*
Ellos quieren leer un libro.	*They want to read a book.*
Podemos bailar bien.	*We are able to dance well.*
Sí, sabemos cantar bien también.	*Yes, we know how to sing well also.*

You can even string three verbs together in one sentence!

| Susana quiere poder hablar español. | *Susan wants to be able to speak Spanish.* |
| Él quiere poder correr en el maratón. | *He wants to be able to run in the marathon.* |

Exercise 6.2

Complete the following sentences with the correct verb form, using the infinitive provided.

1. El muchacho _____ nadar y las amigas de

   él _____ bailar. (saber)

2. No sabemos donde estamos porque siempre _____ las direcciones. (perder)

3. ¿Qué _____ Ud. durante la primavera? (hacer)

4. Yo _____ una pluma y él _____ un libro

   difícil. Nosotros _____ mucha tarea para la clase. (tener)

5. El gerente _____ a la casa a las ocho y media los lunes.
   (volver)

6. Los estudiantes _____ la pregunta. (entender)

7. Yo _____ viajar porque tengo mucho dinero. (poder)

8. Nosotros _____ los pájaros en el parque. (ver)

9. Federico _____ los libros a la biblioteca. (devolver)

10. Yo _____ los platos en la mesa. (poner)

11. La turista _____ estar en los Estados Unidos el miércoles.
    (querer)

Exercise 6.3

Translate the following English sentences into Spanish.

1. *I know where there is an inexpensive restaurant on Fifth Avenue.*

   _____

2. *Carlos doesn't want to make a date with the dentist.*

   _____

3. *We don't want to clean the apartment today.*

   _____

4. *I see a gray cat and a blue bird.*

   _____

5. *She understands the ideas, but she doesn't want to talk.*

   _____

6. *Who is able to sing and dance at the party?*

   _____

7. *I do the homework at eight o'clock on Mondays.*

   _____

8. *We want to return to work on Tuesday.*

   _____

-Ir Verbs

Irregular verbs that end in **-ir** have three possible changes in their stem. The endings are the same as those you have learned for the regular verbs: add **-o**, **-es**, **-e**, **-imos**, **-ís**, **-en** to the stem.

Stem Change e > ie

mentir *to lie*

yo m**ie**nto	nosotros mentimos
tú m**ie**ntes	vosotros mentís
él m**ie**nte	ellos m**ie**nten

preferir *to prefer*

yo pref**ie**ro	nosotros preferimos
tú pref**ie**res	vosotros preferís
ella pref**ie**re	ellas pref**ie**ren

venir *to come*

yo **vengo**	nosotros venimos
tú v**ie**nes	vosotros venís
Ud. v**ie**ne	Uds. v**ie**nen

NOTE: **Venir** also has an irregular **yo** form.

Stem Change e > i

pedir *to ask for, to request*

yo pido	nosotros pedimos
tú pides	vosotros pedís
Ud. pide	Uds. piden

repetir *to repeat*

yo repito	nosotros repetimos
tú repites	vosotros repetís
él repite	ellos repiten

seguir *to follow, to continue*

yo sigo	nosotros seguimos
tú sigues	vosotros seguís
ella sigue	ellas siguen

servir *to serve*

yo sirvo	nosotros servimos
tú sirves	vosotros servís
Ud. sirve	Uds. sirven

sonreír *to smile*

yo sonrío	nosotros sonreímos
tú sonríes	vosotros sonreís
él sonríe	ellos sonríen

Stem Change o > ue

dormir *to sleep*

yo d**ue**rmo	nosotros dormimos
tú d**ue**rmes	vosotros dormís
él d**ue**rme	ellos d**ue**rmen

Stem Change in the *yo* Form Only

oír *to hear*

yo o**ig**o	nosotros oímos
tú oyes	vosotros oís
ella oye	ellas oyen

NOTE: **Oyes**, **oye**, and **oyen** reflect a spelling change (that clarifies the pronunciation) rather than a stem change.

salir *to leave, to exit, to go out*

yo sal**g**o	nosotros salimos
tú sales	vosotros salís
Ud. sale	Uds. salen

 # Exercise 6.4

Complete the following sentences with the correct form of the appropriate verb. Choose from the verbs listed below; use each verb only once.

dormir, mentir, oír, preferir, repetir, salir, seguir, servir, venir

1. ¿Por qué _____ Ud. la pregunta si ellas saben la respuesta?

2. La niña _____ mucho y sus padres están enojados con ella.

3. La fiesta es horrible; hay mucho ruido y humo. Ana quiere

   _____ .

4. Nosotros _____ ocho horas cada noche y podemos trabajar bien durante el día.

5. Ella no sabe donde vive María, pero ella tiene un mapa y puede

   _____ las direcciones a la casa.

6. Ellos _____ a Nueva York a ver los museos.

7. ¿Pueden Uds. _____ bien las voces de los estudiantes?

8. ¿Qué _____ Ud. hacer, jugar al tenis o nadar?

9. A las nueve de la mañana, la cafetería abre y los camareros

_____ el desayuno.

Exercise 6.5

Respond aloud to the following questions.

1. ¿A qué hora almuerza Ud.? ¿Come Ud. mucho?

2. ¿Duerme Ud. bien? ¿Tiene Ud. sueños dulces?

3. ¿Tienes las llaves del edificio donde trabajas?

4. ¿Cuál prefiere Ud. beber, el vino blanco o el vino tinto?

5. ¿Qué hace Ud. el fin de semana?

6. ¿Quiénes sonríen más, los hombres, las mujeres, o los niños?

7. ¿Sabe Ud. jugar al tenis?

8. ¿Dónde pones los platos, los tenedores, las cucharas y los cuchillos?

Exercise 6.6

Complete the following sentences with the correct form of the appropriate verb. Choose from the verbs listed below.

almorzar, cerrar, dormir, empezar, encontrar, entender,
estar, hacer, hay, jugar, poder, poner, preferir, recordar,
saber, salir, seguir, ser, servir, tener, venir, ver, volver

1. A las ocho de la mañana, los empleados abren la puerta de la oficina

y entran. A las ocho de la noche, ellos _____ la puerta

y _____.

2. Los muchachos estudian todo el día en la escuela. A las tres de la tarde,

si hace sol, ellos _____ al béisbol.

3. A mediodía, nosotros _____ en un restaurante económico
con los amigos del trabajo.

4. La maestra _____ las lecciones a las seis.

5. ¿Quién _____ la letra de las canciones?

6. Ella _____ la pregunta pero no _____
la respuesta correcta.

7. Yo toco el piano pero _____ tocar la guitarra.

8. Yo _____ mil dólares en el banco y cien dólares en la mano.

9. ¿Por qué quiere él _____ presidente?

10. Nosotros _____ el camino a la casa de Sara.

11. Los dos niños _____ nueve horas cada noche.

12. No puedo _____ un hotel barato en la ciudad.

13. Laura _____ a la oficina porque quiere hablar con el jefe.

14. Nosotros _____ cansados porque tenemos que trabajar.

15. ¿_____ Ud. preparar una torta deliciosa para la fiesta?

16. En el campo, yo _____ los árboles y los pájaros;

en la ciudad, yo _____ los edificios altos.

17. ¿Por qué no _____ manzanas rojas en el supermercado?

18. El viaje es largo y queremos _____ a casa.

19. Yo _____ las cucharas, los cuchillos y los tenedores

en la mesa y Teresa _____ la comida.

20. Ellos prefieren _____ la tarea a las diez de la noche;

yo _____ la tarea a las siete de la mañana.

Exercise 6.7

Translate the following Spanish sentences into English.

1. ¿En qué piso viven los amigos de Pablo? ¿Son ellos de Perú?
¿Hablan bien el inglés?

_____

_____

2. ¿De qué habla Ud.? ¿Con quién hablan Uds.?

_____

3. Sebastián sale de la casa de Carla a las ocho de la mañana.
   Llega a la oficina a las nueve. Él trabaja ocho horas. ¿A qué hora
   puede llegar a la casa de Carla?

   _____

   _____

4. ¿Por qué hay un árbol en la casa?

   _____

5. Ser o no ser.

   _____

6. Al mediodía, entramos en el edificio y subimos al tercer piso;
   a las tres de la tarde, bajamos al primer piso y salimos.

   _____

   _____

 # Reading Comprehension

El tren

El tren llega a tiempo como siempre. Llega a las cuatro y veintiséis.
Subo al tren con algunas personas y viajo a la ciudad.

Cerca de mí, una mujer duerme. Ella descansa completamente.
Pienso que tiene sueños dulces. Un hombre lee un periódico. Las noticias
son interesantes hoy; él lee con mucho interés. ¿Qué lee? ¿Está interesado
en los deportes o los negocios o los eventos internacionales? Es imposible
saber. Un niño grita y después sonríe. Un hombre a mi lado escribe
cartas de amor. Otras personas hablan por teléfono. Hablan y hablan.
Ellos tienen muchos amigos. Trato de escuchar las conversaciones.
A veces, quiero hablar con alguien pero prefiero viajar sola con mis libros
y mis cuadernos.

El tren llega a la ciudad a las cinco y cuatro. Camino con la muchedumbre hacia las salidas. La estación del tren es grande y hermosa.
Hay restaurantes en el sótano y farmacias y tiendas en el primer piso.
Salgo de la estación. No hay mucho sol, menos mal. La gente pasa.
El tiempo pasa. ¿Qué hago ahora, con muchas posibilidades? (Prefiero
el campo donde hay menos decisiones.) ¿Qué hago yo después de mi viaje
en el tren? Hay teatro y cine, conciertos y museos. Puedo comer en un

buen restaurante o escuchar música gratis en el parque. ¿En qué dirección camino? No, es mejor volver al tren; en el tren todo es seguro. Siempre sale y llega a su destino. El próximo tren sale precisamente a las cinco y veinte. Afortunadamente, hay tiempo.

Es la hora pico. Corro con la muchedumbre al tren. Subimos. Tomamos asiento. Abrimos los libros, las revistas, los periódicos y descansamos, contentos de estar de nuevo en el tren.

Verbos (Verbs)

estar seguro	*to be sure*
hablar por teléfono	*to speak by (on the) phone*
llegar a tiempo	*to arrive on time*
pensar en	*to think about*
ser imposible	*to be impossible*
ser seguro	*to be safe*
subir al tren	*to get on the train*
tomar asiento	*to take a seat*

Nombres

la hora pico	*the rush hour*
la muchedumbre	*the crowd*
la salida	*the exit*
el sótano	*the basement*
el teatro	*the theater*

Preposiciones (Prepositions)

cerca de mí	*near me*
a mi lado	*at my side*

Adverbios

a veces	*at times*
afortunadamente	*fortunately*
completamente	*completely*
de nuevo	*again*
después de + *infinitive*	*after (doing something)*
gratis	*free* (in cost)
hacia	*toward*
menos mal	*luckily*
mejor	*better*

Preguntas

After you have read the selection, answer the following questions in Spanish.

1. ¿Es largo el viaje a la ciudad?

   _____

2. ¿Cómo son los pasajeros que viajan en el tren?

   _____

3. ¿Sabe Ud. si el personaje principal es hombre o mujer? ¿Cómo sabe Ud.?

   _____

4. Después de salir de la estación, ¿en qué piensa el personaje?

   _____

5. ¿Qué decide hacer?

   _____

6. ¿Pasa el personaje mucho tiempo en la ciudad?

   _____

7. ¿Por qué vuelve al tren?

   _____

7

Ir and the Future

Ir (to go)

The conjugation of **ir** (English *to go*) is irregular in the present tense.

yo **voy**	*I am going, I go*	nosotros **vamos**	*we are going, we go*
tú **vas**	*you are going, you go*	vosotros **vais**	*you are going, you go*
él **va**	*he is going, he goes*	ellos **van**	*they are going, they go*
ella **va**	*she is going, she goes*	ellas **van**	*they are going, they go*
Ud. **va**	*you are going, you go*	Uds. **van**	*you are going, you go*

Vamos a la ciudad.	*We are going to the city.*
¿Vas tú a la playa los domingos?	*Do you go to the beach on Sundays?*
Ellas van a la tienda.	*They are going to the store.*
¿Adónde van ellos?	*(To) where are they going?*
Voy al banco los miércoles.	*I go to the bank on Wednesdays.*
¿Quieres ir con nosotros?	*Do you want to go with us?*
Quiero ir al supermercado.	*I want to go to the supermarket.*

A Word About the Verb *ir*
Whether this verb is translated *to go* or *to be going* depends on the context of the sentence.

Exercise 7.1

Complete the following sentences with the correct form of **ir**.

1. El hombre y la mujer _____ al trabajo a las siete de la mañana.

2. Nosotros _____ al cine los sábados.

3. ¿Quiere Ud. _____ con nosotros?

4. La estudiante _____ a la escuela los martes.

5. Los niños quieren _____ al circo porque quieren ver los elefantes.

6. Yo _____ al gimnasio porque quiero hacer ejercicio.

7. ¿_____ tú al campo los fines de semana?

8. Ernesto no quiere _____ a España pero Mariana sí quiere

_____ .

The Future with the Verb *ir*

Ir + **a** + an infinitive is used to express future time. The English equivalent is *to be going to (do something).*

> Ellos **van a cantar** esta noche.   *They are going to sing tonight.*
> **Vamos a decidir** más tarde.   *We are going to decide later.*

To form a question using this construction, place the subject of the sentence either directly after the conjugated form of **ir** or after the infinitive.

> ¿**Van** ellos **a cantar** esta noche?   *Are they going to sing tonight?*
> ¿**Van a cantar** ellos esta noche?   *Are they going to sing tonight?*
> ¿A qué hora **va a llegar** el tren?   *At what hour is the train going to arrive?*

Often the subject pronoun is not necessary.

> ¿**Vas a viajar** a España?   *Are you going to travel to Spain?*
> **Vamos a salir** ahora.   *We are going to leave now.*

 ## Key Vocabulary

The following frequently used **-ar** verbs will help enhance your ability to communicate. As you learn them, remember to practice them aloud.

aceptar	*to accept*	cruzar	*to cross*
apagar	*to turn off*	dibujar	*to draw*
arreglar	*to arrange, to fix*	disfrutar	*to enjoy*
cambiar	*to change*	doblar	*to turn, to fold*
celebrar	*to celebrate*	explicar	*to explain*

firmar	to sign	pintar	to paint
gozar	to enjoy	preparar	to prepare
llorar	to cry	repasar	to review
manejar	to drive	terminar	to finish
marcar	to dial, to mark	tirar	to throw
necesitar	to need	usar	to use
parar	to stop	viajar	to travel

Exercise 7.2

*Complete the following sentences with the appropriate form of the Spanish verb or expression. Remember that the Spanish preposition **a** follows the verb **ir**.*

EXAMPLES   Elena __va a viajar__ (*to be going to travel*) a Portugal.

Ella ___necesita___ (*to need*) aprender el portugués.

1. ¿Dónde _____ (*to be going to be*) Marí y Sara
   a las diez esta noche?

2. Samuel _____ (*to be going to sign*) un documento
   mañana.

3. Mañana, yo _____ (*to be going to finish*) la tarea.

4. ¿Quién _____ (*to be going to buy*) los tiquetes
   para el viaje?

5. Nosotros _____ (*to be going to celebrate*)
   el cumpleaños de Ana el sábado.

6. Él no _____ (*to be going to accept*) la invitación.

7. Nosotros _____ (*to be going to enjoy*) el verano
   este año porque nosotros _____ (*to go*) a Chile.

8. Esta noche yo _____ (*to be going to cook*).
   No quiero _____ (*to go*) a un restaurante.

9. ¿Quién _____ (*to be going to turn off*) las luces?

10. ¿Cómo _____ (*to be going to spend*) Uds. el día
    de acción de gracias?

Idioms

Idioms are expressions that do not translate directly from one language to another. Instead of saying, for example, how old someone or something *is*, Spanish uses the verb **tener**, *to have*.

Yo tengo treinta años.   *I am thirty years old.* (literally,
                                                          I have thirty years.)

Idioms with the Verb *tener*

Indeed, there are many Spanish idioms that use the verb **tener**.

tener ____ años	*to be ____ years old*
tener calor	*to be hot*
tener celos	*to be jealous*
tener cuidado	*to be careful*
tener la culpa	*to be at fault*
tener dolor de (cabeza, estómago, etc.)	*to have a (head)ache, (stomach)ache, etc.*
tener envidia	*to be envious*
tener éxito	*to be successful, to have success*
tener frío	*to be cold*
tener ganas de	*to want, to desire*
tener hambre	*to be hungry*
tener la palabra	*to have the floor*
tener lugar	*to take place*
tener miedo de	*to be afraid of*
tener prisa	*to be in a hurry*
tener que ver con	*to have to do with*
tener rabia	*to be in a rage, to be very angry*
tener razón	*to be right*
tener sed	*to be thirsty*
tener sueño	*to be sleepy*
tener suerte	*to be lucky, to have luck*
tener vergüenza	*to be ashamed*

Exercise 7.3

Answer the following questions aloud in Spanish.

1. ¿Cuántos años tienes?

2. ¿Tiene Ud. frío en el invierno donde vive?

3. ¿Es necesario tener cuidado en las calles de una ciudad grande?

4. ¿Tiene Ud. dolor de cabeza ahora?

5. ¿En qué profesión tiene Ud. éxito?

6. ¿Tiene Ud. ganas de tomar una cerveza fría o prefiere el vino blanco?

7. ¿A qué hora tiene Ud. hambre?

8. ¿Tiene Ud. miedo del agua? ¿Sabe Ud. nadar?

Exercise 7.4

*Complete the following sentences with the appropriate idiom of **tener** in the correct form. Use each idiom no more than once.*

1. Si Uds. _____, ¿comen mucho?

2. Si una persona _____, bebe agua.

3. Siempre gano los premios; yo _____, ¿es verdad?

4. Los muchachos quieren mirar televisión hasta las diez, pero los padres _____ y quieren dormir.

5. En el invierno, nosotros _____ en las montañas. Vamos de vacaciones al Caribe y si _____ nadamos en el océano.

6. ¿Quién quiere hablar? Estamos listos para escuchar las nuevas ideas. Irene _____.

7. ¿_____ tú _____ de hablar delante de mucha gente en una conferencia grande?

8. Yo _____. ¡Quiero salir ahora!

9. Él no tiene mucho dinero pero _____ en la vida.

10. Janet _____ de cabeza y no puede ir al trabajo.

11. ¿Es importante _____ en situaciones peligrosas?

12. Irene tiene una buena respuesta. Ramón tiene una respuesta excelente. No sabemos quien _____ .

13. ¿Dónde _____ la fiesta?

14. Nosotros _____ de ir a la playa el sábado.

15. ¿Cuántos _____ el hermano de Rafael?

16. Es una respuesta excelente, pero ¿qué _____ la pregunta?

Other Idioms

acabar de + infinitive *to have just (done something)*

yo acabo de llegar	*I have just arrived*
tú acabas de cantar	*you have just sung*
él acaba de salir	*he has just left*
nosotros acabamos de decidir	*we have just decided*
vosotros acabáis de pagar	*you have just paid*
ellos acaban de volver	*they have just returned*

NOTE: The present tense of **acabar de** + infinitive is translated in English as the present perfect tense + *just*.

dejar de + infinitive *to stop (doing something)*

yo dejo de fumar	*I stop smoking*
tú dejas de comer	*you stop eating*
ella deja de bailar	*she stops dancing*
nosotros dejamos de trabajar	*we stop working*
vosotros dejáis de beber	*you stop drinking*
ellas dejan de estudiar	*they stop studying*

tener que + infinitive *to have to (do something)*

yo tengo que ir	*I have to go*
tú tienes que cocinar	*you have to cook*
él tiene que hablar	*he has to speak*
nosotros tenemos que caminar	*we have to walk*
vosotros tenéis que escuchar	*you have to listen*
ellos tienen que descansar	*they have to rest*

tratar de + infinitive *to try to (do something)*

yo trato de leer	*I try to read*
tú tratas de limpiar	*you try to clean*
Ud. trata de contestar	*you try to answer*
nosotros tratamos de escribir	*we try to write*
vosotros tratáis de correr	*you try to run*
Uds. tratan de nadar	*you try to swim*

volver a + infinitive *to do (something) again*

yo vuelvo a leer	*I read again*
tú vuelves a cocinar	*you cook again*
Ud. vuelve a mentir	*you lie again*
nosotros volvemos a conversar	*we speak again*
vosotros volvéis a cantar	*you sing again*
Uds. vuelven a ganar	*you win again*

 ## Exercise 7.5

Complete the following letter with the appropriate idiomatic expression. Choose from the expressions listed below.

acabar de, dejar de, tener que, tratar de

Queridos amigos,

Yo _____ (1.) llegar a Lisboa en Portugal. La ciudad

es bonita pero no entiendo el portugués. Yo _____ (2.)

aprender a hablar el idioma si quiero gozar del país. Voy a

_____ (3.) empezar las clases mañana. No debo

_____ (4.) viajar porque aprendo mucho del país y

de la gente.

Hasta pronto.

Useful Words: *que* and *para*

The Relative Pronoun *que*

Spanish **que** (English *that, which,* or *who*) is the most common relative pronoun in everyday speech. **Que** can refer to persons or things, either singular or plural.

El programa que miro los viernes es interesante.	*The program that I watch on Fridays is interesting.*
Los platos, que acabo de comprar, son verdes.	*The plates, which I have just bought, are green.*
Ella tiene un amigo que vive en el campo.	*She has a friend who lives in the countryside.*

The relative pronoun **que** can also be used after prepositions. As the object of a preposition, **que** refers to a thing or things only. It does not refer to a person or persons.

El libro en que escribimos es viejo.	*The book in which we write is old.*
No entiendo el tema de que habla.	*I don't understand the theme of which you speak.*
Ella tiene un bastón con que caminar.	*She has a cane with which to walk.*

The Conjunction *que*

One of the uses of conjunctions is to join two sentences into a single sentence. Spanish **que** (English *that*) used as a conjunction may join a main clause and a dependent (or subordinate) clause to form a sentence or question.

El maestro sabe que los estudiantes entienden.	*The teacher knows that the students understand.*
Él piensa que la lección es fácil.	*He thinks that the lesson is easy.*
Veo que el tren viene.	*I see that the train is coming.*

A Word About *que*

The English word *that*, whether it is used as a relative pronoun or as a conjunction, is often omitted. For example, it is correct in English to say either *the program I see* or *the program **that** I see*, and to say *I think the lesson is easy* or *I think **that** the lesson is easy.* In Spanish, **que** is never omitted.

The Preposition *para*

Para has two meanings in English.

- *for*

José tiene dos libros para la clase.	*Joe has two books for the class.*
La pregunta es para María.	*The question is for María.*
Mañana, el barco sale para Cuba.	*Tomorrow the boat sails for Cuba.*
Los guantes son para el invierno.	*The gloves are for the winter.*
¿Hay una carta para nosotros?	*Is there a letter for us?*
Ella va a estudiar para el examen.	*She is going to study for the exam.*

- *in order to*

Comemos para vivir.	*We eat in order to live.*
Ella baila para estar alegre.	*She dances in order to be happy.*
Él estudia para ser doctor.	*He studies in order to be a doctor.*
Corro para llegar a tiempo.	*I run in order to arrive on time.*
Sara hace ejercicios para cantar.	*Sarah does exercises in order to sing.*

 Exercise 7.6

Complete the following sentences by translating the English phrase in parentheses.

1. Ella viene a la clase _____ (*in order to learn*).

2. Yo sé _____ (*that she is here*).

3. El hombre _____ (*who lives here*) es guapo.

4. ¿Piensa Ud. _____ (*that I should go*)?

5. Él practica _____ (*in order to play*) el piano.

6. ¿_____ (*for whom*) es la pregunta?

7. Las llaves _____ (*that I need*) están en el carro.

8. ¿Tiene Ud. una habitación _____ (*for two persons*)?

Key Vocabulary

These words will help enhance your ability to communicate. As you learn them, remember to practice them aloud.

Las partes del cuerpo (Parts of the Body)

la articulación	*the joint*	la mejilla	*the cheek*
la barba	*the beard*	la muñeca	*the wrist*
la barbilla	*the chin*	el muslo	*the thigh*
la boca	*the mouth*	las nalgas	*the buttocks*
el brazo	*the arm*	la nariz	*the nose*
el cabello	*the hair*	la nuca	*the nape*
la cabeza	*the head*	el oído	*the inner ear*
la cadera	*the hip*	el ojo	*the eye*
la cara	*the face*	la oreja	*the ear*
la ceja	*the eyebrow*	el párpado	*the eyelid*
la cintura	*the waist*	el pecho	*the chest*
el codo	*the elbow*	el pelo	*the hair*
la columna	*the spine*	la pestaña	*the eyelash*
el cuello	*the neck*	el pie	*the foot*
el dedo	*the finger*	la piel	*the skin*
el dedo del pie	*the toe*	la pierna	*the leg*
el diente	*the tooth*	el pulgar	*the thumb*
las encías	*the gums*	la quijada	*the jaw*
la espalda	*the back*	la rodilla	*the knee*
la frente	*the forehead*	los senos	*the breasts*
la garganta	*the throat*	el talón	*the heel*
el hombro	*the shoulder*	el tobillo	*the ankle*
la lengua	*the tongue*	la uña	*the nail*
la mano	*the hand*		

Dentro del cuerpo (Inside the body)

las amígdalas	*the tonsils*	el hueso	*the bone*
la arteria	*the artery*	el músculo	*the muscle*
el cerebro	*the brain*	el pulmón	*the lung*
el corazón	*the heart*	el riñón	*the kidney*
las costillas	*the ribs*	la sangre	*the blood*
el estómago	*the stomach*	el tendón	*the tendon*
el hígado	*the liver*	las venas	*the veins*

In Spanish, the definite articles **el**, **la**, **los**, and **las** are used more frequently than the possessive adjective, especially with parts of the body. In English we would use a possessive adjective (*my, your, his, her, our, their*).

Ella tiene un problema en **el pie**.	*She has a problem with **her foot**.*
Él tiene dolor d**el tobillo** y no puede caminar bien.	*He has a pain in **his toe** and can't walk well.*
El niño tiene **las manos** sucias.	*The boy has dirty hands. (**His hands** are dirty.)*
Tenemos veinte dedos; diez en **las manos** y diez en **los pies**.	*We have twenty digits: ten on **our hands** and ten on **our feet**.*

La familia

As you learn the names for family members, you will see that the plural takes the masculine form when it includes more than one male or a male and female pair. For example, **el padre** means *the father*; **la madre** means *the mother*. The *father* and *mother* together are the *parents*, which in Spanish is expressed as **los padres**.

los bisabuelos	*the great-grandparents*
el bisabuelo	*the great-grandfather*
la bisabuela	*the great-grandmother*
los abuelos	*the grandparents*
el abuelo	*the grandfather*
la abuela	*the grandmother*
los padres	*the parents*
el padre	*the father*
la madre	*the mother*
los parientes	*the relatives*
el pariente	*the (male) relative*
la pariente	*the (female) relative*
el tío, la tía	*the uncle, the aunt*
el esposo / el marido, la esposa	*the husband, the wife*
el hijo, la hija	*the son, the daughter*
el hermano, la hermana	*the brother, the sister*
el nieto, la nieta	*the grandson, the granddaughter*
el primo, la prima	*the (male) cousin, the (female) cousin*
el sobrino, la sobrina	*the nephew, the niece*
el suegro, la suegra	*the father-in-law, the mother-in-law*

el yerno, la nuera	*the son-in-law, the daughter-in-law*
el cuñado, la cuñada	*the brother-in-law, the sister-in-law*
el padrastro, la madrastra	*the stepfather, the stepmother*
el padrino, la madrina	*the godfather, the godmother*
el ahijado, la ahijada	*the godson, the goddaughter*

Time Expressions with *hacer*

To ask *how long* someone has been doing something, Spanish uses the present tense. The translation of this construction is equivalent to the present perfect tense in English. The action begins in the past and continues into the present.

¿**Cuánto tiempo hace que** + verb in the present tense

¿**Cuánto tiempo hace que** Ud. vive aquí?	*How long have you been living here?* (literally, *How much time does it make that you live here?*)
¿Cuánto tiempo hace que él estudia el francés?	*How long has he been studying French?*
¿Cuánto tiempo hace que Uds. viajan?	*How long have you been traveling?*
¿Cuánto tiempo hace que la muchacha mira televisión?	*How long has the girl been watching television?*

To answer the question of *how long* someone has been doing something, Spanish uses the following expression.

Hace + length of time + **que** + verb in the present tense

Hace quince años **que** yo vivo aquí.	*I have been living here for fifteen years.* (literally, *It makes fifteen years that I live here.*)
Hace un mes que él estudia el francés.	*He has been studying French for a month.*
Hace seis semanas que viajamos.	*We have been traveling for six weeks.*
Hace una hora que ella mira televisión.	*She has been watching television for an hour.*

A Word About "How Long"

The **hace** + the length of time + **que** + the verb in the present tense construction looks complicated because the English translation uses the present
perfect tense. But in Spanish, whenever you want to express *how long* someone has been doing something, just use the present tense.

Exercise 7.7

*Complete the following sentences with the correct form of the appropriate verb.
Choose from the infinitives listed below; use each verb no more than once.*

abrir, beber, cerrar, cocinar, comer, correr, deber, dormir,
empezar, estar, hacer, ir, jugar, nadar, perder, saber, salir,
ser, tener que, trabajar, tratar, vivir

1. María y Tomás van a España. El viaje va a _____ fantástico.

2. Susana practica para poder _____ en el maratón.

3. ¿Vas a _____ arroz con pollo para la familia?

4. La parte de la cabeza que _____ entre el pelo y los ojos
   es la frente.

5. Nosotros _____ los ojos para dormir.

6. Yo _____ la boca para hablar, pero las palabras

   no _____.

7. Enrique _____ de estudiar pero prefiere jugar al tenis.

8. Para aprender bien, los estudiantes _____ que asistir
   a la clase.

9. ¿Qué _____ Ud. si tiene sed? ¿_____ agua
   o jugo?

10. Ella quiere _____ a Sudamérica. Ella _____
    en Canadá.

11. La película popular _____ a las siete. Nosotros

    _____ comprar los tiquetes a las seis.

12. Yo soy ingeniero y _____ en el décimo piso del edificio.

13. El hombre fuerte _____ ocho horas cada noche;

    él _____ vegetales y pescado; _____

en la piscina del gimnasio en el invierno, y él _____

al béisbol en el verano.

14. ¿Quién _____ la historia de los Estados Unidos?

15. Ella siempre _____ las llaves de la casa.

Exercise 7.8

Complete the following sentences with the correct form of **ir**.

1. El hombre quiere _____ al partido de béisbol.

   Él _____ siempre los domingos.

2. ¿Por qué no _____ tú al cine con Elena? Ella es una mujer simpática.

3. Nosotros _____ a comprar un carro para el cumpleaños de Pablo.

4. ¿Adónde _____ Uds.?

5. Yo _____ a la escuela los lunes y los miércoles. Los martes,

   _____ a la biblioteca para estudiar.

Exercise 7.9

Complete the following sentences with the correct form of the appropriate verb or expression. Choose from the list below; use each option no more than once.

bajar, cocinar, estar, ganar, hacer, hay, leer, llegar, perder, preferir,
regresar, saber, salir, ser, subir, tener calor, tener frío, tener hambre,
tener miedo, tener razón, tener sed, tener sueño, tomar, venir, volver

1. Son las doce de la noche. Carlos no puede dormir bien y

   _____. Tomás _____ y quiere comer.

2. ¿Quiere Ud. _____ aquí a Nueva York a ver una obra de teatro?

3. Ella no quiere _____ una cita con el doctor porque

   _____ de las inyecciones.

4. Los hijos de Bernarda _____ de la casa a las siete y media de la mañana. Ellos _____ a casa a las cuatro.

5. El viajero _____ los periódicos y las revistas porque quiere _____ las noticias del día.

6. ¿Cuántas guerras _____ en el mundo?

7. El hermano de Alicia siempre _____ el bus para llegar al trabajo, pero Alicia _____ caminar.

8. Miguel piensa que va a _____ mucho dinero este año.

9. Yo trato de _____ a tiempo a la clase.

10. Los dos amigos _____ de Perú. El apartamento de ellos _____ en la calle cuarenta y dos con la avenida doce.

11. Vivo en el décimo piso. Yo _____ y _____ en el ascensor.

12. A las seis de la noche, Elena _____ a casa y empieza a _____ una comida para la familia.

13. Si yo _____, llevo un suéter extra.

14. Si ella _____, va a la playa porque quiere nadar.

15. ¿Bebe Ud. mucho si _____?

16. No jugamos bien al tenis y siempre _____ el juego.

17. Julia piensa que el sol es importante. Ramón piensa que la luna es más importante. ¿Quién _____?

Exercise 7.10

Complete the following sentences with the appropriate part of the body in each blank.

1. Ella tiene _____ corto. Tiene _____ azules y una sonrisa hermosa.

2. La nariz y las cejas son partes de _____.

3. Es difícil correr si tenemos dolor del _____.

4. Comemos con _____. Vamos al dentista para cuidar

   _____.

5. Si yo tengo una infección y no puedo oír bien, la infección está

   en _____.

6. Si una persona toma mucho alcohol, va a tener problemas

   en _____.

7. Si una persona tiene asma, el problema está en _____.

8. El tobillo, el pie, y la _____ son partes de la pierna.

9. Tengo dolor del _____ y no quiero comer.

10. Sonreímos con _____.

Exercise 7.11

Review **ser** *and* **estar**, *then complete the following sentences.*

1. ¿Quién _____ aquí?

2. Los guantes del hombre _____ verdes.

3. Ella quiere _____ con su familia en Navidad.

4. ¿Cómo sabes quién _____ ella?

5. _____ o no _____. Es la cuestión.
   (la cuestión = *the issue*)

6. El muchacho _____ contento si no tiene que ir
   a la escuela.

7. ¿Estás donde quieres _____?

8. Nosotros _____ buenos amigos.

9. Jorge _____ un buen hombre.

10. La fiesta _____ en la casa de Manuel.

11. ¿Cuál _____ la fecha de hoy? ¿Qué día _____
    hoy?

12. Yo _____ de Filadelfia. ¿De dónde _____
    Uds.?

Exercise 7.12

Complete the following sentences with the appropriate family member in Spanish. Use each term no more than once.

1. Graciela tiene sesenta y seis años y tiene dos _____.
   El nombre de uno es Enrique; la otra es Felicia.

2. Enrique tiene treinta años. Felicia tiene treinta y dos años. Ellos son

   _____.

3. Enrique tiene una _____ bonita de treinta y un años.
   Ellos tienen dos hijos.

4. Felicia tiene un _____ flaco de treinta y cuatro años.
   Ellos tienen dos hijas.

5. Los hijos de Enrique y Felicia son jóvenes. Ellos son los

   _____ de Graciela.

6. Los hijos de Enrique y Felicia están contentos porque Graciela es muy

   simpática y ella es la _____ de ellos.

7. El hermano de Felicia es el _____ de los niños de ella.

8. La hermana de Enrique es la _____ de los niños de él.

9. El hermano del esposo de Felicia es el _____ de ella.

10. La hermana del esposo de Felicia es la _____ de ella.

11. El padre de la esposa de Enrique es el _____ de él.

12. La madre de la esposa de Enrique es la _____ de él.

13. El padre del padre de Felicia es el _____ de ella.

14. Todos son _____ de ellos.

Reading Comprehension

La cita

La sala de espera de este doctor es muy grande porque trabaja solo.
Debe tener mucho éxito porque tiene tres secretarias que contestan
sus llamadas, hacen las citas, dan consejos sobre los seguros médicos y
organizan su horario. Confieso que la sala de espera es común; tiene una
mesa como cualquier otra, con revistas de moda para las mujeres y revistas
de deportes para los hombres. Hay una mesita con una lámpara en cada
rincón del cuarto. Son las dos menos quince. Tomo asiento y escojo una
de las revistas.

    Un hombre amable entra. Él debe tener la primera cita de la tarde.
En seguida, una viejecita llega con su hija y toman asiento cerca de mí.
Logro escuchar su conversación. La madre tiene dolor de cabeza; su
hija no camina bien. Un hombre con el brazo roto entra; después,
un muchacho que tiene problemas con el tobillo, una mujer con dolor
del cuello y de la espalda, y un hombre simpático con dolor del estómago.
Algunos están tranquilos, pero la mayoría de ellos están inquietos. Miran
sus relojes a menudo; tratan de leer pero no pueden; tratan de hacer
conversación para pasar el tiempo. Mientras tanto, la gente llega y llega
y llega. Parece que no va a caber ninguna persona más en la sala pequeña.
Pero vienen más y más hasta llenar todo el cuarto con pacientes.

    Son las dos y media. Por fin, el doctor emerge de su oficina.
La secretaria empieza a leer los nombres que están en su lista. Al escuchar
su nombre, cada persona desaparece en la oficina por un rato, sale del
consultorio, hace otra cita antes de volver a casa. Sigue así toda la tarde.

    La secretaria ve que todavía estoy aquí. Tenemos esta conversación:

LA SECRETARIA	¿Cuál es su nombre?
YO	Me llamo Isabel.
LA SECRETARIA	¿Cuál es su apellido?
YO	Pereira. Mi apellido es Pereira.
LA SECRETARIA	Pero su nombre no aparece en la lista.
YO	No tengo una cita hoy. Estoy bien de salud.
LA SECRETARIA	¿Quiere Ud. hacer una cita?
YO	No, estoy bien, gracias.
LA SECRETARIA	La oficina cierra a las seis. Ud. tiene que salir.
YO	Está bien.

Verbos

aparecer	*to appear*	escoger	*to choose*
caber	*to fit*	lograr	*to achieve,*
confesar	*to confess*		*to succeed in* (+ infinitive)
desaparecer	*to disappear*	llenar	*to fill*
emerger	*to emerge*	ver	*to see*

Expresiones verbales

al escuchar	*upon listening, upon hearing*
dar consejos	*to give advice*
estar inquieto	*to be nervous, fidgety*
estar tranquilo	*to be calm*
parece	*it seems*
sigue así	*it continues in this way*

Nombres

el apellido	*the last name, the surname*
la cita	*the appointment*
el consultorio	*the doctor's office*
el horario	*the schedule*
la llamada	*the phone call*
la mayoría	*the majority*
la moda	*the style, the fashion*
el nombre	*the name*
el paciente	*the patient*
el personaje	*the character*
el reloj	*the watch*
el rincón	*the corner*
la sala de espera	*the waiting room*
la secretaria	*the secretary*
los seguros médicos	*medical insurance*

Adjetivos

común	*common*
roto	*broken*
solo	*alone*

Expresiones

a menudo	*frequently*
al final	*at the end*

al principio	*at the beginning*
antes de + *infinitive*	*before (doing something)*
como cualquier otra	*like any (whatever) other*
en seguida	*right away*
mientras tanto	*meanwhile*
por fin	*at last*
por un rato	*for a little while*

Preguntas

After you have read the selection, answer the following questions in Spanish.

1. ¿Cuál es el nombre del personaje principal?

   _____

2. ¿Cómo es la sala de espera?

   _____

3. ¿Cómo están los pacientes?

   _____

4. ¿Qué pasa a las dos y media?

   _____

5. ¿Cómo puede ser la sala grande al principio del cuento y pequeña al final?

   _____

6. Si Isabel no tiene una cita con el doctor y si no está enferma, ¿por qué está ella en la oficina del doctor?

   _____

8

Adjectives and Adverbs

Possessive Adjectives

Possessive adjectives in Spanish agree in gender and number with the noun they modify. Possessive adjectives precede the noun they modify.

mi, **mis** *my*

Mi hermana quiere ir a España.	*My sister wants to go to Spain.*
Mis amigos quieren ir a Portugal.	*My friends want to go to Portugal.*

tu, **tus** *your* (**tú** form)

Tu libro está en la mesa.	*Your book is on the table.*
Tus lápices están en la silla.	*Your pencils are on the chair.*

su, **sus** *your* (**Ud.** form), *his, her, their*

In Spanish, there is only one form for the third-person possessive: the **su** and **sus** form. **Su** is used before a singular noun to show possession; **sus** is used with a plural noun. Because **su/sus** can be very ambiguous, the form that you have already learned and used—the noun + **de** + the pronoun— can be used to clarify the meaning.

Pedro y Linda están aquí.	*Peter and Linda are here.*
Necesito su carro.	*I need his/her/their car.*
¿El carro de él o el carro de ella?	*His car or her car?*
Sus ideas son fantásticas.	*Your/his/her/their ideas are fantastic.*
¿Las ideas de quién?	*Whose ideas?*
Las ideas de Uds.	*Your ideas.*
Ellos viven en las montañas.	*They live in the mountains.*
Su casa es grande.	*Their house is big.*

| Ella escribe mucho. | *She writes a lot.* |
| Sus artículos son interesantes. | *Her articles are interesting.* |

nuestro, **nuestra**, **nuestros**, **nuestras** *our*

Nuestro tren viene.	*Our train is coming.*
Nuestra fiesta va a ser fantástica.	*Our party is going to be fantastic.*
Nuestros libros son viejos.	*Our books are old.*
Nuestras computadoras son nuevas.	*Our computers are new.*

vuestro, **vuestra**, **vuestros**, **vuestras** *your* (**vosotros** form)

Like **vosotros**, this form is used only in Spain. It is explained here so that you will be aware of it, but when you need a word for *your* in Spanish, use **su** or **sus**.

Vuestro amigo es de España.	*Your friend is from Spain.*
Vuestra casa está en Madrid.	*Your house is in Madrid.*
¿Son españoles vuestros maestros?	*Are your teachers Spanish?*
Vuestras amigas son españolas.	*Your friends are Spanish.*

 ## Exercise 8.1

Complete the sentences using **mi**, **mis**, **tu**, **tus**, **su**, **sus**, **nuestro**, **nuestros**, **nuestra**, *or* **nuestras**.

1. Soy estudiante; _____ libros están en la mesa.

2. Él es un profesor excelente; _____ ideas son interesantes.

3. Ellos son abogados; _____ clientes pueden ser culpables o inocentes.

4. Nuestro hermano es profesor; _____ padres enseñan también.

5. Ella es mi abuela; _____ casa está en Florida.

6. El cuñado de Cecilia es carpintero; _____ nombre es Manuel.

7. Uds. son estudiantes; _____ libros son nuevos.

8. Liliana está en Texas; _____ hermanas están en Arizona.

9. Vivo con cuatro amigos y dos gatos; _____ casa es grande.

10. Somos principiantes; _____ tarea no es fácil.

11. Mis primos escriben libros; _____ trabajo es interesante.

12. La hija de Beatriz es doctora; _____ hijo es arquitecto.

Demonstrative Adjectives

In Spanish, there are three demonstrative adjectives; they agree in number and gender with the nouns they modify.

	Masculine	Feminine

- Near the speaker

| *this* | este | esta |
| *these* | estos | estas |

- Near the listener

| *that* | ese | esa |
| *those* | esos | esas |

- Far from both speaker and listener

| *that (over there)* | aquel | aquella |
| *those (over there)* | aquellos | aquellas |

Este periódico es interesante.	*This newspaper is interesting.*
Esta revista es interesante también.	*This magazine is interesting also.*
Estos hombres son fuertes.	*These men are strong.*
Estas mujeres son fuertes también.	*These women are strong also.*
Ese piano es viejo.	*That piano is old.*
Esa guitarra es nueva.	*That guitar is new.*
Esos libros son caros.	*Those books are expensive.*
Esas plumas son costosas.	*Those pens are costly.*
Aquel traje es feo.	*That suit (over there) is ugly.*
Aquella blusa es más bonita.	*That blouse (over there) is prettier.*
Aquellos árboles son enormes.	*Those trees (over there) are enormous.*
Aquellas casas son pequeñas.	*Those houses (over there) are small.*

Neuter Demonstrative Pronouns

Neuter demonstrative pronouns refer to an object that is not known, a statement, or a general idea.

esto	*this*
eso	*that*
aquello	*that (farther away in place or time)*

¿Qué es esto? ¿Qué es eso?	*What is this? What is that?*
Aquello no es necesario.	*That is not necessary.*

 Exercise 8.2

Complete the following sentences using demonstrative adjectives.

EXAMPLE   ¿Quién es __*ese*__ hombre que está con Julia? (*that*)

1. _____ revista que tú lees es interesante, pero _____ artículo tiene más información. (*this/that*)

2. ¿Piensa Ud. que _____ camisas son hermosas, o prefiere Ud. _____ camisas azules? (*these/those*)

3. ¿En qué sitio prefieren Uds. comer, en _____ restaurante o en _____ cafetería? (*that* [*over there*]/*that* [*over there*])

4. _____ falda es bonita, pero voy a comprar _____ pantalones porque son más cómodos. (*this/those*)

5. _____ mujeres corren en el maratón. (*those* [*over there*])

6. ¿Por qué mira Ud. _____ programas en televisión si son repeticiones? (*those*)

7. _____ mes va a ser maravilloso. (*this*)

Adjectives of Nationality

When an adjective of nationality ends in a consonant, **-a** is added to form the feminine.

español	*Spanish*
el restaurante español	*the Spanish restaurant*
la comida española	*the Spanish meal*

inglés	*English*
el hombre inglés	*the English man*
la mujer inglesa	*the English woman*
francés	*French*
el vino francés	*the French wine*
la cerveza francesa	*the French beer*
alemán	*German*
el escritor alemán	*the German writer* (m.)
la escritora alemana	*the German writer* (f.)
japonés	*Japanese*
el muchacho japonés	*the Japanese boy*
la muchacha japonesa	*the Japanese girl*
holandés	*Dutch*
el niño holandés	*the Dutch child* (m.)
la niña holandesa	*the Dutch child* (f.)

In all other cases, the adjectives of nationality will follow the rules you have already learned. Adjectives that end in **-o** change to **-a** when describing a feminine noun.

el hombre cubano	*the Cuban man*
la mujer cubana	*the Cuban woman*
el muchacho chileno	*the Chilean boy*
la muchacha chilena	*the Chilean girl*
el niño norteamericano	*the North American child* (m.)
la niña norteamericana	*the North American child* (f.)
el amigo suizo	*the Swiss friend* (m.)
la amiga suiza	*the Swiss friend* (f.)

Adjectives that end in vowels other than **-o** do not change.

el hombre canadiense	*the Canadian man*
la mujer canadiense	*the Canadian woman*
el niño hindú	*the Hindu child* (m.)
la niña hindú	*the Hindu child* (f.)
el hombre israelí	*the Israeli man*
la mujer israelí	*the Israeli woman*

Country	Nationality	Country	Nationality
Alemania	alemán	Irlanda	irlandés
Arabia Saudita	saudí/saudita	Israel	israelí
(la) Argentina	argentino	Italia	italiano
Austria	austriaco	Jamaica	jamaiquino
Bélgica	belga	Japón	japonés
Bolivia	boliviano	Marrueco	marroquí
(el) Brasil	brasileño	México	mexicano
(el) Canadá	canadiense	Nicaragua	nicaragüense
Chile	chileno	Noruega	noruego
China	chino	Nueva Zelanda	neocelandés
Colombia	colombiano	Pakistán	pakistaní
Corea	coreano	(el) Panamá	panameño
Costa Rica	costarricense	(el) Paraguay	paraguayo
Cuba	cubano	(el) Perú	peruano
Dinamarca	danés	Polonia	polaco
(el) Ecuador	ecuatoriano	Portugal	portugués
Egipto	egipcio	Puerto Rico	puertorriqueño
Escocia	escocés	(la) República	dominicano
España	español	Dominicana	
(los) Estados	norteamericano/	Rusia	ruso
Unidos	estadounidense	El Salvador	salvadoreño
Finlandia	finlandés	Siria	sirio
Francia	francés	Sudán	sudanés
Grecia	griego	Suecia	sueco
Guatemala	guatemalteco	(la) Suiza	suizo
Haití	haitiano	Tailandia	tailandés
Holanda	holandés	Taiwán	taiwanés
Honduras	hondureño	Turquía	turco
Hungría	húngaro	(el) Uruguay	uruguayo
(la) India	hindú	Venezuela	venezolano
Inglaterra	inglés	Vietnám	vietnamita
Irak/Iraq	iraquí	Yemen	yemení
Irán	iraní		

Continent		Continent	
África	africano	Australia	australiano
Antártica	antártico	Europa	europeo
el Ártico	ártico	Norteamérica	norteamericano
Asia	asiático	Sudamérica	sudamericano

Adjectives That Precede a Noun

In Chapter 1, you learned that adjectives follow the nouns they describe. Now you will learn the few adjectives that precede the noun they modify. Remember that adjectives agree in number and gender with the noun they describe.

Two frequently used adjectives, **bueno** and **malo**, drop the **-o** before a masculine singular noun.

bueno *good*

Este niño es un **buen** estudiante.	*This child is a good student.*
Su hermana es una **buena** estudiante.	*His sister is a good student.*
Ellos son **buenos** estudiantes.	*They are good students.*
Ellos tienen **buenas** maestras.	*They have good teachers.*

malo *bad*

Ella tiene un **mal** perro.	*She has a bad dog.*
Su amiga tiene una **mala** idea.	*Her friend has a bad idea.*
Ellas tienen tres **malos** gatos.	*They have three bad cats.*
Son **malas** situaciones.	*They are bad situations.*

 Bueno and **malo** can follow the noun as well as precede it. The use is less frequent, though, and the description loses intensity.

El hombre bueno.	*The (fairly) good man.*

Adjectives That Express Quantity

mucho *a lot of, much, many*

Él no tiene **mucho** dinero.	*He doesn't have a lot of money.*
Tiene **muchos** amigos.	*He has a lot of friends.*
Ellas preparan **mucha** comida para **muchas** personas.	*They prepare a lot of food for a lot of people.*

poco *a little bit, a few, not much, not many*

Hay **poco** dinero en este banco y hay **pocos** clientes.	*There is not much money in this bank and not many clients.*
Poca gente vive en esta calle y hay **pocas** casas.	*Not many people live on this street, and there are few houses.*

bastante, **suficiente** *enough*

> Ellos ganan **suficiente** dinero
> y tienen **bastante** trabajo.

> *They earn enough money and*
> *they have enough work.*

ambos *both*

> España y Portugal son bellos.
> Los viajeros van a visitar
> **ambos** países.

> *Spain and Portugal are beautiful.*
> *The travelers are going to visit*
> *both countries.*

cada *each*

> **Cada** casa tiene dos baños.
> **Cada** apartamento tiene una
> cocina.

> *Each house has two bathrooms.*
> *Each apartment has a kitchen.*

> NOTE: **Cada** has the same form for both masculine and feminine.

varios *several*

> **Varios** restaurantes sirven tacos.
> **Varias** tiendas venden burritos.

> *Several restaurants serve tacos.*
> *Several stores sell burritos.*

alguno *some*

> Él va a volver **algún** día.
> ¿Hay **alguna** farmacia cerca?
> **Algunos** pensamientos son buenos.
> **Algunas** ideas son malas.

> *He is going to return some day.*
> *Is there some pharmacy nearby?*
> *Some thoughts are good.*
> *Some ideas are bad.*

> NOTE: **Alguno** drops the **-o** before a masculine noun.

otro *other, another*

> Él quiere **otro** carro.
> Ella quiere **otra** casa.
> Él tiene **otros** problemas difíciles.
> Ella va a comprar **otras** cosas.

> *He wants another car.*
> *She wants another house.*
> *He has other difficult problems.*
> *She is going to buy other things.*

> NOTE: **Un** and **una** do not precede any form of **otro** and **otra**.

todo *all, every*

> Ella lee **todo** el día.
> **Todo** el mundo está aquí.
> Leo **toda** la información.
> Él escribe **todos** los días.
> Ella hace **todas** las preguntas.

> *She reads all day.*
> *Everyone (all the world) is here.*
> *I read all the information.*
> *He writes every day (all the days).*
> *She asks all the questions.*

Adjectives That Express *Next*, *Only*, and *Last*

próximo *next*

Vamos a viajar el **próximo** año.	*We are going to travel next year.*
La **próxima** lección es interesante.	*The next lesson is interesting.*
¿Qué va a pasar en los **próximos** años y en las **próximas** generaciones?	*What is going to happen in the next years and in the next generations?*

único *only*

Ricardo es el **único** mexicano aquí.	*Ricardo is the only Mexican here.*
Ella es la **única** española.	*She is the only Spaniard.*

último *last, final*

El **último** mes del año es diciembre.	*The last month of the year is December.*
Hoy es la **última** clase del semestre.	*Today is the last class of the semester.*

Adjectives Whose Meaning Depends on Position

Some adjectives have different meanings depending on whether they precede or follow the noun they modify.

Preceding the Noun	Following the Noun
antiguo	
su antiguo novio *her former boyfriend*	una civilización antigua *an ancient civilization*
cierto	
cierto día *a certain day*	una cosa cierta *a sure thing*
grande	
el gran hombre *the great man* la gran mujer *the great woman*	el hombre grande *the big man* la mujer grande *the big woman*

NOTE: **Grande** shortens to **gran** before any singular noun.

pobre	
el pobre niño *the poor, unfortunate little boy*	el hombre pobre *the poor man (without money)*

mismo

el mismo libro *the same book*   el profesor mismo
la misma idea *the same idea*   *the professor himself*

viejo

los viejos amigos   los amigos viejos
  the longtime friends   *the old friends (in years)*

When **mismo** *follows* a noun or pronoun, it *intensifies* the word it describes. For example:

esta casa misma *this very house*
yo mismo *I myself*
el doctor mismo está enfermo *the doctor himself is sick*
ahora mismo *right now*

Exercise 8.3

Complete the following sentences by using the appropriate adjective of nationality.

1. Micaela es de España y habla español porque su padre es español;

   ella habla francés porque su madre es _____.

2. Pensamos que la comida _____ es deliciosa.
   El sushi y el sashimi son platos típicos.

3. Hay mucha arte en Guatemala. ¿Son artistas _____?

4. Para entrar en los Estados Unidos, el ciudadano _____
   tiene que cruzar la frontera entre el Canadá y los Estados Unidos.

5. _____ tienen la reputación de ser poetas.
   La gente de Nicaragua trabaja duro y escribe poesía.

6. Costa Rica es un país con muchos parques nacionales.

   _____ visitan los parques todo el año.

7. Este hombre de India es _____. Su esposa es

   _____ también.

8. Soy portuguesa. Mi hermano es _____ también.

Exercise 8.4

Complete the following sentences using the adjectives from the list below. Use each adjective only one time. Answers may vary.

> alguno, ambos, bastante, bueno, cada, malo, mucho, otro,
> poco, próximo, suficiente, todo, último, único, varios

1. Carlos lee todo el día; quiere leer _____ los libros de la biblioteca.

2. Ella es la _____ persona en la clase que no tiene una computadora.

3. Es necesario tomar _____ agua para estar bien.

4. Hay dos películas que ella quiere comprar, pero no tiene

    _____ dinero para comprar _____ videos.

5. El _____ mes del año es diciembre.

6. El pianista practica el piano dos horas _____ día.

7. Queremos ir a un _____ restaurante para comer bien.

8. No es una _____ idea pasar el día en la playa.

9. Hay _____ revistas y _____ periódicos en la librería.

10. La librería tiene _____ libros sobre la historia de los aztecas, pero tiene más libros sobre la historia de los incas.

11. El _____ tren sale a las nueve y veinte de la mañana.

12. Loreta no está contenta porque el bus no viene y su carro viejo no

    es bueno. Ella quiere comprar _____ carro nuevo.

13. Hay _____ palabras en este artículo que puedo entender.

Exercise 8.5

In each sentence, place one of the following adjectives either before or after the noun, according to the meaning of the sentence: **antiguo, cierto, grande, pobre, mismo, viejo**.

1. Mi amiga y yo asistimos a la _____ clase _____.

2. Atenas y Roma son _____ ciudades _____.

3. El _____ hombre _____ no tiene dinero.

4. La _____ niña _____ está triste porque no tiene amigos.

5. ¿Quién es una _____ mujer _____ de nuestra generación?

6. Somos _____ amigas _____. Pasamos mucho tiempo juntas.

Comparative Adjectives

The comparative structure expresses *more than, less than,* or *the same as.*

- More than

  más + adjetivo + **que**

  Julia es **más** fuerte **que** Juan.
  La revista es **más** interesante **que** el libro.

  more + adjective + ***than***

  Julia is stronger than John.
  The magazine is more interesting than the book.

- Less than

  menos + adjetivo + **que**

  El libro es **menos** interesante **que** la revista.
  Las camisas son **menos** caras **que** los vestidos.

  less + adjective + ***than***

  The book is less interesting than the magazine.
  The shirts are less expensive than the dresses.

- The same as

  tan + adjetivo + **como**

  Estas tortas son **tan** dulces **como** esos pasteles.
  ¿Es el perro **tan** inteligente **como** el gato?

  as + adjective + ***as***

  These cakes are as sweet as those pastries.
  Is the dog as intelligent as the cat?

Superlative Adjectives

- The most/the least

el (la) más + adjetivo + **de**	(*the*) *most* + adjective + *of*
el (la) menos + adjetivo + **de**	(*the*) *least* + adjective + *of*

NOTE: In the superlative structure, Spanish **de** can be translated as *in*.

¿Quién es la persona **más** fuerte **de** su familia?	*Who is the strongest person in your family?*
¿Cuál es la clase **menos** interesante **de** la escuela?	*Which is the least interesting class in the school?*

Irregular Comparatives and Superlatives

bueno	*good*
mejor	*better*
el mejor, la mejor	*the best* (sing.)
los mejores, las mejores	*the best* (pl.)

Esta torta es buena.	*This cake is good.*
El pastel que Ud. tiene es mejor.	*The pastry that you have is better.*
Estos postres son los mejores de todos.	*These desserts are the best of all.*

malo	*bad*
peor	*worse*
el peor, la peor	*the worst* (sing.)
los peores, las peores	*the worst* (pl.)

Él es malo.	*He is bad.*
Ella es peor.	*She is worse.*
Ella es la peor de su escuela.	*She is the worst in her school.*

joven	*young*
menor	*younger*
el menor, la menor	*the youngest* (sing.)
los menores, las menores	*the youngest* (pl.)

NOTE: **Menor** refers only to people: **mi hermano menor**. If you want to compare *trees*, for example, just use the regular comparative structure: **Estos árboles son menos viejos que aquellos árboles.**

El niño es joven.	*The child is young.*
Su hermano es menor.	*His brother is younger.*

Su hermana es la menor de su familia.	*His sister is the youngest in their family.*

viejo	*old*
mayor	*older*
el mayor, la mayor	*the oldest* (sing.)
los mayores, las mayores	*the oldest* (pl.)

NOTE: **Mayor** refers only to people: **mi hermana mayor**. If you want to compare *buildings*, for example, just use the regular comparative structure: **Estos edificios son más viejos que aquellos edificios.**

Ella es vieja.	*She is old.*
Su madre es mayor.	*Her mother is older.*
Su abuela es la mayor de todas.	*Her grandmother is the oldest of all.*

Comparing Nouns

- **más** + nombre + **que**   *more* + noun + ***than***
  menos + nombre + **que**   *less* + noun + ***than***

Tengo **más** lápices **que** María.	*I have more pencils than Maria.*
Ella tiene **menos** libros **que** yo.	*She has fewer books than I.*

- **tanto** + nombre + **como**   *as much* + noun + ***as***

  as many + noun + ***as***

  NOTE: **Tanto** is an adjective and agrees with the noun it modifies.

Él corre **tantos** metros **como** su hijo.	*He runs as many meters as his son.*
Ella trabaja **tantas** horas **como** Ud.	*She works as many hours as you.*
José tiene **tanta** música **como** Sara.	*Joe has as much music as Sarah.*
Él tiene **tanto** pelo **como** su tío.	*He has as much hair as his uncle.*

Comparing Verbs

más que	*more than*
menos que	*less than*
tanto como	*as much as*

Yo estudio **más que** tú.	*I study more than you.*
Tú lees **menos que** yo.	*You read less than I.*
Ella aprende **tanto como** él.	*She learns as much as he.*

Exercise 8.6

Complete the following sentences, using the words in parentheses.

1. Esta película es buena; es _____ de todas. (*the best*)

2. Su carro es caro, pero no es _____ como mi carro. (*as expensive*)

3. El apartamento de María es _____ del edificio. (*the biggest*)

4. Nuestra clase de matemáticas es _____ que la clase de historia. (*more interesting*)

5. Uds. tienen _____ exámenes como nosotros. (*as many*)

6. Su casa es _____ que mi apartamento. (*smaller*)

7. Ella es _____ que él, pero él no es el estudiante _____ de la clase. (*taller/tallest*)

8. Estas películas son _____ que los programas de televisión. (*more exciting*)

9. Mi hermana _____ está _____ que mi hermano _____. (*younger/happier/older*)

10. Las calles son _____ que las avenidas. (*less wide*)

11. ¿Piensa Ud. que los caballos son _____ como los perros? (*as intelligent*)

12. Esa casa roja es _____ que la casa amarilla. (*older*)

13. Yo leo _____ tú. (*more than*)

14. Él sabe _____ nosotros. (*less than*)

15. Ellos viven en el sitio _____ del país. (*most beautiful*)

16. Este restaurante sirve _____ comida de la ciudad. (*the best*)

17. Pienso que Mónica es _____ que Martina. (*older*)

18. Anita tiene dos años. Ella es _____ de su familia. (*the youngest*)

19. La comida hindú es _____ que la comida china. (*spicier*)

20. El baño está _____ que el comedor. (*cleaner*)

21. Somos _____ que nuestros vecinos. (*more affectionate*)

22. ¿Quién es _____ político de los Estados Unidos?

    ¿Quién es _____? (*the best/the worst*)

23. Isabel piensa que el sol es _____ que la luna.

    Ramón piensa que la luna es _____. (*more important*)

24. Estoy _____ que ellos. (*sadder*)

25. Los padres están _____ que sus hijos. (*more tired*)

26. Ella tiene _____ energía como sus estudiantes. (*as much*)

27. Las muchachas juegan _____ deportes como los muchachos. (*as many*)

28. Ellas cantan _____ que sus hermanos. (*better*)

29. Vendo _____ cigarrillos que compro. (*less*)

30. Ellos ganan _____ dinero que Pedro. (*more*)

Adverbs

Adverbs describe verbs or adjectives. In Spanish, adverbs are formed by adding **-mente** to the *feminine form* of the adjective. The suffix **-mente** corresponds to the English suffix *-ly*.

To change the adjective **perfecto** to an adverb, use the feminine form **perfecta** and add **-mente**. The result is the adverb **perfectamente**.

Adjective		Adverb	
claro	*clear*	claramente	*clearly*
rápido	*rapid*	rápidamente	*rapidly*
lento	*slow*	lentamente	*slowly*
franco	*frank*	francamente	*frankly*
honesto	*honest*	honestamente	*honestly*
íntimo	*intimate*	íntimamente	*intimately*
último	*last*	últimamente	*lastly*

If an adjective does not end in **-o**, it has only one form for both masculine and feminine. To form an adverb from these adjectives, simply add **-mente** to the adjective.

Adjective		Adverb	
alegre	*happy*	alegremente	*happily*
feliz	*happy*	felizmente	*happily*
triste	*sad*	tristemente	*sadly*
fácil	*easy*	fácilmente	*easily*
frecuente	*frequent*	frecuentemente	*frequently*

If there are two adverbs in a series, only the final one will add **-mente**. The first one in the series takes the feminine form of the adjective.

Él camina frecuente y alegremente.	*He walks frequently and happily.*
Él corre lenta y tristemente.	*He runs slowly and sadly.*
Hablo clara y concisamente.	*I speak clearly and concisely.*
Ella vive tranquila y libremente.	*She lives calmly and freely.*

 Exercise 8.7

Change the following adjectives to their corresponding adverbial form.

1. sincero (*sincere*)   _____ (*sincerely*)

2. loco (*crazy*)   _____ (*crazily*)

3. total (*total*)   _____ (*totally*)

4. verdadero (*true*)   _____ (*truly*)

5. inocente (*innocent*)   _____ (*innocently*)

6. cariñoso (*affectionate*)   _____ (*affectionately*)

7. completo (*complete*)   _____ (*completely*)

8. normal (*normal*)   _____ (*normally*)

Adverbs That Do Not Take the Suffix -*mente*

Adverbs of Quantity

mucho	*a lot*	más	*more*
tanto	*so much*	menos	*less*
poco	*a little bit*	demasiado	*too much*
casi	*almost*		

Adverbs That Tell How Something Is Done

bien	*well*	mejor	*better*
mal	*badly*	peor	*worse*

Adverbs of Time and Place

a veces	*sometimes*	cerca	*nearby*
ahora	*now*	en lo alto	*up, up there*
ahora mismo	*right now*	lejos	*far off*
siempre	*always*	adelante	*in front*
todavía	*still, yet; no, not yet*	al fondo	*in back,*
ya	*already*		*at the bottom*
ya no	*no longer*	atrás	*in back*
temprano	*early*	arriba	*up, upstairs*
tarde	*late*	abajo	*down, downstairs*
aquí, allí	*here, there*	adentro	*inside*
acá, allá	*here, there*	afuera	*outside*

NOTE: **Acá** and **allá** are usually used with verbs of motion.

Adverbs of Direction

a la derecha	*to the right*
a la izquierda	*to the left*
derecho, recto	*straight ahead*

Ya sé que ella está **aquí**.	*I already know that she is here.*
Él **siempre** hace bien su tarea.	*He always does his homework well.*
Los niños cocinan **poco**.	*The children cook a little bit.*
¿Por qué no vienes **acá**?	*Why don't you come here?*
María llega **temprano**.	*María arrives early.*
Su amiga llega **tarde**.	*Her friend arrives late.*
A la derecha, hay una iglesia.	*To the right, there is a church.*
A la izquierda, hay un banco.	*To the left, there is a bank.*

Exercise 8.8

Complete the following sentences with the adverb in parentheses.

1. Llego al trabajo a las siete de la mañana; _____ llego

    _____. (*always/early*)

2. Para hablar _____ el español, tengo que pronunciar

    _____. (*well/clearly*)

3. ¿Corre ella _____? (*slowly*)

4. Todo el mundo quiere vivir _____. (*happily*)

5. Simón y Teresa viajan cada mes. Viajan _____.
    (*frequently*)

6. ¿Puede Ud. comer después de su operación? _____.
    (*not yet*)

7. ¿Necesita Ud. ayuda con sus problemas? _____.
    (*no longer*)

8. ¿Dónde están los niños? ¿Están _____ o

    _____? (*upstairs/downstairs*)

9. El hombre camina _____ y _____.
    (*quickly/happily*)

10. La muchacha _____ firma sus cartas

    _____. (*always/affectionately*)

11. Los adolescentes comen _____. (*a lot*)

12. _____, hay un río. (*straight ahead*)

13. ¿A que hora llegamos _____? (*there*)

14. Hablo _____ y _____. (*honestly/sincerely*)

Some adverbs can be replaced by **con** or **sin** + the corresponding noun. The most common such adverbs are the following.

con cuidado	*with care* (instead of *carefully*)
sin cuidado	*without care* (instead of *carelessly*)
con cariño	*with affection* (instead of *affectionately*)
con dificultad	*with difficulty*
sin dificultad	*without difficulty*
con inteligencia	*with intelligence* (instead of *intelligently*)

Exercise 8.9

Translate the following sentences into Spanish.

1. *My younger brother is ten years old.*

   _____

2. *He understands this chapter, but he doesn't want to learn all the words.*

   _____

   _____

3. *I know why his sister wants to go to Spain. Her relatives are there.*

   _____

4. *Every year at Thanksgiving, we cook too much.*

   _____

5. *Juan always loses his gloves.*

   _____

6. *His grandmother is older than his grandfather.*

   _____

7. *The last month of the year is December; the first month is January.*

   _____

8. *We have a good class; we learn a lot.*

   _____

9. *Your book has just arrived.*

   _____

10. *I know that my cat is smarter than your dog.*

    _____

11. *These trees are older than those trees over there.*

    _____

12. *We listen to the same sad songs every day.*

    _____

13. *Do you think that the president of the United States is a great man?*

    _____

14. *Are you coming to our party on Friday? It begins at nine o'clock at night.*

_____

_____

15. *Carolina is as tall as Enrique; her sister is the tallest of all.*

_____

16. *This book is the most interesting book in the library.*

_____

17. *Which is the most dangerous animal in the world?*

_____

18. *I am the only person in the family who knows how to play tennis. Sometimes I win; sometimes I lose.*

_____

_____

Exercise 8.10

Translate the following sentences into English.

1. El señor Gómez hace su trabajo con dificultad.

_____

2. Ella habla sinceramente, y su amigo responde humildemente.

_____

3. Esta mujer siempre explica todo claramente.

_____

4. Francamente, no quiero salir esta noche. Prefiero leer y escribir tranquilamente.

_____

_____

5. Bernardo va siempre al mismo restaurante. Él piensa que es el mejor restaurante de la ciudad.

_____

_____

Reading Comprehension

La fiesta

Esta noche hay una fiesta en la casa de una conocida. Tengo la invitación encima del piano que ya no toco. No sé si quiero ir. La fiesta empieza a las ocho. Pienso que los invitados van a llegar a las nueve. (No sé porque las invitaciones siempre llevan la hora equivocada. Si ella sabe que vamos a llegar después de las nueve, ¿por qué escribe que empieza a las ocho?)

¿Cómo imagino la fiesta? Primero hay música. Con mucho cuidado, los anfitriones ponen música alegre. La casa está limpia y hay entremeses y bocadillos en la mesa. Hay mucho que beber también: vino y cerveza, vodka y tequila. Hay soda y gaseosa, agua mineral y jugo para la gente que no quiere tomar alcohol. Después de mucha preparación, todo está listo.

Al entrar, los invitados sonríen y ponen las botellas de vino que llevan consigo en la mesa. La gente empieza a hablar, un poquito al principio, y mientras que toman, hablan más y más y en voz más y más alta. Ponen la música en alto volumen y algunas parejas empiezan a bailar. Las personas que saben la letra de las canciones cantan. Todo el mundo está muy alegre. Pasan unas horas y la anfitriona va a la cocina. Apagan las luces; ella vuelve con una torta de chocolate con velas y todos los amigos cantan 'Cumpleaños Feliz'.

Voy a mi alcoba a mirar mi vestuario. Mi cuarto es muy tranquilo, con una brisa que viene del mar. Las paredes son de un color azul celeste que produce calma. El ambiente es relajante, un ambiente de quietud. Es una habitación cómoda donde descanso, leo y miro la televisión todas las noches. Son las ocho ya. Va a empezar mi programa favorito en media hora.

Verbos

apagar	*to turn off*	imaginar	*to imagine*
al entrar	*upon entering*	sonreír	*to smile*

Nombres

el ambiente	*the atmosphere*	la brisa	*the breeze*
el anfitrión/	*the host/*	la conocida	*the acquaintance*
la anfitriona	*the hostess*	el entremés	*the appetizer*
el bocadillo	*the snack*	el invitado	*the guest*
la botella	*the bottle*	la letra	*the words* (of a song)

la pareja	the couple	el vestuario	the closet,
la soda, la gaseosa	the soda		the wardrobe
la vela	the candle		

Preposiciones

| acerca de | about |
| encima de | on top of |

Expresiones

la hora equivocada	the wrong hour
consigo	with themselves
en alto volumen	loudly

Preguntas

After you have read the selection, answer the following questions in Spanish.

1. ¿A qué hora empieza la fiesta?

   _____

2. ¿Cuál es la actitud de Isabel acerca de la fiesta después de recibir la invitación?

   _____

3. ¿Toca ella su piano?

   _____

4. ¿Dónde tiene lugar la fiesta?

   _____

5. ¿Qué hace la gente en la fiesta?

   _____

6. ¿Piensa Ud. que ella va a ir a la fiesta?

   _____

Negatives and Prepositions

Negatives

You already know how to make a sentence negative by placing **no** directly before the first verb.

Yo canto.	*I sing.*
Yo **no** canto.	*I don't sing.*
Yo **no** quiero cantar.	*I don't want to sing.*

The following list of negative words adds to this base.

nada	*nothing*
nadie	*no one*
nunca	*never*
jamás	*never*
ninguno	*not one*

Learn the affirmative words also.

algo	*something*
alguien	*someone*
a veces, algunas veces	*sometimes*
siempre	*always*
alguno	*some*

nada *nothing*

To form a negative sentence, **no** precedes the first verb and **nada** follows it.

No tengo **nada** en mi bolsa.	*I have nothing in my bag.*
Ella **no** entiende **nada**.	*She doesn't understand anything.*

¿Tienen Uds. algo para ella?   *Do you have something for her?*
No, **no** tenemos **nada**.   *No, we have nothing.*

If you have two verbs in the sentence, **no** precedes the first verb and **nada** follows the second verb.

Ella **no** quiere hacer **nada**.   *She doesn't want to do anything.*
No vamos a escribir **nada**.   *We are not going to write anything.*

A Word About Negatives

You can see that Spanish, unlike English, uses a double negative. In fact, a Spanish sentence can include three or four negatives. The more negatives you use, the more negative the sentence becomes.

Algo can sometimes be used as an adverb to mean *somewhat.*

El libro es algo interesante.   *The book is somewhat interesting.*

Nada can be used as an adverb to mean *not at all.*

El libro no es nada interesante.   *The book is not interesting at all.*

nadie *no one*

No precedes the verb and **nadie** follows it.

¿Hay alguien aquí?   *Is there someone here?*
No, **no** hay **nadie**.   *No, there is no one.*
No viene **nadie** a mi fiesta.   *No one is coming to my party.*

Nadie can also be placed directly before the first verb. In this case, **no** is not used.

Nadie quiere cocinar esta noche.   *No one wants to cook tonight.*
Nadie sabe donde está el tren.   *No one knows where the train is.*

nunca, jamás *never*

No precedes the verb and **nunca** or **jamás** follows it. Both **nunca** and **jamás** mean *never.*

Ella **no** habla **nunca**; es muy   *She never talks; she is very shy.*
   tímida.
Él **no** baila **jamás**.   *He never dances.*

Nunca and **jamás** can also be placed directly before the first verb with no change in the meaning.

El niño **nunca** practica el piano.

The boy never practices the piano.

Jamás bebo café con azúcar.

I never drink coffee with sugar.

ninguno *not one, no*

No precedes the verb and **ninguno** follows it.

Ninguno is the only negative expression in the list above that is an adjective. This means that it must agree in number and gender with the noun it modifies. **Ninguno** shortens to **ningún** before a masculine singular noun. **Ninguno** is not used in the plural unless the noun it modifies is always used in the plural, such as **vacaciones**.

No hay **ningún** hotel en esta ciudad.

There is no hotel in this city.

No tenemos **ninguna** idea.

We have no (not one) idea.

No tenemos **ningunas** vacaciones en agosto.

We don't have any vacation in August.

Ninguno may also precede the noun. In this case, **no** is not used.

Ningún muchacho va a la playa.
Ninguna persona llega tarde para la clase.

Not one boy is going to the beach.
Not one person arrives late for the class.

Exercise 9.1

Answer the following questions in the negative.

EXAMPLE   ¿Entiende ella todo? No, ___*ella no entiende nada.*___

1. ¿Aprenden Uds. algo en México? No, _____

2. ¿Cuántas personas van a su fiesta? _____

3. ¿Escuchas siempre las noticias? No, _____

4. ¿Tienen ellos muchos enemigos? No, _____

5. ¿Hay un hospital aquí? No, _____

6. ¿Vas a viajar? No, _____

7. ¿Es la película algo cómica? No, _____

8. ¿Bailas a veces? No, _____

More Negative Expressions

no... ni... ni... *neither . . . nor . . .*

Él **no** fuma **ni** cigarrillos **ni** cigarros.	*He smokes neither cigarettes nor cigars.*
Ella **no** compra **ni** revistas **ni** periódicos.	*She buys neither magazines nor newspapers.*

no más que *not more than* (with numbers)

Él **no** tiene **más que** cien dólares en el banco.	*He doesn't have more than one hundred dollars in the bank.*

NOTE: In an affirmative sentence, **más de** is used.

Él tiene **más de** cien dólares en el banco.	*He has more than 100 dollars in the bank.*

tampoco *neither, either*

Ella nunca va al cine.	*She never goes to the movies.*
Yo **no** voy **tampoco**.	*I don't go either.*

ni... tampoco *not . . . either*

Él no entiende la lección.	*He doesn't understand the lesson.*
Ni yo **tampoco**.	*Neither do I.*

sino *but rather*

Sino is used in the second clause of a sentence in which the first clause is negative.

Yo no soy profesor, **sino** estudiante.	*I am not a teacher, but rather a student.*
Ellos no son cubanos, **sino** españoles.	*They are not Cubans, but rather Spaniards.*
No vendemos, **sino** compramos.	*We don't sell, but rather we buy.*

de nada, **por nada** *you're welcome, think nothing of it*
no hay de que *you're welcome, don't mention it*

Gracias por el regalo.	*Thanks for the gift.*
De nada. / No hay de que.	*You're welcome.*

ya no *no longer*

Ella **ya no** quiere trabajar.	*She no longer wants to work.*

ahora no *not now*

> ¿Puede Ud. pagar la cuenta?　*Can you pay the bill?*
> **Ahora no.**　*Not now.*

todavía no *not yet*

> ¿Están Uds. listos?　*Are you ready?*
> **Todavía no.**　*Not yet.*

ni siquiera *not even*

> Él **ni siquiera** sabe escribir.　*He doesn't even know how to write.*

sin + infinitive + **nada** *without* + gerund + *anything*

> Él contesta **sin** saber **nada.**　*He answers without knowing anything.*

no es para tanto *it's not such a big deal*

> Elena no cocina bien, pero su esposo piensa que **no es para tanto**.　*Elena doesn't cook well, but her husband thinks that it's not such a big deal.*

casi nunca *almost never, hardly ever*

> María toca el piano, pero **casi nunca** practica.　*María plays the piano, but she almost never practices.*

más que nada *more than anything*

> Silvia quiere viajar **más que nada**.　*Sylvia wants to travel more than anything.*

nada más *nothing more, that's all*

> Paula tiene una casa en las montañas, **nada más**.　*Paula has a house in the mountains, nothing more.*

In Spanish, unlike English, the more negatives you use, the more negative the sentence becomes.

> **No** recibo **nunca ninguna** carta de **nadie**.　*I never receive any letter from anybody.*
> Él **jamás** pide **nada** a **nadie**.　*He never asks anything of anybody.*
> Ellos **no** quieren viajar **nunca jamás**.　*They don't want to travel ever again.*

Exercise 9.2

Rewrite the following sentences in the negative.

EXAMPLE   Yo como siempre.
            Yo no como nunca.

1. Yo tengo más de treinta dólares en mi cartera.

   _____

2. Siempre estamos contentos.

   _____

3. Hago mucho hoy.

   _____

4. Quiero ir también.

   _____

5. Este programa es algo interesante.

   _____

6. ¿Quieres tomar algo?

   _____

7. ¿Hay alguna farmacia aquí? [Write a negative response.]

   _____

8. ¿Tiene ella muchas amigas? [Write a negative response.]

   _____

9. El novio siempre limpia el apartamento.

   _____

10. Ella estudia todo el tiempo.

    _____

11. Muchas mujeres quieren bailar con él.

    _____

12. Alguien vive en la casa blanca.

    _____

Exercise 9.3

Answer the following questions aloud, using a negative expression.

1. No quiero ir al cine con Luisa. ¿Quieres ir tú?

2. ¿Quién cocina para Ud.?

3. ¿Es el programa algo interesante?

4. Ellos siempre van de vacaciones en el verano. ¿Y Ud.?

5. ¿Con quién hablas a las seis de la mañana?

6. ¿Por qué siempre corres al tren?

Prepositions

A preposition shows the relationship of a noun or a pronoun to some other word in a sentence, clause, or phrase. You already know the most commonly used prepositions.

a	*at, to*	en	*in, on*
con	*with*	para	*for, in order to*
de	*of, from, about*	sin	*without*

In general, prepositions are followed by verbs in the infinitive form, nouns, or pronouns.

- Followed by an infinitive of a verb

  Ella estudia **para aprender**.   *She studies in order to learn.*
  Él habla **sin pensar**.   *He speaks without thinking.*

  An infinitive that follows a preposition in Spanish is often translated with the English gerund (*thinking*, for example). In Spanish, the verb is always the infinitive (for example, **pensar**, *to think*).

- Followed by a noun

  Él tiene un libro **para la clase**.   *He has a book for the class.*

- Followed by a pronoun

  El libro es **para ella**.   *The book is for her.*

Prepositions Followed by Verbs or Nouns

antes de *before*

Antes de nadar, ella quiere comer.	*Before swimming, she wants to eat.*
Antes de la clase, ellos estudian.	*Before the class, they study.*

después de *after*

Después de correr, ellos tienen sed.	*After running, they are thirsty.*
Después de la comida, él va a casa.	*After the meal, he goes home.*

en vez de *instead of*

En vez de correr, él prefiere caminar.	*Instead of running, he prefers to walk.*

además de *in addition to*

Además de ser valiente, ella es simpática.	*In addition to being brave, she is nice.*

a pesar de *in spite of*

A pesar de estar enfermo, él va al trabajo.	*In spite of being sick, he goes to work.*

Prepositions Followed by Nouns or Pronouns

contra	*against*	según	*according to*
durante	*during*	sobre	*above, on top of, about* (a theme or topic)
entre	*between, among*		
excepto	*except*	hasta	*until*
hacia	*toward*	desde	*since; from* (a point of departure in place or time)
salvo	*except*		

Hacia can be combined with an adverb with the following meanings.

hacia atrás	*toward the rear*
hacia adelante	*toward the front*
hacia arriba	*upward*
hacia abajo	*downward*

Sobre means *on top of, about* a theme or topic. It can also mean *about* in the sense of *approximately.*

El sartén está sobre la estufa.	*The pan is on top of the stove.*
El autor escribe sobre la historia.	*The author writes about history.*
Vamos al cine sobre las ocho.	*We are going to the movies about eight o'clock.*

Desde means *from* if you have a specific point of departure in terms of place or time.

Veo el río desde mi ventana.	*I see the river from my window.*
Ella trabaja desde las siete de la mañana hasta las tres de la tarde.	*She works from seven o'clock in the morning until three in the afternoon.*

In addition to simple prepositions, there are many compound prepositions that are followed by nouns or pronouns. The list below includes both types.

al lado de	*next to*
alrededor de	*around*
cerca de	*near*
debajo de	*underneath*
bajo	*under* (more figurative than **debajo de**)
delante de	*before, in front of* (physical location)
ante	*before, in front of, in the presence of*
dentro de	*inside of*
detrás de	*behind*
tras	*after* (in a set of expressions)
encima de	*on top of*
enfrente de, frente a	*in front of, opposite, facing, across from*
fuera de	*outside of*
junto a, pegado a	*close to, right next to*
lejos de	*far from*

Pronouns That Follow Prepositions

You have already learned that subject pronouns follow prepositions.

para él	*for him*	para Ud.	*for you* (sing.)
para ella	*for her*	para Uds.	*for you* (pl.)
para ellos	*for them* (m.)	para nosotros	*for us*
para ellas	*for them* (f.)	para vosotros	*for you*

The only exceptions appear in the first-person and second-person singular.

para **mí**	*for me*
para **ti**	*for you*

There are a few situations, however, where the subject pronouns **tú** and **yo** are used after prepositions. Note the following expressions.

entre tú y yo	*between you and me*
menos tú y yo	*except you and me*
excepto tú y yo	*except you and me*
según tú	*according to you*
incluso yo	*including me*
salvo yo	*except me*

The only preposition that combines with a pronoun is **con**.

conmigo	*with me*
contigo	*with you*
consigo	*with yourself, with himself, with herself, with themselves*

The Preposition *por*

Por has the following meanings.

- *through, by*

El ladrón sale por la ventana.	*The robber leaves through the window.*
Preferimos viajar por avión.	*We prefer to travel by plane.*
Él manda mensajes por correo electrónico.	*He sends messages by e-mail.*

- *because of, on account of, for the sake of, out of*

La planta es verde por la clorofila.	*The plant is green because of the chlorophyll.*
Él está triste por el mal clima.	*He is sad because of the bad weather.*
Ella no quiere hablar por miedo.	*She doesn't want to talk out of fear.*
Ellas aprenden bien por ti.	*They learn well because of you.*

- *in exchange for; in place of* (suggests a substitution)

Pago diez dólares por este vestido.	*I pay $10 (in exchange) for this dress.*

| El estudiante enseña por el profesor. | *The student teaches for (instead of) the teacher.* |

- *per*

| Él gana quinientos dólares por semana. | *He earns $500 per week.* |
| Recibe mil doscientos dólares por mes. | *He receives $1,200 per month.* |

- *for* (before a period of time)

Cada día, corro por una hora.	*Each day, I run for an hour.*
Cada noche, leo por media hora.	*Each night, I read for a half hour.*
Ella tiene ganas de estudiar el español por dos años.	*She wants to study Spanish for two years.*

Por adds the idea of motion to prepositions of location.

| El niño corre por debajo de la mesa. | *The child runs under the table.* |
| El gato salta por encima del sofá. | *The cat jumps over the sofa.* |

Por appears in some common expressions.

por acá, por aquí	*around here*
por allá, por allí	*around there*
por ahora	*for now*
por casualidad	*by chance*
por lo común	*usually*
por costumbre	*usually*
por ejemplo	*for example*
por eso	*therefore, for this reason*
por favor	*please*
por fin	*finally*
por lo menos	*at least*
por poco	*almost*
por primera vez	*for the first time*
por supuesto	*of course*
por todas partes	*everywhere*
por la mañana	*in the morning* (imprecise time)
por la tarde	*in the afternoon*
por la noche	*in the evening*

Por and *para* Compared

Remember that **para** means *for.*

El regalo es para su hijo.   *The gift is for her son.*
Tengo una pregunta para ella.   *I have a question for her.*

Para is also used to express a specific time limit or deadline in the future. In this context, it can be translated as *for, by, on,* or *before.*

Necesito la blusa para el viernes.   *I need the blouse for Friday.*

Por is translated as simple *for* only when **por** precedes a quantity of time.

Voy a viajar por varios meses.   *I am going to travel for several months.*

Ella mira televisión por una hora.   *She watches television for an hour.*
Dormimos por ocho horas cada   *We sleep for eight hours every night.*
   noche.

With the exception of their English translations as *for,* the meanings of **por** and **para** do not overlap. Again, **por** means *for* only when it precedes a period of time. **Para** means *for* in almost all other cases.

Queremos una habitación para   *We want a room for two persons*
   dos personas por una noche.   *for one night.*
El tren sale para el Canadá.   *The train is leaving for Canada.*

 Exercise 9.4

Complete the following sentences with the correct prepositions and pronouns.

1. ¿Quieres salir _____ a las cinco? (*with me*)

2. No quiero salir _____. (*without you*)

3. ¿Tiene Ud. confianza _____? (*in him*)

4. Ella lleva su bolsa _____. (*with her*)

5. Este regalo es _____. (*for them*)

6. _____, ¿quién cocina mejor? (*between him and her*)

7. _____, esta película es horrible. (*between you and me*)

8. Los niños corren _____. (*toward us*)

9. El hombre quiere hablar _____, pero yo no quiero hablar

_____. (*with me/with him*)

10. Hay una estatua _____. (*near him*)

11. Julia no quiere tocar el piano _____. (*in front of them*)

12. Primero, ella quiere practicar _____. (*in front of us*)

13. Este hombre siempre está sentado _____. (*behind her*)

14. La familia de Pedro vive _____ pero vive _____.
(*far from him/near me*)

Exercise 9.5

Complete the following sentences with the Spanish for the words in parentheses.

1. _____, las muchachas van a practicar el piano.
(*before lunch*)

2. _____, quieren mirar televisión. (*after dinner*)

3. _____, vamos a la playa. (*after eating*)

4. _____ a su trabajo, ella toma su desayuno.
(*before going*)

5. _____ temprano, ella llega tarde. (*in spite of
leaving*)

6. El muchacho baila _____ la música. (*without
listening to*)

7. Ella estudia _____. (*in order to learn*)

8. ¿Están las llaves _____ la ventana o _____
la puerta? (*underneath/on top of*)

9. Vamos al teatro que está _____ la tercera avenida. (*near*)

10. El padre corre _____ su hija. (*toward*)

11. ¿Cuándo sale el tren _____ Madrid? (*for*)

12. Hay muchos árboles _____ la casa lujosa. (*behind*)

13. La radio habla _____ la situación mundial. (*about*)

14. Tomás va a estar de viaje _____ seis meses. (*for*)

15. No quiero hablar _____ la clase. (*in front of*)

16. Vamos al cine una vez _____ semana. (*per*)

17. Ellos prefieren viajar _____ tren _____ tres horas. (*by/for*)

18. El rió está _____ las montañas. (*far from*)

19. Ella no quiere ir a Alaska _____ el frío. (*because of*)

20. Practico el piano _____ tocar bien. (*in order to*)

Exercise 9.6

Translate the following sentences into English.

1. Ella nunca habla contra sus amigos.

   _____

2. Los zapatos de Sara están debajo de su cama.

   _____

3. Australia está lejos de los Estados Unidos.

   _____

4. La escuela está entre la iglesia y el banco.

   _____

5. Puedo ver el río desde mi ventana.

   _____

6. Ella duerme ocho horas cada noche. Ella duerme desde las once hasta las siete.

   _____

7. Bajo la ley, ¿quién tiene protección?

   _____

8. Pongo un libro encima del otro.

   _____

9. Antonio nunca canta sin nosotros.

   _____

10. El testigo tiene que aparecer ante el juez.

    _____

11. Los niños hablan mucho de la película.

    _____

12. El autor escribe sobre la historia y los derechos humanos.

    _____

13. El cine está lejos del mercado.

    _____

Exercise 9.7

Translate the following sentences into Spanish.

1. _I enter the store through the door._

   _____

2. _Everyone wants to go except Samuel._

   _____

3. _All the men dance except Pablo._

   _____

4. _My garden is next to my neighbor's garden._

   _____

5. _We walk toward the park._

   _____

6. _There is a bus stop in front of Laura's house._

   _____

7. _According to the news, a lot of people are not going to vote._

   _____

8. _There are comfortable chairs around the swimming pool._

   _____

9. _Day after day, they work a lot._

   _____

10. _James' house is behind the school._

    _____

11. *Are you going to study for the test?*

_____

12. *She doesn't want to travel out of fear.*

_____

 # Reading Comprehension

El circo

Aunque ella tiene cuarenta años, mi amiga Leonora quiere trabajar
en un circo. Es verdad que ella es soltera y maestra y tiene el verano libre
pero no entiendo por qué ella no quiere ir al Caribe o a cualquier sitio
relajante. Ella piensa que va a ser una gran aventura. Hay una gira del
circo por el noreste de los Estados Unidos y ella va a pasar todo el verano
con ellos.

Yo soy soltera también y tengo el verano libre, pero no tengo el menor
interés en el circo. ¡Es absurdo! ¿Qué hay que hacer en un circo? Según
Leonora, ella va a vender tiquetes por la mañana. Después de almorzar,
va a mirar algunos ensayos y a hablar con los trapecistas. Desde las dos
de la tarde hasta las siete, ella y sus colegas van a vender más tiquetes por
teléfono y en persona. A eso de las ocho de la noche, al escuchar la música
que indica que el circo va a empezar, Leonora va a cerrar la oficina y salir
para ir a ver la función. El colmo es que va a ganar solamente trescientos
dólares por semana. Ella sale mañana. Por mi parte, prefiero pasar el
verano aquí. Es bonito, hace buen tiempo y tengo otras amigas. De todos
modos, ella va a volver pronto.

Vocabulario

aunque	*although*	libre	*free* (as in time)
el circo	*the circus*	el noreste	*the northeast*
el colega	*the colleague*	qué hay que hacer	*what is there to do*
el colmo	*the limit*	el sitio	*the place*
el ensayo	*the rehearsal*	soltera	*single*
la gira	*the tour*	el tiquete	*the ticket*
indicar	*to indicate*	de todos modos	*anyway*
el interés	*the interest*	el trapecista	*the trapeze artist*

Nombres

la caja	*the box*	las noticias	*the news*
el correo	*the post office*	la parada	*the bus stop*
los derechos humanos	*the human rights*	la película	*the film*
		el/la testigo	*the witness*
el/la juez	*the judge*	el vecino	*the neighbor*
la ley	*the law*		

Preguntas

After you have read the selection, answer the following questions in Spanish.

1. ¿Cuántos años tiene Leonora?

   _____

2. ¿Por qué quiere ir al circo?

   _____

3. ¿Qué va a hacer Leonora durante el día?

   _____

4. ¿Cuánto va a ganar ella por semana en el circo?

   _____

 # Key Vocabulary

These words will help enhance your ability to communicate. As you learn them, remember to practice them aloud.

Nature

el alba (*f.*)	*the dawn*	el mar	*the sea*
el cielo	*the sky*	las montañas	*the mountains*
la colina	*the hill*	el monte	*the hill*
el desierto	*the desert*	la nieve	*the snow*
la estrella	*the star*	las nubes	*the clouds*
la inundación	*the flood*	el ocaso	*the sunset*
el lago	*the lake*	el océano	*the ocean*
la lluvia	*the rain*	la puesta del sol	*the sunset*
la luna	*the moon*	el relámpago	*the lightning*
la madrugada	*the dawn, early morning*	el río	*the river*
		el sol	*the sun*

el temblor	*the tremor*	la tormenta	*the storm*
la tempestad	*the storm*	el trueno	*the thunder*
el terremoto	*the earthquake*	el viento	*the wind*
la tierra	*the earth*		

Weather

¿Qué tiempo hace?	*What's the weather like?*
Hace buen tiempo.	*The weather is good.*
Hace mal tiempo.	*The weather is bad.*

Hace calor.	*It's hot.*	Hay estrellas.	*The stars are out.*
Hace frío.	*It's cold.*	Hay luna.	*The moon is out.*
Hace fresco.	*It's cool.*	Hay neblina.	*It's foggy.*
Hace sol.	*It's sunny.*	Hay nubes.	*It's cloudy.*
Hace viento.	*It's windy.*	Hay polvo.	*It's dusty.*
		Hay lodo.	*It's muddy.*

Exercise 9.8

Answer the following questions aloud in Spanish.

1. No comemos a las siete. ¿A qué hora comen Uds.?

2. Los libros no están en la mesa, sino en el piso. ¿Por qué están los libros en el piso?

3. ¿Qué haces por costumbre los sábados por la noche?

4. Después de hacer ejercicio, ¿en qué parte del cuerpo tienes dolor?

5. ¿Vive Ud. en un apartamento o en una casa? ¿En qué piso vive?

6. ¿Quiere Ud. viajar o prefiere Ud. ahorrar su dinero?

7. Si Ud. tiene hambre, ¿qué come? Si Ud. tiene sed, ¿qué bebe?

8. Enrique tiene ocho años. Su hermano tiene diez años y su hermana tiene doce. ¿Quién es el mayor de su familia?

9. ¿Va Ud. a la playa en el verano?

10. ¿Qué haces tú si tu amigo quiere ir a un restaurante en particular y quieres ir a otro?

Exercise 9.9

Regular and irregular verbs. *Complete the following sentences with the correct conjugation of the verbs in parentheses.*

1. Él no _____ jugo de naranja; _____ jugo de manzana. (*to drink/to drink*)

2. El niño no _____ bien el piano, porque no _____ nunca. (*to play/to practice*)

3. No _____ ningún buen hotel en la ciudad. (*there is*)

4. ¿_____ Uds. al campo con sus primos el domingo? (*to go*)

5. Yo _____ que él va a _____ un buen abogado si él estudia. (*to know/to be*)

6. Fernando _____ a Nueva York. ¿Cuántos amigos de él _____ en la ciudad? (*to want to go/to live*)

7. Yo _____ mi casa casi todos los días. No _____ limpiar mi casa los sábados. (*to clean/have to*)

8. Los dos amigos quieren _____ de fumar. (*to stop*)

9. ¿Cuál _____ su número de teléfono? (*to be*)

10. Nosotros _____ que el primo de Carlos _____ con nuestro hermano. (*to know/to be*)

11. La clase _____ a las seis. Nosotros _____ de la clase a las ocho. (*to begin/to leave*)

12. En la clase, estudiamos mucho y _____ la lección. (*to understand*)

13. ¿Dónde _____ las llaves que tú siempre pierdes? (*to be*)

14. ¿Quién _____ contestar las preguntas? (*to be able*)

15. La verdad es que ella _____ bien, pero nunca _____. (*to try to cook/to have success*)

16. ¿Qué _____ Ud. durante el día? (*to do*)

17. Toda la familia _____ a España todos los años. (*to travel*)

18. Ella _____ el piano y él _____ la flauta.
    Los domingos _____ al béisbol. (*to play/to play/to play*)

19. ¿Quién _____ la cuenta? (*to be going to pay*)

20. Mi amiga está en Portugal y no quiere _____ a los Estados Unidos. (*to return*)

21. Mi amiga _____ dolor de estómago. ¿Piensa Ud. que

    _____ a un médico? (*to have/ought to go*)

22. El carro de Juan es viejo. Él va a _____ otro. (*to buy*)

23. _____ a mi casa el sábado? ¿Qué quieres

    _____ para el desayuno? (*to come/to have*)

24. Si nadie quiere _____, ¿por qué tanta gente va a la playa?
    (*to swim*)

25. Ellos _____ en el maratón cada año en Boston. (*to run*)

Exercise 9.10

Prepositions and verbs. *Complete the following sentences with the Spanish for the words in parentheses.*

1. _____, las muchachas van a practicar la canción.
   (*before singing*)

2. _____, Raúl quiere ir al cine. (*after resting*)

3. _____ a las ocho, salimos a las seis y media.
   (*in order to arrive*)

4. _____, vamos a la playa. (*after eating*)

5. ¿Va ella a la fiesta _____ enferma todo el día?
   (*after being*)

6. Enrique baila _____ la música. (*without listening to*)

7. _____ duro, este hombre no tiene éxito.
   (*in spite of working*)

8. Ellos leen el periódico _____ al trabajo.
   (*before going*)

9. _____ algunas cervezas, Uds. deben comer algo.
   (*before having*)

10. _____ su tarea, el estudiante decide jugar.
    (*instead of doing*)

11. Ella quiere viajar _____ seis meses. (*for*)

12. Voy a pasar _____ la ciudad antigua en mayo. (*through*)

13. Necesito una habitación _____ una persona

    _____ tres días. (*for/for*)

14. El tren sale _____ México mañana, pero ella prefiere viajar

    _____ avión. (*for/by*)

Exercise 9.11

Numbers, telling time, adverbs, prepositions, and comparisons. *Complete the following sentences with the Spanish for the words in parentheses.*

1. Mi primo vive entre la _____ y

   la _____ avenida. (*sixth/seventh*)

2. Él llega _____ si camina _____.
   (*rapidly/to the left*)

3. ¿Por qué vive ella en el _____ piso? (*eighth*)

4. _____ el _____ tren llega de
   Los Angeles. (*at 10:45/third*)

5. Hay un buen restaurante en la calle _____ con

   la _____ avenida. (*34th/third*)

6. Ella siempre pierde sus llaves. _____ están

   _____ su mesa. _____ están

   _____ el carro. (*at times/underneath/frequently/in*)

7. Su hermana _____ nunca lee el periódico y nunca
   sabe nada. (*older*)

8. Mi hermano _____ está feliz porque nuestra tía viene
   de Texas. (*younger*)

9. Si estoy en la _____ avenida,

   ¿debo ir _____, _____,

   o _____ para llegar a la librería? (*seventh/to the right/
   to the left/straight ahead*)

10. Los domingos, mi amiga duerme _____.
    (*until 11:00 A.*)

11. Mi amigo no trabaja los domingos, pero su trabajo empieza

    _____ los lunes. (*at 8:00 A.M.*)

12. La película empieza _____ esta noche. (*at 7:45*)

13. Ella es _____ mujer de la familia que va a una
    universidad. (*the first*)

14. Las calles de México son _____ que las calles
    de España. (*narrower*)

15. Carla es _____ su hermano, pero su hermano

    es _____ ella. (*taller than/older than*)

16. El doctor piensa que el pollo es bueno, pero el pescado

    es _____ para la salud del paciente. (*better*)

17. El niño está triste pero su madre está _____ él.
    (*sadder than*)

18. Ella vive con sus tres hermanos _____. (*younger*)

19. Sara va al gimnasio porque quiere ser _____

    su _____ amiga. (*stronger than/best*)

20. ¿Cuál es la _____ película del año? (*worst*)

Exercise 9.12

Translate the following sentences into Spanish.

1. *My niece is going to be 13 years old next week.*

    _____

2. *The girls are hungry and thirsty, and no one knows how to cook.*

    _____

3. *Not one child wants to go to the dentist. I don't know why everyone
   is afraid to go.*

    _____

    _____

4. *The film begins at eight o'clock. We have to arrive at seven thirty.*

_____

5. *She thinks that he ought to try to run every day in order to be stronger.*

_____

_____

6. *She always goes to Las Vegas in the winter. She loses frequently. But today she is lucky and wins one hundred dollars.*

_____

_____

7. *That church is old. It is much older than this temple.*

_____

8. *I try to speak with my friends in Spanish. I have a lot to learn. I should study every morning.*

_____

_____

9. *Carla spends a lot of time in the store. She looks at the clothes, but she leaves without buying anything.*

_____

_____

10. *How many earthquakes are there in California each year?*

_____

11. *Who is here? It is I.*

_____

12. *George is a good man.*

_____

13. *Elena and her friends are intelligent.*

_____

14. *His grandmother and grandfather are happy because their grandchildren are well.*

_____

_____

Exercise 9.13

On a separate sheet of paper, write the English translation of the following infinitives from Part I.

1. abrir	28. dejar de	55. llegar	82. repasar
2. acabar de	29. descansar	56. llenar	83. repetir
3. aceptar	30. describir	57. llevar	84. romper
4. ahorrar	31. devolver	58. llorar	85. saber
5. almorzar	32. dibujar	59. manejar	86. salir
6. apagar	33. disfrutar	60. marcar	87. seguir
7. aparecer	34. doblar	61. mentir	88. ser
8. aprender	35. dormir	62. meter	89. servir
9. arreglar	36. empezar	63. mirar	90. sonreír
10. bailar	37. encontrar	64. nadar	91. subir
11. bajar	38. entender	65. necesitar	92. tener que
12. beber	39. entrar	66. oír	93. tener
13. cambiar	40. escribir	67. parar	94. terminar
14. caminar	41. escuchar	68. pasar	95. tirar
15. cantar	42. estar	69. pensar	96. tocar
16. celebrar	43. estudiar	70. perder	97. tomar
17. cerrar	44. explicar	71. pintar	98. trabajar
18. cocinar	45. firmar	72. poder	99. tratar de
19. comer	46. fumar	73. poner	100. usar
20. compartir	47. ganar	74. practicar	101. vender
21. comprar	48. gozar	75. preferir	102. venir
22. comprender	49. hablar	76. prender	103. ver
23. contestar	50. hacer	77. preparar	104. viajar
24. correr	51. ir	78. querer	105. vivir
25. cruzar	52. jugar	79. recibir	106. volver
26. deber	53. leer	80. recordar	107. votar
27. decidir	54. limpiar	81. regresar	

Reading Comprehension

El trabajo

No voy al trabajo hoy, ni mañana, ni pasado mañana. No tengo ganas.
Mi oficina es demasiado oscura. Cuando entro, finjo que estoy bien y que
entiendo como funcionan todas las máquinas que están allí, pero en
realidad, no entiendo nada. El cambio de un año a otro es impresionante.
Ahora no hay espacio ni para mis plantas ni para mis fotos. Hay una
computadora encima de la mesa y una impresora entre la máquina de
facsímile y la contestadora. El papel está debajo de la mesa; mis plumas y
mis lápices están al lado de la computadora. Yo sé que tengo que aprender
a usar todo para tener éxito en este nuevo mundo de la tecnología.

Durante el día, si mi jefe quiere hablar conmigo, él no sale de su
oficina. (Él está a solo veinte pasos de mi oficina.) Ya no habla conmigo
cara a cara. ¡No! Él manda un correo electrónico desde su oficina. Ya no
escucho su voz bella y expresiva. Ya no viene a mi cuartito para conversar
conmigo, ni discutimos las noticias del día, ni tomamos un café juntos.
Ahora él no busca razones para venir a mi oficina.

Son las doce. Ahora él prepara las facturas y los depósitos para la
semana. Almuerza rápidamente para volver a su computadora. Casi no
descansa. Todos los empleados salen a las cinco, pero él siempre trabaja
hasta las seis. Tengo mucho que hacer en la casa, pero si hago un gran
esfuerzo, puedo terminar antes de las cinco. Al fin y al cabo, no voy a
llamar a la oficina; es mejor ir a saludar a mis colegas.

Verbos

buscar	*to look for*	llamar	*to call*
conversar	*to converse*	mandar	*to send*
discutir	*to discuss*	saludar	*to greet*
fingir	*to pretend*		
funcionar	*to function,*		
	to work		

Nombres

el cambio	*the change*	el correo	*e-mail*
la computadora	*the computer*	electrónico	
la contestadora	*the answering*	el cuartito	*the little room*
	machine		(**-ito** makes the
			room smaller)

el depósito	*the deposit*	la máquina	*the fax machine*
el empleado	*the worker*	de facsímile	
el esfuerzo	*the effort*	el mundo	*the world*
el espacio	*the space*	las noticias	*the news*
la factura	*the invoice, bill*	la razón	*the reason*
la impresora	*the printer*	la voz	*the voice*
el jefe	*the boss*		

Adjetivos

impresionante	*impressive*
oscuro	*dark*

Expresiones

al fin y al cabo	*after all*
cara a cara	*face to face, in person*
está a sólo veinte pasos	*he is only twenty steps away*
pasado mañana	*the day after tomorrow*
tengo mucho que hacer	*I have a lot to do*
todo lo necesario	*all that is necessary*

Preguntas

After you have read the selection, answer the following questions in Spanish.

1. ¿Dónde está Isabel al empezar este cuento? ¿Por qué no quiere ir al trabajo?

   _____

2. ¿Quiere ella aprender todo lo necesario de la tecnología?

   _____

3. ¿Cómo es su relación con su jefe?

   _____

4. ¿En qué piensa Isabel durante el día?

   _____

5. ¿Qué va a hacer a las cinco?

   _____

6. ¿Piensa Ud. que Isabel está contenta?

   _____

II

Objects, Reflexive Verbs, and the Present Subjunctive

10

The Indirect Object

Gustar and the Indirect Object

Gustar means *to be pleasing to* and is used to express the idea of *liking* in Spanish.

Me gusta and *me gustan*

Me is the indirect object pronoun that means *to me*. In Spanish, there is no exact translation of *I like*. Compare the English construction with the Spanish construction.

Singular Noun as the Subject

English Construction	*I like this class.*
Spanish Construction	**Me gusta** esta clase.
	To me is pleasing this class.

Esta clase is a singular noun—the subject.
Gusta is the verb and agrees with the singular subject.
Me is the indirect object pronoun—the person to whom the action is occurring.

Me gusta la música.	*The music is pleasing to me.*
Me gusta el libro.	*The book is pleasing to me.*
Me gusta esta idea.	*This idea is pleasing to me.*
Me gusta la cerveza.	*The beer is pleasing to me.*
Me gusta el chocolate.	*Chocolate is pleasing to me.*

NOTE: In the Spanish construction, subjects retain their articles (**el**, **la**, **los**, **las**) even when the English translation doesn't include them (for example, **el chocolate**, English *Chocolate*—not *The chocolate*—in the example above).

A Word About Practicing Orally
It is essential to practice orally **me gusta** and all the forms to follow. The more
you practice, the more natural it becomes.

Plural Noun as the Subject

If the subject of the sentence is a plural noun, **gusta** becomes **gustan** to
agree with the plural subject.

English Construction	*I like the books.*
Spanish Construction	**Me gustan** los libros.
	To me are pleasing the books.

Los libros is the plural noun—the subject.
Gustan is the verb and agrees with the plural subject.
Me is the indirect object pronoun—the person to whom the action is
    occurring.

Me gustan las fiestas.	*The parties are pleasing to me.*
Me gustan los deportes.	*Sports are pleasing to me.*
Me gustan los perros.	*Dogs are pleasing to me.*

Verb as the Subject

Me gusta is also used when the subject is a verb. The verb form is the infinitive, no matter what the English translation is. When an infinitive is the
subject, the singular **gusta** is used.

English Construction	*I like to swim.*
Spanish Construction	**Me gusta** nadar.
	To me is pleasing to swim.

Me gusta comer.	*To eat is pleasing to me.*
Me gusta bailar.	*To dance is pleasing to me.*
Me gusta ir al cine.	*To go to the movies is pleasing to me.*
Me gusta escribir y leer.	*To write and to read are pleasing*
	to me.

NOTE: **Gusta** remains singular even if it is followed by a series of verbs.

The only forms of **gustar** that you will need are the third-person singular,
gusta, and the third-person plural, **gustan**.

To make a sentence negative, simply place **no** before the indirect object.

No me gustan las cucarachas.   *Cockroaches are not pleasing to me.*
No me gusta cocinar.   *To cook is not pleasing to me.*

Review
- If the subject of the sentence is a singular noun or a verb, use **gusta**.

  Me gusta el hotel.
  Me gusta viajar.

- If the subject is a plural noun, use **gustan**.

  Me gustan las vacaciones.

- If the sentence is negative, place **no** before the indirect object.

  No me gustan los ratones.

Te gusta and *te gustan*

Te is the indirect object pronoun that means *to you*. When you use **te**, you are speaking in the familiar **tú** form.

English Construction   *You like his car.*
Spanish Construction   **Te gusta** su carro.
                              To you is pleasing his car.

Singular Noun as the Subject

Te gusta mi idea.   *My idea is pleasing to you.*
¿Te gusta la puesta del sol?   *Is the sunset pleasing to you?*
¿Te gusta el teatro?   *Is theater pleasing to you?*
¿Te gusta España?   *Is Spain pleasing to you?*

Plural Noun as the Subject

Te gustan las flores rojas.   *Red flowers are pleasing to you.*
¿Te gustan las lecciones?   *Are the lessons pleasing to you?*
¿Te gustan tus cursos?   *Are your courses pleasing to you?*

Verb as the Subject

Te gusta viajar.   *To travel is pleasing to you.*
Te gusta descansar.   *To rest is pleasing to you.*
Te gusta cantar y bailar.   *To sing and dance is pleasing to you.*

Le gusta **and** *le gustan*

Le is the indirect object pronoun that means *to him* (**a él**), *to her* (**a ella**), or *to you* (**a Ud.**).

English Construction	*He likes the wine.*
Spanish Construction	**Le gusta** el vino.
	To him is pleasing the wine.

Because **le** means *to him, to her,* and *to you,* it can have any of the following meanings.

The wine is pleasing to him.
The wine is pleasing to her.
The wine is pleasing to you.

To clarify this ambiguity, the sentence must begin with a prepositional phrase that clarifies the meaning of the indirect object pronoun **le**.

A él le gusta el vino.	*The wine is pleasing to him.*
A él le gusta cantar.	*Singing is pleasing to him.*
A él le gustan los libros.	*Books are pleasing to him.*
A ella le gusta el vino rosado.	*Rosé wine is pleasing to her.*
A ella le gusta escribir cartas.	*Writing letters is pleasing to her.*
A ella le gustan las montañas.	*The mountains are pleasing to her.*
A Ud. le gusta la cerveza.	*The beer is pleasing to you.*
A Ud. le gusta tomar un descanso.	*To take a break is pleasing to you.*
A Ud. le gustan las playas.	*Beaches are pleasing to you.*

You can also insert proper names and nouns in the prepositional phrase.

A Fernando le gusta la verdad.	*The truth is pleasing to Fernando.*
A María le gusta bailar.	*To dance is pleasing to Maria.*
A Roberto le gustan los carros nuevos.	*New cars are pleasing to Robert.*

Singular nouns can be inserted in the prepositional phrases.

A la mujer le gusta leer.	*To read is pleasing to the woman.*
Al hombre le gusta cocinar.	*To cook is pleasing to the man.*

Nos gusta and *nos gustan*

Nos is the indirect object pronoun that means *to us*.

English Construction	*We like to speak Spanish.*
Spanish Construction	**Nos gusta** hablar español.
	To us is pleasing to speak Spanish.

Nos gusta la torta de chocolate.	*Chocolate cake is pleasing to us.*
Nos gusta comer en el parque.	*To eat in the park is pleasing to us.*
Nos gustan nuestros maestros.	*Our teachers are pleasing to us.*

Les gusta and *les gustan*

Les is the indirect object pronoun that means *to them* (**a ellos**, **a ellas**) and *to you* (**a Uds.**).

English Construction	*They like the film.*
Spanish Construction	**Les gusta** la película.
	To them is pleasing the film.

Because **les** means both *to them* and *to you*, the meaning of this sentence can be either of the following.

The film is pleasing to them.
The film is pleasing to you (pl.).

To clarify this ambiguity, the sentence must begin with a prepositional phrase that clarifies the meaning of **les**.

¿**A Uds. les gusta** el café negro?	*Is black coffee pleasing to you?*
¿**A Uds. les gusta** el presidente?	*Is the president pleasing to you?*
A ellas les gustan los hoteles.	*Hotels are pleasing to them.*
A ellos les gusta dormir bien.	*To sleep well is pleasing to them.*

Nouns and proper names can be inserted in the prepositional phrases.

A Sara y Enrique les gusta nadar.	*To swim is pleasing to Sara and Henry.*
A los niños les gustan los juguetes.	*Toys are pleasing to the children.*
A las niñas les gustan las lecciones.	*The lessons are pleasing to the girls.*

If you want to add emphasis to the constructions of **me gusta** and **te gusta**, add **a mí**, which emphasizes **me**, and **a ti**, which emphasizes **te**.

A mí me gusta el café.   *Coffee is pleasing to me.*
A ti te gusta el vino.   *Wine is pleasing to you.*

There is no ambiguity in these examples. **A mí** and **a ti** give the feeling of the emphasized pronoun in English: ***I*** *like coffee.* ***You*** *like wine.*

Exercise 10.1

Pronounce the examples aloud so you can become familiar with the sound.

Singular Subject	Singular Subject	Plural Subject
Me gusta el hotel.	Me gusta viajar.	Me gustan los hoteles.
Te gusta la clase.	Te gusta correr.	Te gustan las clases.
Le gusta el libro.	Le gusta escribir.	Le gustan los libros.
Nos gusta la comida.	Nos gusta comer.	Nos gustan las comidas.
Les gusta el programa.	Les gusta leer.	Les gustan los programas.

Exercise 10.2

Complete the following sentences. Choose the correct indirect object pronoun, as indicated by the prepositional phrase in parentheses, then choose either **gusta** *or* **gustan**, *depending on whether the subject is singular or plural.*

EXAMPLES   (A mí) __me gusta__ el helado.

(A él) __le gustan__ las galletas.

(A nosotros) __nos gusta__ el postre.

1. (A mí) _____ el café con azúcar.

2. (A ella) _____ el café negro.

3. (A María) _____ el té.

4. (A mí) _____ escribir libros.

5. (A mis amigos) _____ cocinar.

6. (A Susana y a Miguel) _____ viajar.

7. (A ellos) _____ comer en buenos restaurantes.

8. (A mí) _____ ir al teatro.

9. (A ti) _____ ir al cine.

10. (A nosotros) _____ salir los sábados.

11. (A Guillermo) _____ los restaurantes japoneses.

12. (A su amiga) _____ los restaurantes hindúes.

13. (A Uds.) _____ los restaurantes franceses.

14. (A mí) _____ las playas del Caribe.

15. (A ti) _____ las piscinas grandes.

16. (A tu hermana) _____ la ciudad.

17. (Al hermano de José) _____ el campo.

18. (A nosotros) _____ viajar.

19. (A Cecilia y a su familia) _____ conversar.

20. (A los niños) _____ aprender todo.

21. (A los adolescentes) _____ jugar deportes.

22. ¿(A Uds.) _____ el alcalde de su ciudad?

Verbs like *gustar*

You have just learned a very important form, not only to express the idea of *I like*, but for other verbs as well. The following verbs are used with an indirect object.

agradar *to be pleasing to* (very close in meaning to **gustar**)

¿No te agrada nadar?	*Isn't swimming pleasing to you?*
Me agrada vivir en el campo.	*To live in the country is pleasing to me.*

convenir *to suit someone, to be convenient (for)*

¿Te conviene tomar ese trabajo?	*Does it suit you to take that job?*
No nos conviene viajar ahora.	*It does not suit us to travel now.*

doler *to be painful, to hurt*

Me duele la cabeza.	*My head hurts me.*
Te duelen los dientes.	*Your teeth hurt you.*
¿A Uds. les duelen los pies si caminan mucho?	*Do your feet hurt you if you walk a lot?*

NOTE: In Spanish, the possessive adjective is not used with parts of the body and the indirect object pronoun.

encantar *to be enchanting to, to like very much*

Le encanta viajar.	*To travel is enchanting to him. (He loves traveling.)*
Le encanta visitar España.	*To visit Spain is enchanting to him.*

NOTE: **Encantar** is much stronger than **gustar**. **Encantar** cannot be used in the negative.

faltar *to be lacking* (something), *to be missing* (something)

A ellos les falta disciplina.	*They lack discipline.*
Aquí falta luz.	*Here there is no light.*

NOTE: **Faltar** can be used without the indirect object pronoun.

fascinar *to fascinate, to be fascinating (to)*

Nos fascina el baile flamenco.	*Flamenco dance fascinates us.*
Me fascinan estos dibujos.	*These drawings are fascinating to me.*

hacer falta *to need* (something)

Me hace falta tomar unas vacaciones.	*I need to take a vacation.*

importar *to be important to, to matter*

No me importa.	*It is not important to me.*
A Sandra le importan sus amigos.	*Sandra's friends are important to her.*
No importa.	*It doesn't matter. / Never mind.*

NOTE: **Importar** can be used without the indirect object pronoun.

interesar *to be interesting (to)*

Les interesa estudiar.	*To study is interesting to them.*
Me interesa ir a museos.	*It interests me to go to museums.*

molestar *to bother, to annoy*

¿Le molesta si alguien fuma? *Does it bother you if someone smokes?*

A él no le molesta nada. *Nothing bothers him.*

parecer *to seem, to appear to be*

Me parece que es una buena escuela. *It seems to me that it is a good school.*

Parece que va a llover. *It seems that it is going to rain.*

NOTE: **Parecer** can be used without the indirect object pronoun.

quedar *to be left over, to remain*

Nos quedan veinte minutos. *We have 20 minutes left.*

No me queda mucho dinero. *I don't have much money left.*

¿Cuántas páginas nos quedan por leer? *How many pages are left for us to read?*

NOTE: **Quedar por** + an infinitive = *to remain to be.*

sobrar *to have more than enough of* (something)

Me sobra comida para mañana. *I have more than enough food for tomorrow.*

tocarle a alguien *to be someone's turn*

Cada vez que me toca a mí, gano. *Every time it's my turn, I win.*

Cada vez que le toca a él, pierde. *Every time it's his turn, he loses.*

Exercise 10.3

Complete the following sentences with the correct prepositional phrase, according to the words in parentheses.

EXAMPLE ___A él___ le gusta nadar. (*to him*)

1. _____ le gusta el tenis. (*to her*)

2. ¿_____ le gustan todos los deportes? (*to you*)

3. _____ me gusta leer, pero me encanta escribir. (*to me*)

4. Yo sé que _____ te gusta estudiar, pero _____ les gusta ir a fiestas. (*to you/to them*)

5. Parece que _____ le gusta cocinar. (*to no one*)

6. ¿_____ le gusta limpiar su apartamento? (*to whom*)

Exercise 10.4

Change the following singular sentences to plural. Make sure both the subject and the verb are plural. The indirect object pronoun will remain the same.

EXAMPLE   Me gusta su idea.   *Me gustan sus ideas.*

1. Les encanta ese carro rojo. _____

2. Te agrada el programa. _____

3. Me gusta la silla. _____

4. Nos importa nuestro amigo. _____

5. Le fascina esa computadora. _____

Exercise 10.5

Translate the following sentences into English.

EXAMPLE   Me gusta viajar.   *Traveling / To travel is pleasing to me.*

1. A Susana le duele la cabeza. _____

2. Me falta un lápiz con que escribir. _____

3. ¿Por qué no te gusta bailar? _____

4. Nos fascinan los viajes exóticos. _____

5. A ella le interesan las noticias del día.

   _____

6. ¿A Ud. le molesta su perfume? _____

7. ¿A Uds. les importan las lecciones? _____

8. ¿Te conviene seguir tus estudios este año?

   _____

9. A él no le gusta manejar en la lluvia.

   _____

10. A ella no le gusta el clima caliente. _____

Exercise 10.6

Answer the following questions aloud in Spanish.

1. ¿A Ud. le duele la cabeza después de trabajar todo el día?

2. ¿Qué les conviene estudiar ahora?

3. ¿Cuántos libros nos quedan por leer?

4. ¿Por qué a Uds. les fascina hablar español?

5. ¿Les gustan los carros grandes que usan mucha gasolina?

6. ¿Te interesa la tecnología?

7. ¿Qué le encanta hacer?

8. En su familia, ¿a quién le gusta jugar al baloncesto? ¿A quién le gusta bailar?

9. ¿Te importa saber de la política?

10. ¿A Uds. les fascina viajar?

The Indirect Object Pronoun

Review the indirect object pronouns.

me		*to me*
te		*to you* (sing., familiar)
le	a Ud.	*to you* (sing., formal)
	a él	*to him*
	a ella	*to her*
nos		*to us*
os		*to you* (pl., familiar; used only in Spain)
les	a Uds.	*to you* (pl., formal)
	a ellos	*to them* (m.)
	a ellas	*to them* (f.)

So far, you have learned the indirect object with verbs like **gustar**. Now make sure you know what an indirect object is in other sentences as well. For example, *I give the gift **to him***. In this sentence, *to him* is the indirect object.

The indirect object receives the action of the verb indirectly. It answers questions about to whom or for whom an action is done.

In order to have an indirect object in a sentence, there must be a direct object, either real or implied. In the example above, *the gift* is the direct object.

The translation of the indirect object is *to me, to you, to him, to her, to us, to them.*

A Word About Indirect Objects
Be sure to practice the indirect object orally as much as you can. The structure of Spanish and English is quite different here, so take your time and practice.

Verbs that commonly take indirect objects follow.

cobrar *to charge* (money)		**comprar** *to buy*	
yo cobro	nosotros cobramos	yo compro	nosotros compramos
tú cobras	vosotros cobráis	tú compras	vosotros compráis
Ud. cobra	Uds. cobran	él compra	ellos compran

contar *to relate, to tell a story, to count;* **contar con** *to count on, to rely on*		**contestar** *to answer*	
yo cuento	nosotros contamos	yo contesto	nosotros contestamos
tú cuentas	vosotros contáis	tú contestas	vosotros contestáis
él cuenta	ellos cuentan	ella contesta	ellas contestan

dar *to give*		**decir** *to say, to tell*	
yo doy	nosotros damos	yo digo	nosotros decimos
tú das	vosotros dais	tú dices	vosotros decís
él da	ellos dan	ella dice	ellas dicen

enseñar *to teach*		**enviar** *to send*	
yo enseño	nosotros enseñamos	yo envío	nosotros enviamos
tú enseñas	vosotros enseñáis	tú envías	vosotros enviáis
Ud. enseña	Uds. enseñan	él envía	ellos envían

hacer *to do, to make*		**preguntar** *to ask* (a question)	
yo hago	nosotros hacemos	yo pregunto	nosotros preguntamos
tú haces	vosotros hacéis	tú preguntas	vosotros preguntáis
Ud. hace	Uds. hacen	él pregunta	ellos preguntan

prestar *to lend*	
yo presto	nosotros prestamos
tú prestas	vosotros prestáis
ella presta	ellas prestan

traer *to bring*	
yo traigo	nosotros traemos
tú traes	vosotros traéis
Ud. trae	Uds. traen

vender *to sell*	
yo vendo	nosotros vendemos
tú vendes	vosotros vendéis
ella vende	ellas venden

Position of the Indirect Object Pronoun

The indirect object pronoun can be placed in either of two positions in a sentence or phrase.

Indirect Object Pronoun Placed Directly Before the First Verb

In the first position, the indirect object pronoun is placed *directly before the first verb* in a sentence or question.

Carlos **me escribe** una carta.	*Charles writes a letter to me.*
Carlos **te escribe** una carta.	*Charles writes a letter to you.*
Yo **le escribo** una carta.	*I write a letter to you.* / *I write a letter to him.* / *I write a letter to her.*
Carlos **os escribe** una carta.	*Charles writes a letter to you.*
Yo **les escribo** una carta.	*I write a letter to you.* / *I write a letter to them.*

Remember that the indirect object pronoun **le** is ambiguous. It means *to him, to her, to you.* Out of context, there is no way to know what the meaning is. So a prepositional phrase is added to clarify the meaning.

María **le escribe** una carta **a Ud.**	*Maria writes a letter to you.*
María **le escribe** una carta **a él.**	*Maria writes a letter to him.*
María **le escribe** una carta **a ella.**	*Maria writes a letter to her.*

Remember also that a proper noun can be inserted in the clarifying prepositional phrase.

María **le escribe** una carta **a Juan.**	*Maria writes a letter to John.*
María **le escribe** una carta **a Susana.**	*Maria writes a letter to Susana.*

A noun can also be inserted in the prepositional phrase.

María **le escribe** una carta **a su hermana**.	*Maria writes a letter to her sister.*
María **le escribe** una carta **a mi amigo**.	*Maria writes a letter to my friend.*
Juan **le escribe** una carta **a su padre**.	*John writes a letter to his father.*
Juan **le escribe** una carta **a su primo**.	*John writes a letter to his cousin.*

Like **le**, **les** is ambiguous. It means *to you* (**a Uds.**) and *to them* (**a ellos, a ellas**). A prepositional phrase is added to clarify the meaning. A proper noun or a noun can also be used as a clarifier.

Juan **les escribe** una carta **a Uds.**	*John writes a letter to you.*
Juan **les escribe** una carta **a ellas**.	*John writes a letter to them.*
Él **les escribe** una carta **a sus hermanos**.	*He writes a letter to his brothers.*
Juan **les escribe** una carta **a Ana y José**.	*John writes a letter to Ana and Joseph.*

With the verbs **comprar** and **hacer**, the translation of the indirect object pronoun is *for me, for you, for him, for her, for us, for them.*

Él **me compra** flores.	*He buys flowers for me.*
Yo **le compro** flores a él.	*I buy flowers for him.*
Te hago un favor.	*I do (for) you a favor.*

Exercise 10.7

Using the new verbs, complete the following sentences with the correct verb and indirect object pronoun. Add clarifiers when necessary.

1. Julia _____ dos tarjetas cada semana. (*to write/to me*)

2. José y Maria _____ tarjetas desde Barcelona. (*to write/to us*)

3. Carlos _____ la lección de hoy. (*to give/to me*)

4. Yo _____ si mi tarea está en tu casa. (*to ask/you*)

5. Él _____ que su hermana vive en Nueva York. (*to say/to me*)

6. Ella _____ su bolígrafo. (*to lend/to him*)

7. Nosotros _____ a hablar español. (*to teach/
to Ana y José*)

8. Ellos _____ café con leche a mi oficina. (*to bring/to us*)

9. Yo _____ los resultados de la elección. (*to tell/to him*)

10. Yo _____, "¿Cuánto _____
Ud.?" (*to ask/the cab driver, to charge/me*)

Exercise 10.8

*Complete the following sentences with the correct verb and indirect object pronoun.
Notice that these sentences include two verbs. Practice placing the indirect object
pronoun directly before the first verb.*

EXAMPLES Juan __*me quiere dar*__ una lámpara. (*to want to give/to me*)

Juan __*me va a dar*__ una lámpara. (*to be going to give/to me*)

1. Alicia _____ una alfombra.
(*to want to give/to me*)

2. El maestro _____ el francés.
(*to want to teach/to his students*)

3. Mis primos _____ un carro para mi
cumpleaños. (*to be going to buy/for me*)

4. Yo _____ mi computadora vieja.
(*to want to sell/to you*)

5. ¿Tienes frío? Yo _____ una chaqueta.
(*to be able to bring/to you*)

6. Ud. _____ la verdad. (*ought to tell/him*)

7. ¿Quién _____ las lecciones de hoy?
(*to be able to teach/us*)

8. ¿_____ Ud. el favor de limpiar mi casa?
(*to be able to do/for me*)

9. Yo _____ buenas direcciones, pero no sé
donde estoy. (*to want to give/to you*)

10. Ellos siempre _____ cómo estoy. (*to ask/me*)

Indirect Object Pronoun Attached to the Infinitive

In the second position, the indirect object pronoun is *attached to the infinitive* if there is an infinitive in the sentence or question.

Let us say, for example, that a sentence includes a phrase that has an infinitive but no other form of a verb. In that type of phrase, any indirect object pronoun *must* be attached to the infinitive.

Antes de prestarte dinero,...	*Before lending you money, . . .*
Después de enseñarnos el francés,...	*After teaching us French, . . .*
En vez de escribirme una carta,...	*Instead of writing a letter to me, . . .*

In other cases, sentences may include a phrase with more than one verb, one of which is an infinitive. You may also attach an indirect object pronoun to the infinitive in this type of phrase.

¿Puede Ud. **hacerme** el favor de cerrar la ventana?	*Can you do me the favor of closing the window?*
Pedro quiere **darte** un libro.	*Peter wants to give you a book.*
Vamos a **enseñarle** a pintar.	*We are going to teach him to paint.*
Ella quiere **traernos** café.	*She wants to bring coffee to us.*
El niño va a **decirles** la verdad.	*The boy is going to tell them the truth.*

Exercise 10.9

Complete the following sentences by attaching the indirect object pronoun to the infinitive. Use the words within parentheses as well as the prepositional phrases in the sentences for clarification.

1. Ella _____ un cuento esta noche.
   (*to want to tell/to me*)

2. Patricia _____ a Ud. su guitarra.
   (*to be going to lend*)

3. ¿Quién _____ a su familia?
   (*to be going to write*)

4. Nosotros _____ a sus amigos la casa.
   (*to be going to sell*)

5. Yo _____ a Uds. mi bicicleta. (*to want to lend*)

Exercise 10.10

Some of the following sentences have two verbs; some have one. Complete the sentences with the correct verb or verbs and indirect object pronoun. The verbs in this lesson are very important, so try to memorize them as you do the following exercise.

1. Si tienes frío, yo _____ un suéter.
   (*to give/to you*)

2. El camarero _____ al hombre un vaso de agua.
   (*to bring/to him*)

3. Manuel _____ a cocinar.
   (*to want to teach/to us*)

4. Nosotros _____ el viernes.
   (*to be going to write/to them*)

5. Tú _____ tus libros todo el tiempo.
   (*to lend/to me*)

  Review the positions of the indirect object pronoun.

- Directly before the first verb
- Attached to the infinitive

Whether the indirect object pronoun is placed directly before the first verb or is attached to the infinitive, the meaning is exactly the same. Practice the indirect object pronouns and the verbs aloud as much as you can.

Yo **te quiero escribir** una carta. Yo **quiero escribirte** una carta.	*I want to write you a letter.*
Él **me va a vender** un carro. Él **va a venderme** un carro.	*He is going to sell me a car.*
Ellos **nos quieren contar** un cuento. Ellos **quieren contarnos** un cuento.	*They want to tell us a story.*
Les debemos decir a Uds. la verdad. **Debemos decirles** a Uds. la verdad.	*We ought to tell you the truth.*

Exercise 10.11

Translate the following sentences into English.

1. Me puede decir, ¿por qué a Sandra no le gusta tocar la guitarra?

   _____

2. El amigo de Elena le presta a Ud. sus libros.

   _____

3. Elena le da a su hermano los bolígrafos que él necesita.

   _____

4. Las lecciones de música no son caras. El maestro les cobra a sus estudiantes quince dólares por hora.

   _____

   _____

5. Me fascina jugar al tenis, pero más me conviene nadar.

   _____

6. El doctor no está en su consultorio. No sé si quiere hablar conmigo.

   _____

7. Entre tú y yo, tenemos que decidir quien va a contarles a los niños el cuento.

   _____

   _____

8. ¿Por qué el abogado les hace preguntas a los testigos si ya sabe las respuestas?

   _____

   _____

9. ¿Puede Ud. venderme rápidamente dos maletas? Voy a viajar mañana.

   _____

10. Ella nos quiere llamar el día de acción de gracias.

    _____

11. A ella le gusta celebrar el día del amor y la amistad.

    _____

12. ¿Les conviene tomar sopa de pollo cuando Uds. están enfermos?

_____

13. Le digo a ella que su idea es buena.

_____

14. A ella no le gusta el café; su colega siempre le trae el té.

_____

15. El camarero le trae al hombre un vaso de agua. Él les trae a los jovencitos un vaso de leche.

_____

_____

Exercise 10.12

Translate the following sentences, then answer the questions orally in Spanish.

EXAMPLE ¿Es esta lección difícil? _Is this lesson difficult?_

(Oral) _Sí, es difícil, pero me gusta aprender._

1. ¿Quiere Ud. viajar conmigo el año que viene? ¿Tiene Ud. vacaciones? ¿Adónde quiere ir?

_____

2. ¿Dónde te gusta comer? ¿Prefieres comer en un restaurante o en casa?

_____

3. ¿A Ud. le molesta la contaminación de las ciudades grandes?

_____

4. ¿Te gusta bailar? ¿A quién le gusta bailar contigo?

_____

5. A ellos no les gusta el restaurante en la calle cuarenta y dos con la novena avenida. ¿Sabe Ud. la razón?

_____

_____

6. Es el cumpleaños de Susana. ¿Le debo traer flores?

_____

7. Les decimos a los niños que es importante estudiar. ¿Por qué no nos prestan atención?

_____

_____

8. Le presto dinero a María porque ella es una buena amiga y siempre me devuelve el dinero. ¿Les presta Ud. dinero a sus amigos?

_____

_____

9. ¿Qué le contesta Ud. al muchacho si él le dice que él tiene miedo de nadar?

_____

_____

10. Ellos quieren darte un carro para celebrar el nuevo año pero tienen solamente quinientos dólares. ¿Qué deben hacer?

_____

_____

11. Tenemos hambre. ¿Quién nos va a enseñar a cocinar?

_____

12. ¿Dónde estoy? ¿Me puedes dar buenas direcciones?

_____

13. Tu mejor amigo quiere darte un buen regalo. Él quiere hacerte el favor de limpiar tu apartamento. ¿Cuántos cuartos tienes?

_____

_____

14. El niño le pregunta a Ud., "¿por qué hay nubes en el cielo?" ¿Sabe Ud. la razón?

_____

_____

Exercise 10.13

Translate the following sentences from English to Spanish.

1. *Every year he gives a gift to his girlfriend.*

   _____

2. *Carla never tells me her secrets.*

   _____

3. *Henry doesn't want to lend money to us.*

   _____

4. *Who is going to buy books for the children?*

   _____

5. *After writing to his friends, he is going to the movies.*

   _____

6. *They charge us too much. We charge them little.*

   _____

7. *Why don't you answer the students? They ask you many questions.*

   _____

8. *We are going to give a dog to Peter and Rosa.*

   _____

9. *I'll bring you coffee if you bring me tea.*

   _____

10. *I tell you that the train is coming.*

   _____

11. *Why do you teach us German if we want to learn French?*

   _____

12. *She listens to everything, but says nothing to you.*

   _____

13. *Susan's aunt tells her that she wants to go to Mexico for her vacation. She tells me that she wants to go to Paris.*

   _____

   _____

14. *After studying a lot, do your eyes hurt?*

_____

15. *Everyone wants to go to the football game except me.*

_____

 # Reading Comprehension

Ir de compras

A mi amigo Julio y a mí nos gusta ir de compras. Nos fascina pasear en el carro a regiones en las afueras. Durante el día, nos encanta probar la comida típica del área. Al entrar en un restaurante, el camarero nos dice "¿En qué puedo servirles?" y le preguntamos, "¿qué clase de comida nos recomienda?" Él nos recomienda los mariscos y nos da unos minutos para decidir. Después de un rato, nos dice, "Disculpe, están Uds. listos para ordenar?" Julio le pregunta cuánto cuesta la langosta. "No hay" nos contesta. Escogemos, pues, crema de almejas, cangrejo con ajo y camarones. Después de la comida deliciosa, continuamos alegremente nuestro viaje turístico.

Vocabulario

ir de compras	*to go shopping*
pasear en el carro	*to take a ride*
las afueras	*outskirts, suburbs*
probar	*to taste, to take a taste*
el área (*f.*)	*the area*
al entrar	*upon entering*
en qué puedo servirles	*how can I serve (help) you*
recomendar	*to recommend*
los mariscos	*seafood*
un rato	*a little while*
disculpe	*excuse me*
están Uds. listos para ordenar	*are you ready to order*
la langosta	*the lobster*
escoger	*to choose*
crema de almejas	*clam chowder*
el cangrejo	*crab*
el ajo	*garlic*
los camarones	*shrimp*

Preguntas

After you have read the selection, answer the following questions in Spanish.

1. ¿Por qué a los dos amigos les gusta ir de compras?

   _____

2. ¿Qué les gusta comer?

   _____

3. ¿Adónde van después de comer?

   _____

 # Reading Comprehension

El viaje

Me gusta viajar porque cuando viajo no soy de aquí ni soy de allá.
Me fascina la idea. Pienso ir a Italia. Me dicen que es un país maravilloso,
el más bello del mundo. Me cuentan que la gente es muy amable y que
gozan de la vida cada día. Me dicen que exactamente a las siete todas las
noches en todas las ciudades y todos los pueblos, la gente sale, los jóvenes
y los viejos, salen de sus casas y dan una vuelta por la ciudad. Después
de caminar por una hora, vuelven a la casa para cenar. ¡Qué imagen más
hermosa! Me parece que me va a gustar Italia.

No me importa que hay mucho que hacer antes de viajar. Primero,
tengo que hacer las reservaciones. Voy a pedir un asiento con ventanilla
porque me encanta mirar el cielo y las nubes por la ventana. Yo sé que
a otras personas les gusta el asiento en el pasillo para poder andar por
el avión sin molestar a nadie.

La parte que me encanta más es la hora de la comida. La azafata nos
pregunta, "¿qué quieren Uds.?" Le contestamos con "pollo, por favor,"
o "pescado," o "prefiero carne, por favor." Nos dan lo que pedimos y por
un rato hay silencio en el avión mientras los pasajeros comen. Si es largo
el viaje, nos muestran una película y también podemos escuchar música
con los audífonos que nos dan. Yo misma prefiero leer o escribir pero
a muchos viajeros les gusta mirar la película mientras otros duermen.

No puedo tardar más. Primero, voy a escoger una buena fecha que
me va a traer suerte. Después voy a comprar un tiquete de ida y vuelta
y un vuelo directo. Finalmente, voy a arreglar solamente una maleta para
no cargar mucho. Yo sé que una buena experiencia me espera.

Verbos y expresiones verbales

andar	*to walk*	escoger	*to choose*
arreglar la maleta	*to pack the suitcase*	esperar	*to await*
cargar	*to carry*	gozar (de)	*to enjoy*
cenar	*to dine*	tardar	*to delay*
dar una vuelta	*to take a walk*		

Nombres

el asiento	*the seat*
los audífonos	*the headphones*
la azafata	*the stewardess, flight attendant*
la imagen	*the image*
el pasillo	*the aisle*
la ventanilla	*the window in a car, boat, or airplane*
el vuelo	*the flight*

Pronombres relativos y conjunciones

lo que	*that which,* often translated as *what*
mientras	*while*

Expresiones

hay mucho que hacer	*there is a lot to do*
ida y vuelta	*round-trip*
por un rato	*for a little while*

Preguntas

After you have read the selection, answer the following questions in Spanish.

1. ¿A Isabel le gusta viajar?

   _____

2. ¿Por qué escoge Italia?

   _____

3. ¿Qué tiene que hacer antes de viajar?

   _____

4. ¿Qué piensa hacer ella durante el viaje? ¿Qué hacen los otros pasajeros?

   _____

5. ¿Piensa Ud. que Isabel va a viajar?

   _____

11

The Direct Object

The Personal *a* and the Direct Object

The direct object receives the action of the verb directly.
The direct object can be a thing.

> I see **the tree**.

The direct object can be a person.

> I see **the woman**.

When the direct object is a person, an untranslated **a** is placed directly before the direct object person. This is called the *personal a*.

Yo veo **a la mujer**.	*I see the woman.*
Vemos **a Pedro**.	*We see Peter.*
Uds. ven **a sus primos**.	*You see your cousins.*

If the direct object person is masculine and singular, the **a** combines with **el** and becomes **al**.

Yo visito **al hombre**.	*I visit the man.*
Tú visitas **al niño**.	*You visit the child.*

Personal **a** is used before **alguien** and **nadie**.

¿Quieres llamar **a alguien**?	*Do you want to call someone?*
No puedo llamar **a nadie**.	*I can't call anyone.*

Personal **a** is not used with **tener**.

Tengo dos hermanas.	*I have two sisters.*
Ella tiene cinco sobrinos.	*She has five nephews.*

Remember that if the direct object is a *thing,* there is no personal **a.**

Yo veo el árbol.	*I see the tree.*
Queremos ver una película hoy.	*We want to see a film today.*
Él espera el tren en la estación.	*He waits for the train in the station.*

Transitive Verbs

Transitive verbs are verbs that take a direct object.

The English translation for many Spanish verbs includes a preposition. That means that for this type of verb, the direct object will immediately follow the verb in Spanish, but it will follow a preposition in English. Look closely at the headings for verbs such as **buscar** *to look **for**.* Study the following examples.

Yo escucho la música.	*I **listen to** the music.*
Ella mira la casa.	*She **looks at** the house.*
Esperamos el tren.	*We **wait for** the train.*

Here is a list of frequently used transitive verbs.

abrazar *to embrace, to hug*

yo abrazo	nosotros abrazamos
tú abrazas	vosotros abrazáis
ella abraza	ellas abrazan

acompañar *to accompany*

yo acompaño	nosotros acompañamos
tú acompañas	vosotros acompañáis
él acompaña	ellos acompañan

amar *to love*

yo amo	nosotros amamos
tú amas	vosotros amáis
ella ama	ellas aman

ayudar *to help*

yo ayudo	nosotros ayudamos
tú ayudas	vosotros ayudáis
Ud. ayuda	Uds. ayudan

besar *to kiss*

yo beso	nosotros besamos
tú besas	vosotros besáis
él besa	ellos besan

buscar *to look for*	
yo busco	nosotros buscamos
tú buscas	vosotros buscáis
ella busca	ellas buscan

conocer *to be acquainted with,* *to know* (a person or place)	
yo conozco	nosotros conocemos
tú conoces	vosotros conocéis
Ud. conoce	Uds. conocen

Conocer means to know a person or place in terms of being acquainted.

Yo conozco a esta mujer.	*I know (am acquainted with) this woman.*
Él conoce Paris.	*He knows Paris.*

Compare this with **saber**, which means to know a fact or to know how to do something.

Ella sabe la verdad.	*She knows the truth.*
Yo sé nadar.	*I know how to swim.*

cuidar *to take care of*	
yo cuido	nosotros cuidamos
tú cuidas	vosotros cuidáis
él cuida	ellos cuidan

dejar *to leave* (something or someone) *behind*	
yo dejo	nosotros dejamos
tú dejas	vosotros dejáis
ella deja	ellas dejan

Dejar means to leave something or someone behind.

Dejo mis llaves en mi casa.	*I leave my keys in my house.*

Compare that with **salir**, which means to exit.

Salgo de mi oficina a las tres.	*I leave my office at three o'clock.*

encontrar *to find*

yo encuentro	nosotros encontramos
tú encuentras	vosotros encontráis
Ud. encuentra	Uds. encuentran

NOTE: **Encontrar** and **hallar** are synonyms and can be used interchangeably.

escuchar *to listen to*

yo escucho	nosotros escuchamos
tú escuchas	vosotros escucháis
ella escucha	ellas escuchan

esperar *to wait for*

yo espero	nosotros esperamos
tú esperas	vosotros esperáis
él espera	ellos esperan

extrañar *to miss* (a person or a place)

yo extraño	nosotros extrañamos
tú extrañas	vosotros extrañáis
ella extraña	ellas extrañan

gritar *to yell at, to scream at*

yo grito	nosotros gritamos
tú gritas	vosotros gritáis
él grita	ellos gritan

hallar *to find*

yo hallo	nosotros hallamos
tú hallas	vosotros halláis
Ud. halla	Uds. hallan

NOTE: **Hallar** and **encontrar** are synonyms and can be used interchangeably.

invitar *to invite*

yo invito	nosotros invitamos
tú invitas	vosotros invitáis
él invita	ellos invitan

llamar *to call*

yo llamo	nosotros llamamos
tú llamas	vosotros llamáis
ella llama	ellas llaman

llevar *to carry, to carry off, to carry away; to wear*

yo llevo	nosotros llevamos
tú llevas	vosotros lleváis
Ud. lleva	Uds. llevan

matar *to kill*

yo mato	nosotros matamos
tú matas	vosotros matáis
él mata	ellos matan

mirar *to look at, to watch*

yo miro	nosotros miramos
tú miras	vosotros miráis
ella mira	ellas miran

querer + **a** + person
to love a person

yo quiero	nosotros queremos
tú quieres	vosotros queréis
Ud. quiere	Uds. quieren

Querer a una persona means *to love a person*. This verb is less strong than **amar**.

> Ella quiere a su amiga.   *She loves her friend.*

Compare that with **amar**, which expresses a deeper love.

> Él ama a su esposa.   *He (deeply) loves his wife.*

recoger *to gather, to pick up*	
yo recojo	nosotros recogemos
tú recoges	vosotros recogéis
ella recoge	ellas recogen

saludar *to greet*	
yo saludo	nosotros saludamos
tú saludas	vosotros saludáis
él saluda	ellos saludan

ver *to see*	
yo veo	nosotros vemos
tú ves	vosotros veis
Ud. ve	Uds. ven

visitar *to visit*	
yo visito	nosotros visitamos
tú visitas	vosotros visitáis
él visita	ellos visitan

Exercise 11.1

Complete the following sentences, using the correct form of the verb and the personal **a**.

EXAMPLES   Nosotros ___*visitamos a Susana*___ cada año en España.
(*to visit Susan*)

Ella ___*ama a su madre*___. (*to love her mother*)

1. Antes de salir de la casa, ella _____.
   (*to kiss her husband*)

2. Carlos quiere _____ el día del amor
   y la amistad. (*to call his friends*)

3. Yo siempre _____ a la tienda.
   (*to accompany my grandmother*)

4. No puedo _____. No sé donde está.
   (*to find my younger brother*)

5. El estudiante del primer año _____.
   (*to miss his family*)

6. En clase, nosotros _____, y prestamos
   atención. (*to look at the teacher*)

7. María y Sofía quieren _____ en el hospital.
   (*to help the patients*)

8. Yo _____ well. (*to know Peter*)

9. Los profesores _____ cada día en el colegio.
   (*to see their students*)

10. Los padres _____.
    (*to take care of their children*)

11. El taxista _____ al hotel.
    (*to take the tourists*)

12. Ella no entiende la lección porque no _____.
    (*to listen to the teacher*)

13. Jorge no puede _____ y está preocupado.
    (*to find his sister*)

14. No sé porque él _____. (*to yell at his boss*)

15. Roberto va a _____ a la fiesta.
    (*to invite Ramona*)

16. Veinte minutos pasan y Teresa no quiere _____
    más. (*to wait for her friend*)

The Direct Object Pronoun

The direct object pronouns **me**, **te**, **nos**, and **os** have the same form as the indirect object pronouns **me**, **te**, **nos**, and **os**. The only new forms are **lo**, **los**, **la**, and **las**.

me	*me*	nos	*us*
te	*you*	os	*you* (used only in Spain)
lo	*him, it* (m., object)	los	*them* (m., persons and objects)
la	*her, it* (f., object)	las	*them* (f., persons and objects)

Make sure you know what the direct objects and direct object pronouns are in all cases. Review the following.

> *I see **the man**.*

In this sentence, *the man* is the direct object.

> *I see **the tree**.*

In this sentence, *the tree* is the direct object.

The direct object pronoun replaces the direct object.

*I see the man. I see **him**.*
*I see the tree. I see **it**.*

Review what you know about direct object pronouns.

- The direct object pronoun replaces the direct object.
- The direct object pronoun can refer to a person or a thing.
- It receives the action of the verb directly.
- It answers the question about what or who received the action.

Position of the Direct Object Pronoun

The direct object pronoun can be placed in either of two positions in a sentence or phrase.

Direct Object Pronoun Placed Directly Before the First Verb

In the first position, the direct object pronoun is placed *directly before the first verb* in a sentence or question.

Ella **me** conoce bien.	*She knows me well.*
Los niños **te** van a escuchar.	*The children are going to listen to you.*
Ellas **nos** saludan los lunes.	*They greet us on Mondays.*
¿**Os** podemos recoger a la una?	*Can we pick you up at one o'clock?*

Direct Object Pronoun Attached to the Infinitive

In the second position, the direct object pronoun is attached to the infinitive. Whether the direct object pronoun is placed before the first verb or attached to the infinitive, the meaning of the sentence is the same.

Ella quiere **visitarme** en México.	*She wants to visit me in Mexico.*
Queremos **invitarte** a la fiesta.	*We want to invite you to the party.*
Debo **llamarlo** ahora.	*I ought to call him now.*
¿Quién quiere **ayudarla**?	*Who wants to help her?*
¿Puedes **esperarnos**?	*Can you wait for us?*
Vamos a **extrañarlos** mucho.	*We are going to miss them a lot.*

The Direct Object Pronoun as a Person

The direct object pronoun needs no clarifiers, since it is clear that **lo** can only mean *him*, **la** can only mean *her*, **los** can only mean *them* (masculine, or masculine and feminine), and **las** can only mean *them* (feminine).

lo	*him*	los	*them* (m.)
la	*her*	las	*them* (f.)

María **lo** ama.	*Mary loves him.*
Jorge **la** besa.	*George kisses her.*
Los conozco de mi viaje a México.	*I know them from my trip to Mexico.*
Yo **las** debo acompañar al tren.	*I ought to accompany them to the train.*

In order to express the direct object pronoun *you* in the **Ud.** and **Uds.** form, the indirect object pronoun **le** and **les** is used in most countries.

Yo **le** conozco, ¿verdad?	*I know you, right?*
¿Puedo **ayudarle**?	*May I help you?*
Les acompañamos al parque.	*We accompany you to the park.*

To make a sentence negative, place **no** before the direct object pronoun.

No lo veo.	*I don't see him.*
Ella **no** me conoce.	*She doesn't know me.*
Ellos **no** nos quieren abrazar.	*They don't want to hug us.*

When the direct object pronoun is attached to the infinitive, place **no** before the first verb.

No quiero escucharlo.	*I don't want to listen to him.*
Él **no** quiere esperarme.	*He doesn't want to wait for me.*
No queremos buscarla.	*We don't want to look for her.*

Exercise 11.2

Complete the following sentences with the correct form of the verb and the direct object pronoun.

1. Ricardo _____ hasta las seis todas las noches.
   (*to wait for me*)

2. Él _____, pero no recuerda de donde.
   (*to know you* [familiar])

3. Nuestros amigos _____ con la tarea.
   (*to be going to help us*)

4. Cecilia y Susana van a viajar mañana. Vamos a _____.
   (*to miss them*)

5. Enrique es un buen estudiante, pero no está en clase hoy.

   Yo _____, pero no _____.

   (*to look for him/to find him*)

6. Francisca quiere a su amigo Pablo. Ella _____ mucho.
   (*to love him*)

7. ¿Quién quiere _____? (*to visit her*)

8. ¿Dónde están las muchachas? _____ Uds.? (*to see them*)

9. ¿Saludan Uds. a sus amigos todos los días? Nosotros no

   _____ nunca. (*to greet them*)

10. Su amigo es simpático. No sé por qué Ud. _____.
    (*to be going to leave him*)

11. Cuando sus padres están ocupados y no pueden cuidar a sus hijos,

    una niñera _____. (*to take care of them*)

12. _____, ella va a preparar la cena. (*after calling him*)

13. ¿Conocen Uds. a mi amiga Ramona? Sí, nosotros _____
    bien. (*to know her*)

14. Ella mira a la profesora y _____. (*to listen to her*)

15. _____ a la fiesta, él tiene que encontrar su número
    de teléfono. (*before inviting her*)

Exercise 11.3

Translate the following sentences into English.

1. Si un hombre acompaña a una mujer hermosa a la reunión, ¿la va a besar?

   _____

2. Nos parece que el muchacho está enfermo y no puede hacer su tarea.
   Decidimos ayudarlo.

   _____

3. Sara siempre llega tarde y no la queremos esperar más.

    _____

4. ¿Extraña Ud. a su familia que vive lejos? ¿La quiere visitar?

    _____

5. Los ingleses van a llegar a los Estados Unidos esta tarde. Vamos a llevarlos del aeropuerto a un buen hotel.

    _____

    _____

 ## Exercise 11.4

Translate the following sentences into Spanish.

1. *I see José, but he doesn't see me.*

    _____

2. *We don't know where the tourists are who are visiting us from Spain.*

    _____

3. *They are going to visit their friends in Canada after selling their boat.*

    _____

The Direct Object Pronoun as a Thing

lo	*it* (m.)	los	*them* (m.)
la	*it* (f.)	las	*them* (f.)

Guillermo compra **el carro**.   *Bill buys the car.*
Él **lo** compra.   *He buys it.*

Let's review what we know about direct object pronouns.

• The direct object pronoun replaces the direct object.
• The direct object pronoun is placed directly before the first verb or attached to the infinitive.

Guillermo vende su carro.   *Bill sells his car.*
Él **lo** vende.   *He sells it.*

Yo tengo la llave.	*I have the key.*
La tengo.	*I have it.*
Comemos los vegetales.	*We eat the vegetables.*
Los comemos.	*We eat them.*
Ella lee las revistas.	*She reads the magazines.*
Ella **las** lee.	*She reads them.*
Veo las flores en el jardín.	*I see the flowers in the garden.*
¿Puedes **verlas** también?	*Can you see them also?*
Él espera el tren a las nueve.	*He waits for the train at nine.*
Tiene que **esperarlo**.	*He has to wait for it.*
Ella no entiende la lección.	*She doesn't understand the lesson.*
Necesita estudiar para	*She needs to study in order to*
entenderla.	*understand it.*
Tengo dos buenos libros en casa.	*I have two good books at home.*
Voy a **leerlos** mañana.	*I am going to read them tomorrow.*

Exercise 11.5

Complete the following sentences with the correct form of the verb and the direct object pronoun.

1. ¿Tiene Ud. el libro rojo? Sí, yo _____, pero yo no

    _____. (*to have it/to want to read it*)

2. Su casa está sucia, pero Pedro no _____.
   (*to want to clean it*)

3. ¿Dónde están nuestros mapas de México? Nosotros siempre

    _____ en el coche, pero hoy no _____.

    (*to have them/to see them*)

4. No sé por qué él tiene tres carros; él _____ pero

    él no _____ tampoco. (*is not able to use them/*

    to want to sell them)

5. Necesitamos cuarenta tenedores, quince cuchillos y ochenta cucharas

    para la fiesta. ¿Quién tiene tiempo para _____?

    (*to buy them*)

6. En el verano, ella busca buenos libros; ella _____ en la biblioteca. (*to find them*)

7. Antes de estudiar la lección, ella está nerviosa. Después de

   _____, tiene más confianza. (*to study it*)

8. Las revistas que recibimos están en la casa pero no podemos

   _____. (*to find them*)

9. Los niños escuchan a sus padres porque sus padres

   _____. (*to love them*)

10. Este hombre tiene mucho dinero debajo de su cama, pero ¿es mejor

    _____ en el banco? (*to have it*)

Review Chart of Indirect and Direct Object Pronouns

Subject Pronoun	Indirect Object Pronoun	Direct Object Pronoun
yo	me	me
tú	te	te
él	le (a él)	lo
ella	le (a ella)	la
Ud.	le (a Ud.)	—
nosotros	nos	nos
vosotros	os	os
ellos	les (a ellos)	los
ellas	les (a ellas)	las
Uds.	les (a Uds.)	—

Notice again that there is no direct object pronoun for *you*. In order to express the direct object *you*, use **le** for the singular and use **les** for the plural.

Quiero ayudarlo.	*I want to help him.*
Quiero ayudarla.	*I want to help her.*
Quiero ayudar**le**.	*I want to help you* (sing.).
Quiero ayudarlos.	*I want to help them.*
Quiero ayudarlas.	*I want to help them.*
Quiero ayudar**les**.	*I want to help you* (pl.).

Exercise 11.6

Test your knowledge. *Complete the following sentences with the correct indirect or direct object pronoun. Place the pronoun before the first verb or attach it to the infinitive.*

1. ¿Conoce Ud. a mi amiga Sara? Sí, _____ conozco. (*her*)

2. ¿Dónde está Mario? ¿_____ ves? (*him*)

3. Ella mira a la profesora y _____ escucha bien. (*her*)

4. A ella _____ gustan las lecciones. (*to her*)

5. ¿Por qué siempre _____ dices mentiras si yo _____ digo la verdad? (*to me/to you*)

6. ¿Pedro _____ va a dar regalos a sus hijos este año? (*to them*)

7. _____ voy a ayudar a cocinar. (*them*)

8. ¿Cuánto tiempo _____ queda? (*us*)

9. ¿_____ escribes a tus padres? (*to them*)

10. Ellos quieren enviar _____ una carta desde Madrid. (*to them*)

11. ¿Por qué _____ haces preguntas si ya sabes la respuesta? (*me*)

12. Los niños quieren dar_____ a sus padres un beso. (*to them*)

13. En vez de invitar_____ al concierto, él decide ir solo. (*her*)

14. Antes de ver_____, ella va al cine. (*them*)

15. ¿Lees el periódico en la mañana o _____ lees en la tarde? (*it*)

16. La comida esta fría y no _____ queremos comer. (*it*)

17. Las lecciones son difíciles, y ella estudia mucho. Después de una hora, ella _____ entiende. (*them*)

18. La maestra repite las preguntas para los estudiantes. Ella _____ repite para practicar la pronunciación también. (*them*)

19. ¿Dónde están mis llaves? Siempre _____ pierdo. No _____ veo. (*them/them*)

20. _____ dan flores pero no _____ gustan. (*to me/to me*)

Exercise 11.7

*Review **gustar** and indirect object pronouns, and then answer the questions orally.*

1. ¿A los hombres les gusta hablar mucho?
2. ¿A los soldados les gusta luchar o prefieren vivir en paz?
3. ¿A los niños qué les gusta hacer?
4. ¿A quién le gusta trabajar mucho? ¿A quién le gusta ir de vacaciones?
5. ¿Por qué a algunas personas no les gusta nada?

Exercise 11.8

Translate the following sentences into Spanish.

1. I see my friends every Saturday. It is pleasing to us to go to the movies.

   _____

2. She looks at the teacher, she listens well, but still she understands nothing.

   _____

   _____

3. Lisa waits for her sister, who always arrives late.

   _____

4. We travel to Ecuador in order to be with our relatives.

   _____

5. The lesson is difficult and he wants to study it for the test.

   _____

6. Can you go to the post office for me? I have a letter for my friend and I want to send it today.

   _____

   _____

7. Do you want to accompany him to the party? He is shy and doesn't want to go alone.

   _____

   _____

8. *Where do you know her from? Do you see her all the time?*

_____

9. *She has new shoes but she never wears them.*

_____

10. *I hardly ever see you.*

_____

 # Reading Comprehension

La bienvenida

¡Es increíble! Aquí estoy en Italia. Hay muchos italianos en el aeropuerto que esperan a los pasajeros. Yo los miro: un hombre besa a una mujer; tres niños corren hacia una mujer y emocionados la besan, y ella, con lágrimas en los ojos, los besa y los abraza. Una mujer le dice a su novio que lo extraña cuando está lejos de ella; él le dice que la ama. Los niños, tan contentos de ver a sus padres de nuevo, saltan de alegría. Los viajeros como yo, sin familia (nadie nos espera porque no conocemos a nadie), recogemos nuestras maletas y seguimos a la aduana. No me molesta esperar un rato. Dentro de poco, sellan mi pasaporte y me dan una bienvenida cariñosa.

Salgo del aeropuerto al sol. Camino hacia los taxistas. Hace fresco y estoy bien. Tomo el primer taxi en la fila, le pregunto al conductor cuanto cobra por el viaje y me parece justo. Me lleva a la plaza central donde hay muchos hoteles interesantes. Pago la tarifa, le doy una propina, y con una sonrisa, me bajo del taxi.

Entro en el hotel que me interesa y le pregunto al dueño cuanto cobra por una noche para una persona. Le digo que quiero una habitación sencilla y tranquila con un baño privado. El dueño, muy simpático, me dice que tiene una habitación hermosa que da a la plaza. Después de verla, la tomo. Él mira mi pasaporte. Escribo mi nombre en el registro, y él me da las llaves. Estoy cansada pero estoy emocionada también. Ya es tarde. Decido comer un pasaboca e ir al cuarto para dormir. Yo sé que voy a tener sueños dulces.

Verbos

abrazar	*to embrace*		recoger	*to pick up*
bajarse de	*to get off*		saltar	*to jump*
dar a (la plaza)	*to face/overlook (the plaza)*		sellar	*to stamp*

Nombres

la aduana	*customs*	el pasaboca	*the snack*
la bienvenida	*the welcome*	la propina	*the tip*
el conductor	*the driver*	un rato	*a little while*
el dueño	*the owner*	el registro	*the register*
la fila	*the line*	la sonrisa	*the smile*
la lágrima	*the tear*	la tarifa	*the fare*
la maleta	*the suitcase*	el viajero	*the traveler*

Conjunción

e   *and*

For reasons of pronunciation, **y** meaning *and* is replaced by **e** before words beginning with **i** or **hi**.

Adjetivos

cariñoso	*affectionate*
emocionado	*excited*

Preguntas

After you have read the selection, answer the following questions in Spanish.

1. ¿Cómo está Isabel al llegar a Italia? Si Ud. piensa que está alegre, ¿por qué? Igualmente, si piensa que está triste, ¿por qué?

   _____

2. ¿Espera ella mucho tiempo en el aeropuerto?

   _____

3. ¿Qué tiempo hace?

   _____

4. ¿Escoge un hotel con cuidado?

   _____

5. ¿Quiere Isabel salir la primera noche? ¿Qué hace?

   _____

12

Reflexive Verbs

A verb is reflexive when the subject and the object refer to the same person. The purpose of the reflexive verb is to show that the action of the verb remains with the subject. This can be seen in the following sentence.

I wash myself.

Subject	Verb	Object
I	*wash*	*myself*

The Reflexive Pronouns

The reflexive pronouns are object pronouns.

me	*myself*		nos	*ourselves*
te	*yourself*		os	*yourselves*
se	*himself, herself, yourself*		se	*themselves, yourselves*

In Spanish reflexive verbs, **-se** is added to the basic infinitive.

To conjugate a reflexive verb, drop the **-se** and place the reflexive pronoun before the conjugated verb. The reflexive verb always has a reflexive pronoun.

lavarse *to wash oneself*

yo **me** lavo	*I wash myself*	nosotros **nos** lavamos	*we wash ourselves*
tú **te** lavas	*you wash yourself*	vosotros **os** laváis	*you wash yourselves*
él **se** lava	*he washes himself*	ellos **se** lavan	*they wash themselves*
ella **se** lava	*she washes herself*	ellas **se** lavan	*they wash themselves*
Ud. **se** lava	*you wash yourself*	Uds. **se** lavan	*you wash yourselves*

193

Compare the reflexive verb with the nonreflexive verb.

| Reflexive | Él se lava. | *He washes **himself**.* |
| Nonreflexive | Él lava el carro. | *He washes **the car**.* |

Some Frequently Used Reflexive Verbs

bañarse *to bathe oneself*

yo me baño	nosotros nos bañamos
tú te bañas	vosotros os bañáis
él se baña	ellos se bañan

dedicarse *to dedicate oneself*

yo me dedico	nosotros nos dedicamos
tú te dedicas	vosotros os dedicáis
ella se dedica	ellas se dedican

defenderse *to defend oneself*

yo me defiendo	nosotros nos defendemos
tú te defiendes	vosotros os defendéis
Ud. se defiende	Uds. se defienden

divertirse *to amuse oneself, to have a good time*

yo me divierto	nosotros nos divertimos
tú te diviertes	vosotros os divertís
él se divierte	ellos se divierten

expresarse *to express oneself*

yo me expreso	nosotros nos expresamos
tú te expresas	vosotros os expresáis
ella se expresa	ellas se expresan

llamarse *to call oneself*

yo me llamo	nosotros nos llamamos
tú te llamas	vosotros os llamáis
Ud. se llama	Uds. se llaman

preguntarse *to ask oneself, to wonder*

yo me pregunto	nosotros nos preguntamos
tú te preguntas	vosotros os preguntáis
él se pregunta	ellos se preguntan

A Word About Reflexive Verbs
It is not necessary to use both the subject pronoun and the reflexive pronoun with reflexive verbs, except in the third person for clarity. From now on, the subject pronouns **yo**, **tú**, **nosotros**, and **vosotros** will be omitted. Practice reflexive verbs aloud with their reflexive pronouns.

Reflexive Verbs Whose English Translations Do Not Necessarily Include *Oneself*

acostarse *to go to bed*

me acuesto	nos acostamos
te acuestas	os acostáis
él se acuesta	ellos se acuestan

despertarse *to wake up, to wake oneself*

me despierto	nos despertamos
te despiertas	os despertáis
Ud. se despierta	Uds. se despiertan

ducharse *to shower, to take a shower*

me ducho	nos duchamos
te duchas	os ducháis
él se ducha	ellos se duchan

dormirse *to fall asleep*

me duermo	nos dormimos
te duermes	os dormís
ella se duerme	ellas se duermen

enfermarse *to get sick*

me enfermo	nos enfermamos
te enfermas	os enfermáis
Ud. se enferma	Uds. se enferman

levantarse *to get up, to raise oneself*

me levanto	nos levantamos
te levantas	os levantáis
él se levanta	ellos se levantan

sentarse *to sit down, to seat oneself*

me siento	nos sentamos
te sientas	os sentáis
ella se sienta	ellas se sientan

vestirse *to get dressed*

me visto	nos vestimos
te vistes	os vestís
Ud. se viste	Uds. se visten

Position of the Reflexive Pronoun

The reflexive pronoun can be placed in either of two positions in a sentence or phrase.

In the first position, the reflexive pronoun is placed directly before the conjugated verb.

Nos despertamos a las ocho.	*We wake up at eight o'clock.*
Nos levantamos a las ocho y media.	*We get up at eight thirty.*

Ellos **se** divierten los fines de semana.	*They have a good time on weekends.*
¿A qué hora **te** acuestas?	*At what time do you go to bed?*

In the second position, the reflexive pronoun is attached to the infinitive.

Ella va a **dedicarse** a la ley.	*She is going to dedicate herself to the law.*
Voy a **bañarme** antes de **acostarme**.	*I am going to bathe myself before going to bed.*
Queremos **expresarnos** bien en español.	*We want to express ourselves well in Spanish.*

Exercise 12.1

Complete the following sentences with the correct form of the appropriate verb. Use each verb only one time.

acostarse, bañarse, dedicarse, despertarse, divertirse, dormirse, ducharse, expresarse, levantarse, llamarse, sentarse

1. Soy enfermera; tengo que _____ a las seis de la mañana.

2. Después de despertarme, _____ y voy a la cocina a preparar mi desayuno.

3. Antes de vestirme, _____ o _____. Me gusta cantar en el baño.

4. A las siete, _____ en la mesa para comer.

5. Tengo dos buenos amigos; _____ Carlos y Julia.

6. Ellos son abogados y _____ a defender a la gente.

7. Trabajamos mucho durante la semana y _____ los fines de semana.

8. Practicamos la gramática de español por horas y horas en conversación y siempre tratamos de _____ bien.

9. Durante la semana, les hablo por teléfono. A mí me gusta leer hasta tarde, pero a ellos les gusta _____ a las once.

10. Me gusta acostarme a las doce. _____ rápidamente.

Reflexive Verbs with Parts of the Body and Clothing

Note that the possessive adjective is not used with reflexive verbs when you are talking about parts of the body or clothing. The definite article is typically used instead.

afeitarse *to shave*

me afeito	nos afeitamos
te afeitas	os afeitáis
él se afeita	ellos se afeitan

cepillarse (los dientes, el pelo)
to brush (one's teeth, one's hair)

me cepillo	nos cepillamos
te cepillas	os cepilláis
ella se cepilla	ellas se cepillan

maquillarse (la cara) *to put makeup on, to make up* (one's face)

me maquillo	nos maquillamos
te maquillas	os maquilláis
Ud. se maquilla	Uds. se maquillan

peinarse (el pelo)
to comb (one's hair)

me peino	nos peinamos
te peinas	os peináis
él se peina	ellos se peinan

pintarse (las uñas) *to put makeup on, to put (nail) polish on*

me pinto	nos pintamos
te pintas	os pintáis
ella se pinta	ellas se pintan

ponerse *to put on* (clothing)

me pongo	nos ponemos
te pones	os ponéis
Ud. se pone	Uds. se ponen

quitarse *to take off* (clothing)

me quito	nos quitamos
te quitas	os quitáis
él se quita	ellos se quitan

Reflexive Verbs That Express Emotion

Regular

alegrarse (de)	*to become happy, to be glad*
animarse	*to cheer up*
asustarse	*to get frightened/scared*
calmarse	*to calm down*
enfadarse (con)	*to get angry*
enojarse (con)	*to get angry*
preocuparse (de)	*to worry*
tranquilizarse	*to calm down*

Reflexive Verbs That Express Movement

Regular

quedarse	*to remain*
mudarse	*to move* (from one place to another)
pararse	*to stand up*

Irregular

caerse *to fall down*	
me caigo	nos caemos
te caes	os caéis
él se cae	ellos se caen

irse *to go away, to leave quickly*	
me voy	nos vamos
te vas	os vais
ella se va	ellas se van

moverse *to move*	
me muevo	nos movemos
te mueves	os movéis
Ud. se mueve	Uds. se mueven

Exercise 12.2

Complete the following sentences with the correct form of the appropriate verb. Use each verb only one time.

afeitarse, alegrarse, caerse, cepillarse, enojarse, mudarse, peinarse, pintarse, ponerse, preocuparse, quedarse, quitarse, tranquilizarse

1. El niño alegre está en el árbol. No tiene miedo de _____.

2. El esposo _____ la barba mientras su esposa _____ las uñas.

3. No entiendo por qué _____ tú si alguien te critica.

4. Al entrar en el apartamento lujoso, nosotros _____ los zapatos.

5. Hace frío y ellos _____ un suéter y una chaqueta.

6. Es un buen hotel, pero no quiero _____ en esta ciudad.

7. El estudiante _____ mucho porque tiene un examen mañana.

8. Voy a _____ a San Francisco; me dicen que es un sitio hermoso.

9. Ella está nerviosa; para _____ ella toma leche caliente.

10. Nosotros _____ mucho de escuchar las buenas noticias.

11. Antes de dormirme, siempre _____ los dientes.

12. Después de despertarse, ellos _____ el cabello.

Reflexive Verbs That Express "To Become"

Ponerse + adjective

> **Ponerse** is the most common expression for *to become*; it is used for physical or emotional changes.

> Me pongo brava al escuchar las noticias.
> *I become angry upon hearing the news.*
>
> Ella se pone roja porque es tímida.
> *She gets red (blushes) because she is shy.*

Volverse + adjective

> **Volverse** is used to express a sudden, involuntary change.

> Hasta los psicólogos se vuelven locos.   *Even the psychologists go crazy.*

Hacerse, **llegar a ser**

> Both **hacerse** and **llegar a ser** are used with nouns expressing profession; they imply effort on the part of the subject.

> Ella se hace doctora.
> *She is becoming a doctor.*
>
> Él llega a ser doctor también.
> *He is becoming a doctor also.*

Most Frequently Used Reflexive Verbs

Regular

arreglarse	*to get ready to go out, to fix oneself up*
aprovecharse (de)	*to take advantage of*
atreverse (a)	*to dare to*
burlarse (de)	*to make fun of*
callarse	*to become quiet*
demorarse	*to delay*
desayunarse	*to have breakfast*
enamorarse (de)	*to fall in love with*
equivocarse	*to make a mistake*

fiarse (en)	*to trust, to have trust in*
fijarse (en)	*to notice*
lastimarse	*to hurt oneself*
llevarse (bien) (con)	*to get along (well) with*
mejorarse	*to get better*
meterse (en)	*to get involved in, to meddle*
portarse (bien/mal)	*to behave oneself (well/badly)*
quejarse (de)	*to complain about*
quemarse	*to burn oneself, to get burned*
reunirse (con)	*to meet with*

Irregular

acordarse (de) *to remember*

me acuerdo	nos acordamos
te acuerdas	os acordáis
él se acuerda	ellos se acuerdan

darse cuenta (de) *to realize*

me doy cuenta	nos damos cuenta
te das cuenta	os dais cuenta
ella se da cuenta	ellas se dan cuenta

encontrarse (con) *to meet*

me encuentro	nos encontramos
te encuentras	os encontráis
Ud. se encuentra	Uds. se encuentran

A Word About Prepositions That Follow Reflexive Verbs

The prepositions that follow certain reflexive verbs in Spanish cannot be omitted even if the English translation does not include them.

| Me fijo mucho **en** los detalles. | *I notice the details a lot.* |
| Él se acuerda **de** ella. | *He remembers her.* |

morirse *to die*

me muero	nos morimos
te mueres	os morís
él se muere	ellos se mueren

parecerse (a) *to resemble, to look like*

me parezco	nos parecemos
te pareces	os parecéis
Ud. se parece	Uds. se parecen

reírse *to laugh*

me río	nos reímos
te ríes	os reís
él se ríe	ellos se ríen

sentirse (bien/mal) *to feel (well/ill) (or any emotion or health condition)*

me siento	nos sentimos
te sientes	os sentís
ella se siente	ellas se sienten

Exercise 12.3

Complete the following sentences with the correct form of the appropriate reflexive verb. Use each verb only one time. Be sure to include prepositions when you need them.

acordarse, aprovecharse, atreverse, burlarse, callarse, demorarse, desayunarse, enamorarse, encontrarse, equivocarse, fiarse, fijarse, meterse, parecerse, ponerse, portarse, quejarse, reírse

1. A la familia le gusta comer juntos en la mañana. Siempre _____ con cereal y jugo antes de salir de la casa.

2. A los adolescentes les gusta ir a la escuela secundaria porque _____ sus amigos todos los días.

3. Muchas personas _____ nerviosas antes de tener un examen.

4. La niña feliz piensa que todo es gracioso; ella _____ todo el tiempo.

5. Él _____ mucho porque habla sin saber nada.

6. Yo no _____ nunca del número de teléfono de mi tío.

7. ¿_____ Ud. de una buena situación?

8. Ella _____ sus vecinos porque hacen mucho ruido.

9. La obra de teatro es interesante; el tiempo pasa rápidamente y la audiencia no _____ la hora.

10. Nadie debe _____ nadie.

11. La hija tiene la misma nariz que su mamá. _____ mucho.

12. No me gusta _____ los problemas de otros.

13. Ella llega tarde porque _____ los trenes durante la hora pico.

14. El hombre soltero _____ locamente de la mujer hermosa.

15. Nosotros _____ para escuchar hablar al experto que habla en voz baja.

16. Carla tiene miedo del agua y no _____ viajar en barco.

17. ¿Piensan Uds. que los adolescentes _____ bien o mal?

18. Él no tiene amigos porque no _____ nadie.

Review Chart of Indirect and Direct Object Pronouns and Reflexive Pronouns

Subject Pronoun	Indirect Object Pronoun	Direct Object Pronoun	Reflexive Pronoun
yo	me	me	me
tú	te	te	te
él	le	lo	se
ella	le	la	se
Ud.	le	le	se
nosotros	nos	nos	nos
vosotros	os	os	os
ellos	les	los	se
ellas	les	las	se
Uds.	les	les	se

Reflexive Verbs with Reciprocal Meanings

The plural forms of reflexive verbs are sometimes used to express the idea of *each other.* If the meaning is unclear, Spanish uses **el uno al otro**, **la una a la otra**, **los unos a los otros**, and **las unas a las otras** for clarification.

ayudarse	*to help each other*
conocerse	*to know each other*
entenderse	*to understand each other*
escribirse	*to write to each other*
hablarse	*to speak to each other*
quererse	*to love each other*
verse	*to see each other*

Elena y Paula se ayudan mucho.	*Helen and Paula help each other a lot.*
Mis amigos se ayudan el uno al otro.	*My friends help each other.*
Nos conocemos bien.	*We know each other well.*
¿Se conocen Uds.?	*Do you know each other?*
Las dos hermanas se entienden bien.	*The two sisters understand each other well.*
Roberto y Sonia se quieren.	*Robert and Sonia love each other.*
Ellos se ven todos los días.	*They see each other every day.*

Se and Impersonal Expressions

In impersonal expressions with **se**, the verb has no personal subject. In English these sentences are translated by subjects such as *one, you, they, people* (in general), or by the passive voice.

The third-person singular or plural of the verb is used in these expressions.

English Construction	*How do you say "hello" in Spanish?*
Spanish Construction	¿Cómo **se dice** "hello" en español?

Se vive bien en este país.　　　　*One lives well in this country.*

Se cree que los italianos son　　　*It is believed (one believes / people*
　románticos.　　　　　　　　　　　*believe) that Italians are romantic.*

Se sabe que él es un buen　　　　 *It is known that he is a good worker.*
　trabajador.

Aquí **se habla** español.　　　{ *One speaks Spanish here.*
　　　　　　　　　　　　　　　 { *Spanish is spoken here.*

No **se permite** nadar aquí.　　*It is not permitted to swim here.*

¿Dónde **se puede** estacionar　 *Where can one park in New York?*
　en Nueva York?

Se prohíbe fumar.　　　　　　*It is prohibited to smoke.*

Exercise 12.4

Complete the story by filling in the blanks with the verbs in parentheses.

Ricardo _____ (1. *wakes up*) a las seis todos los días.

Él _____ (2. *takes a shower*) antes de _____

(3. *to get dressed*). Le gusta _____ (4. *to have breakfast*)

en casa antes de salir para su trabajo. Ricardo _____

(5. *meets with*) sus colegas a las siete y media de la mañana. Todos son

bomberos y _____ (6. *dedicate themselves*) a apagar

incendios. _____ (7. *They help each other*).

_____ (8. *One says*) que los bomberos son héroes;

_____ (9. *they dare to*) a entrar en edificios peligrosos

sin _____ (10. *to worry*). Ellos ayudan a la gente a

_____ (11. *calm down*) y _____ (12. *to feel*)

mejor. De vez en cuando, _____ (13. *they delay*) en apagar
el incendio y el edificio _____ (14. *gets burned*). Ricardo
_____ (15. *stays*) en la estación de bomberos por tres días.
Al regresar a casa, él come algo, _____ (16. *takes a bath*),
_____ (17. *goes to bed*) temprano y _____
(18. *falls asleep*) rápidamente.

 # Reading Comprehension

El encuentro

Me despierto bien. Me gustan las cortinas delgadas porque dejan entrar
la luz de la mañana. Más allá de mi ventana, veo las plantas exuberantes
de verde radiante. Después de ducharme largamente, me pongo un vestido
sencillo pero elegante y salgo del hotel con el libro de turismo en mi bolsa.
Busco un restaurante acogedor para tomar el primer café del día. Entro
en uno que tiene un ambiente agradable y miro todos los pasteles.
No puedo escoger entre el de nata y la torta con crema y fruta; pues,
pido dos pasteles y un café solo, y me los da. Me siento en una mesa
hermosa para dos.

El café está fuerte y delicioso. No hay razón para apresurarme y como
los pasteles tranquilamente. El restaurante se llena; se ve que la gente
es muy amable y habladora. Conversan con todo el cuerpo, sobre todo
con las manos. ¿De qué hablan, tan animados, a esta hora tan temprano
de la mañana?

No conozco a nadie. Pero me parece posible encontrarme a alguien,
a una persona con quien pueda tener una conversación interesante. (Este
restaurante es un buen sitio; no me muevo de aquí por un rato.) Alguien
va a verme, aquí sentada, y en vez de pasar por mi mesa sin decir nada,
me va a decir; "Señorita, está ocupada esta silla?" Yo le voy a contestar con
una sonrisa, "No, Ud. puede sentarse." Y él se sienta complacido. Dentro
de poco somos amigos, y después de tomar otro café y otro pastel, él me
invita a acompañarlo a un museo y tomar un vino con él. Charlamos y nos
reímos y nos divertimos mucho durante nuestra cena de pescado y
camarones. A lo lejos, en la distancia, lo veo venir.

Verbos

apresurarse	*to rush*	escoger	*to choose*
charlar	*to chat*	llenarse	*to fill up*
conversar	*to converse*	moverse	*to move*
dejar	*to let*	pedir	*to ask for, to request*

Nombres

los camarones	*the shrimp*
la nata	*the cream*
el pastel	*the pastry*

Adjetivos

acogedor	*cozy*	hablador(-a)	*talkative*
animado	*energetic, excited*	ocupado	*busy*
complacido	*satisfied*	radiante	*radiant*
delgado	*thin, slim*	sentado	*seated*

Expresiones

a lo lejos	*far away*
más allá de mi ventana	*outside my window*
sobre todo	*above all*

Preguntas

After you have read the selection, answer the following questions in Spanish.

1. ¿Cómo se despierta?

   _____

2. Después de vestirse, ¿adónde va?

   _____

3. ¿Por qué escoge ella una mesa para dos?

   _____

4. Mientras ella come los pasteles, ¿lee Isabel su libro?

   _____

5. ¿Dónde tiene lugar la conversación que ella tiene con el hombre?

   _____

6. Al final de este cuento, ¿está ella sola o acompañada?

   _____

13

The Present Subjunctive

The present subjunctive is a mood in the present tense, widely used in Spanish but rarely used in English. So far you have studied the present tense in the indicative mood, the most frequently used mood in the language. This chapter introduces the present subjunctive. It is important to learn it now so that you can express yourself confidently and freely in the present tense.

The present subjunctive cannot exist alone. Another element in the sentence always causes it to be used. The subjunctive is often needed after the following elements.

- Certain impersonal expressions
- Certain verbs
- Certain conjunctions
- Certain dependent adjective clauses
- Certain expressions

Formation of the Present Subjunctive

- Almost all verbs form the present subjunctive from the first-person singular **yo** form of the present indicative. Drop the **-o** to get the stem for the present subjunctive.

- Verbs that are irregular in the present indicative are irregular in the present subjunctive in the same way.

- There are only six verbs that do not form the present subjunctive from the **yo** form of the present indicative.

-Ar **Verbs**

In order to conjugate both regular and irregular **-ar** verbs in the present subjunctive, you start with the **yo** form of the present indicative. Drop the **-o** and add **-e, -es, -e, -emos, -éis, -en** to the stem.

Infinitive	**yo** Form	Present Subjunctive	
cantar	canto	yo cante	nosotros cantemos
		tú cantes	vosotros cantéis
		él cante	ellos canten
bailar	bailo	yo baile	nosotros bailemos
		tú bailes	vosotros bailéis
		ella baile	ellas bailen
cerrar	cierro	yo cierre	nosotros cerremos
		tú cierres	vosotros cerréis
		Ud. cierre	Uds. cierren
pensar	pienso	yo piense	nosotros pensemos
		tú pienses	vosotros penséis
		ella piense	ellas piensen
recordar	recuerdo	yo recuerde	nosotros recordemos
		tú recuerdes	vosotros recordéis
		él recuerde	ellos recuerden

Note that the first-person singular and the third-personal singular are identical in the present subjunctive.

The first two examples, **cantar** and **bailar**, are regular. The last three, **cerrar**, **pensar**, and **recordar**, are irregular in the present indicative. Note that their stem changes in the present indicative are also present in the present subjunctive, except in the **nosotros** and **vosotros** forms, which are unaffected by stem changes.

A Word About the Present Subjunctive

The formation of the subjunctive comes from the conjugation of the *first-person singular* of the present indicative. Any irregularity that the verb has in the present indicative **yo** form also occurs in the present subjunctive. To learn the subjunctive well, practice the **yo** form of the verbs, because that will be the stem of the present subjunctive.

-*Er* and -*ir* Verbs

In order to conjugate both regular and irregular -**er** and -**ir** verbs in the present subjunctive, you drop the -**o** from the first-person singular of the present indicative and add -**a**, -**as**, -**a**, -**amos**, -**áis**, -**an** to the stem.

-*Er* Verbs

Infinitive	**yo** Form	Present Subjunctive	
comer	como	yo coma	nosotros comamos
		tú comas	vosotros comáis
		él coma	ellos coman
querer	quiero	yo quiera	nosotros queramos
		tú quieras	vosotros queráis
		ella quiera	ellas quieran
poder	puedo	yo pueda	nosotros podamos
		tú puedas	vosotros podáis
		Ud. pueda	Uds. puedan
ver	veo	yo vea	nosotros veamos
		tú veas	vosotros veáis
		él vea	ellos vean

-*Ir* Verbs

Infinitive	**yo** Form	Present Subjunctive	
vivir	vivo	yo viva	nosotros vivamos
		tú vivas	vosotros viváis
		él viva	ellos vivan
mentir	miento	yo mienta	nosotros mintamos
		tú mientas	vosotros mintáis
		ella mienta	ellas mientan
pedir	pido	yo pida	nosotros pidamos
		tú pidas	vosotros pidáis
		Ud. pida	Uds. pidan
dormir	duermo	yo duerma	nosotros durmamos
		tú duermas	vosotros durmáis
		él duerma	ellos duerman

NOTE: In the irregular **-ir** verbs, there is an additional irregularity in the **nosotros** and **vosotros** forms. The stem change **e > ie** or **e > i** has an **-i-** in the **nosotros** and **vosotros** forms. The stem change **o > ue** has a **-u-** in the **nosotros** and **vosotros** forms.

-Er and *-ir* Verbs with *-g-* or *-zc-* in the *yo* Form

In the present subjunctive, certain **-er** and **-ir** verbs carry the irregularity of the first-person singular throughout the conjugation. There are no **-ar** verbs that have this irregularity.

Infinitive	**yo** Form	Present Subjunctive	
conocer	conozco	yo conozca	nosotros conozcamos
		tú conozcas	vosotros conozcáis
		él conozca	ellos conozcan
decir	digo	yo diga	nosotros digamos
		tú digas	vosotros digáis
		ella diga	ellas digan
hacer	hago	yo haga	nosotros hagamos
		tú hagas	vosotros hagáis
		Ud. haga	Uds. hagan
poner	pongo	yo ponga	nosotros pongamos
		tú pongas	vosotros pongáis
		él ponga	ellos pongan
salir	salgo	yo salga	nosotros salgamos
		tú salgas	vosotros salgáis
		ella salga	ellas salgan
tener	tengo	yo tenga	nosotros tengamos
		tú tengas	vosotros tengáis
		Ud. tenga	Uds. tengan
traer	traigo	yo traiga	nosotros traigamos
		tú traigas	vosotros traigáis
		él traiga	ellos traigan
venir	vengo	yo venga	nosotros vengamos
		tú vengas	vosotros vengáis
		ella venga	ellas vengan

Irregular Verbs

There are only six verbs that have a present subjunctive that is not formed from the first-person singular. They are irregular in that they cannot be formed from the **yo** form.

Infinitive	**yo** Form	Present Subjunctive	
dar	doy	yo dé	nosotros demos
		tú des	vosotros deis
		él dé	ellos den
estar	estoy	yo esté	nosotros estemos
		tú estés	vosotros estéis
		ella esté	ellas estén
ir	voy	yo vaya	nosotros vayamos
		tú vayas	vosotros vayáis
		Ud. vaya	Uds. vayan
saber	sé	yo sepa	nosotros sepamos
		tú sepas	vosotros sepáis
		él sepa	ellos sepan
ser	soy	yo sea	nosotros seamos
		tú seas	vosotros seáis
		ella sea	ellas sean
haber	he	yo haya	nosotros hayamos
		tú hayas	vosotros hayáis
		Ud. haya	Uds. hayan

NOTES: **Dé** (the form for both the first- and third-person singular of **dar**) has a written accent to distinguish it from **de** (*of*).

The word **hay** comes from the infinitive **haber**. You will not need this form for any other use at this time.

Verbs with Orthographic Changes

Verbs with orthographic changes are not irregular. The spelling changes simply maintain the sound of the **yo** form. Some of the most common spelling changes are the following.

- Verbs that end in **-gar** change **g** to **gu**.
- Verbs that end in **-car** change **c** to **qu**.
- Verbs that end in **-zar** change **z** to **c**.

Infinitive	**yo** Form	Present Subjunctive	
apagar	apago	yo apague	nosotros apaguemos
		tú apagues	vosotros apaguéis
		él apague	ellos apaguen
buscar	busco	yo busque	nosotros busquemos
		tú busques	vosotros busquéis
		Ud. busque	Uds. busquen
comenzar	comienzo	yo comience	nosotros comencemos
		tú comiences	vosotros comencéis
		ella comience	ellas comiencen
empezar	empiezo	yo empiece	nosotros empecemos
		tú empieces	vosotros empecéis
		él empiece	ellos empiecen
explicar	explico	yo explique	nosotros expliquemos
		tú expliques	vosotros expliquéis
		Ud. explique	Uds. expliquen
llegar	llego	yo llegue	nosotros lleguemos
		tú llegues	vosotros lleguéis
		ella llegue	ellas lleguen
tocar	toco	yo toque	nosotros toquemos
		tú toques	vosotros toquéis
		Ud. toque	Uds. toquen

NOTE: The change **z** > **c** occurs before the vowel **e** without affecting the sound. The consonants **c** (before **i** and **e**), **s**, and **z** all have the same sound.

A Word About Pronunciation of the Present Subjunctive
Like the present indicative, the stress in the present subjunctive tense is on the second to last syllable. As you practice, make sure you pronounce the verbs in this way: **yo <u>can</u>te, tú <u>can</u>tes, él <u>can</u>te, nosotros can<u>te</u>mos, ellos <u>can</u>ten**. If a word carries an accent mark, stress the accented syllable: **vosotros can<u>téis</u>**.

Uses of the Present Subjunctive

Remember that the subjunctive mood cannot exist alone; it must always be caused by some other element in the sentence. This is a mood that expresses wishes, doubts, and what is possible, rather than what is certain. Following are the specific uses of the present subjunctive.

After Certain Impersonal Expressions

A sentence or question may consist of a main clause and a dependent or subordinate clause connected by the Spanish conjunction **que**.

Here is a sentence with a main clause and a subordinate clause in the indicative mood.

Él sabe	= the main clause
que yo cocino bien.	= the dependent clause

However, suppose that the main clause has an impersonal expression, such as **Es dudoso**. This causes the subjunctive to be used in the dependent clause.

Es dudoso que yo **cocine** bien.   *It is doubtful that I cook well.*

Frequently used impersonal expressions are the following.

es bueno (que)	*it is good (that)*
es difícil·(que)	*it is difficult (that)*
es dudoso (que)	*it is doubtful (that)*
es fácil (que)	*it is easy (that)*
es imposible (que)	*it is impossible (that)*
es importante (que)	*it is important (that)*
es malo (que)	*it is bad (that)*
es mejor (que)	*it is better (that)*
es necesario (que)	*it is necessary (that)*
es posible (que)	*it is possible (that)*
es probable (que)	*it is probable (that)*
es preciso (que)	*it is extremely necessary (that)*
es una lástima (que)	*it is a pity (that)*
es urgente (que)	*it is urgent (that)*

Es importante que ella **coma** bien.   *It is important that she eat well.*

Es necesario que **estudiemos**   *It is necessary that we study for*
    para el examen.   *the test.*

Es imposible que él **tenga** razón.	*It is impossible that he is right.*
¿Es posible que ella **venga** mañana?	*Is it possible that she will come tomorrow?*
Es probable que mi amiga me **vea** en el restaurante.	*It is probable that my friend will see me in the restaurant.*
Es un lástima que Pedro no lo **quiera** hacer.	*It is a pity that Peter doesn't want to do it.*
Es dudoso que **viajemos** a España.	*It is doubtful that we will travel to Spain.*

Once you begin a sentence with one of the impersonal expressions above, it is mandatory to use the subjunctive in the dependent clause. You do not have to make any decisions, nor do you have a choice about whether or not to use it. These impersonal expressions in the main clause always trigger the subjunctive in the subordinate clause.

Notice that some of the example sentences and questions above are translated with the future in English. This is because the present subjunctive carries with it a feeling of the future and doubt.

If you wish to make a general statement with an impersonal expression, you need neither a dependent clause nor a subjunctive. You simply use the structure you have already learned, which follows English word order.

Es importante comer bien.	*It is important to eat well.*
¿Es necesario trabajar mucho?	*Is it necessary to work a lot?*
Es posible salir temprano.	*It is possible to leave early.*
Es bueno nadar cada día.	*It is good to swim every day.*

 ## Exercise 13.1

Complete the following sentences with the correct form of the verb in parentheses.

EXAMPLE   Es importante que nuestros amigos __*vengan*__ a la fiesta. (venir)

1. Es posible que él me _____ la verdad. (decir)

2. Es una lástima que Sara no lo _____. (hacer)

3. ¿Es posible que Uds. _____ a mi amigo Raúl? (conocer)

4. Es necesario que nosotros _____ bien. (dormir)

5. Es importante que ella _____ bien las direcciones. (saber)

6. Es necesario que nosotros _____ mucha agua fría en el verano. (tomar)

7. Es dudoso que ellos _____ temprano. (levantarse)

8. ¿Es posible que ella _____ a tiempo? (llegar)

9. Es posible que yo _____ en Francia. (quedarse)

10. Es probable que mucha gente importante _____ en la conferencia. (estar)

11. Es difícil que yo te _____ una buena respuesta. (dar)

12. Es urgente que tú _____ al doctor hoy. (ir)

13. Es dudoso que ellos _____ ricos. (ser)

14. Es importante que los padres les _____ a sus hijos. (leer)

15. La niña acaba de comer. Es imposible que _____ hambre. (tener)

16. Es probable que nosotros le _____ flores al profesor. (traer)

17. Es bueno que Uds. _____ mejor. (sentirse)

After Certain Verbs

Expressing Wishes or Preferences

Verbs that express wishes or preferences *with regard to other people* in the main clause will cause the subjunctive mood in the dependent clause. The subject in the main clause must be different from the subject in the dependent clause.

querer	*to want*
desear	*to desire, to want*
preferir	*to prefer*

Here is a sentence with a main clause and a subordinate clause in the indicative mood.

Él sabe	= the main clause
que yo canto.	= the dependent clause

However, suppose that the main clause has one of the verbs above, such as **Él quiere**. This causes the subjunctive to be used in the dependent clause.

Él quiere que yo **cante**.   { *He wants that I sing.* / *He wants me to sing.* }

The English equivalent does not always show the distinction in moods like Spanish does. But even in the English translation of the above example, it is clear that the person in the main clause, *he*, wants the other person, *me*, to do something.

Quiero que él **baile**.	*I want him to dance.*
Deseamos que ella **esté** bien.	*We want her to be well.*
Ella prefiere que su hijo **juegue** al béisbol.	*She prefers that her son play baseball.*

If there is only one subject for the two verbs in a sentence, there is neither a dependent clause nor a subjunctive.

Yo quiero cantar.	*I want to sing.*
Deseamos descansar.	*We want to rest.*
Ella prefiere dormir.	*She prefers to sleep.*

Expressing Hope, Happiness, Sadness, or Regret

Verbs that express hope, happiness, sadness, or regret with regard to other people in the main clause will cause the subjunctive mood in the dependent clause.

alegrarse de	*to be glad*
esperar	*to hope*
estar contento de	*to be happy*
estar triste de	*to be sad*
gustarle a uno	*to be pleasing*
sentir	*to regret*
tener miedo de, temer	*to be afraid of, to fear*

Me alegro de que Uds. **estén** bien.	*I am glad that you are well.*
Esperamos que Ud. **tenga** un buen fin de semana.	*We hope that you have a good weekend.*
La maestra está contenta de que **hagamos** la tarea.	*The teacher is happy that we do the homework.*
¿Estás triste de que no **podamos** aceptar tu invitación?	*Are you sad that we cannot accept your invitation?*
Me gusta que mi familia **venga** a verme.	*It pleases me that my family is coming to see me.*
Lo siento que Ud. nunca se **gane** la lotería.	*I am sorry that you never win the lottery.*

El líder tiene miedo de que el grupo no **resuelva** el problema.	*The leader fears that the group will not resolve the problem.*
Los padres temen que sus hijos no **quieran** estudiar.	*The parents fear that their children don't want to study.*

If there is only one subject for the two verbs in a sentence, the sentence follows the basic structure that you have learned.

Me alegro de estar aquí.	*I am glad to be here.*
Él espera salir dentro de una hora.	*He hopes to leave within the hour.*
Me gusta ir al cine.	*It pleases me to go to the movies.*
Ella tiene miedo de volar.	*She is afraid of flying.*

Expressing Orders, Requests, or Advice

Verbs that express orders, requests, or advice in the main clause will cause the subjunctive mood in the dependent clause.

aconsejar	*to advise*
decir	*to tell* (someone to do something)
dejar	*to permit, to let*
insistir en	*to insist*
pedir	*to request, to ask for*
permitir	*to permit*
prohibir	*to prohibit*
mandar	*to order*
sugerir	*to suggest*

Te aconsejo que **tomes** el tren.	*I advise you to take the train.*
Ella insiste en que yo **me quede**.	*She insists that I stay.*
Les pedimos que **vayan** de vacaciones.	*We ask them to go on vacation.*
Le sugiero que Ud. **lea** este artículo.	*I suggest that you read this article.*

Dejar, **permitir**, **prohibir**, and **mandar** can be used in two ways.

Les dejo que **entren.** Les dejo entrar.	*I let them enter.*
Te permito que **nades** aquí. Te permito nadar aquí.	*I permit you to swim here.*
Te prohíbo que **fumes** en la casa. Te prohíbo fumar en la casa.	*I prohibit you to smoke in the house.*

| El capitán les manda que los soldados **descansen**. Les manda descansar. | *The captain orders the soldiers to rest. He orders them to rest.* |

Decir is used, as you have learned, to relate a fact. This idea is expressed with the indicative.

| José nos dice que el tren viene. | *Joe tells us that the train is coming.* |
| Ella me dice que le gusta viajar. | *She tells me that she likes to travel.* |

However, when **decir** is used to give an *order*, the subjunctive is used in the dependent clause.

Yo te digo que **vayas** al doctor.	*I tell you to go to the doctor.*
Ud. me dice que yo **me quede.**	*You tell me to stay.*
Les decimos que **se acuesten** ahora.	*We tell them to go to bed now.*
Él nos dice que **tengamos** cuidado.	*He tells us to be careful.*
¿Puede Ud. decirle que me **llame**?	*Can you tell her to call me?*

Notice that when English *to tell* is being used to order someone to do something, the command form is always the conjugation of the verb *to tell* + the infinitive.

An English command is expressed as follows: *He tells me to go.*

Compare that to simply relating a fact: *He tells me that the bus is here.*

Expressing Doubt or Uncertainty

Verbs that express doubt or uncertainty in the main clause will cause the subjunctive mood in the dependent clause.

dudar	*to doubt*
no creer	*not to believe*
no pensar	*not to think*

Ella duda que yo **sepa** tocar el piano.	*She doubts that I know how to play the piano.*
La gente no cree que **sea** la verdad.	*The people don't believe that it is the truth.*
No pensamos que Daniel nos **invite** a la fiesta.	*We don't think that Daniel will invite us to the party.*

Exercise 13.2

Complete the following sentences with the correct form of the present subjunctive.

1. ¿Qué quieres que yo te _____? (decir)
2. Él quiere que su amiga _____ la cuenta. (pagar)
3. Espero que Uds. _____ bien. (sentirse)
4. Ellos se alegran de que el bebé _____. (dejar de llorar)
5. Ellos nos piden que _____ mejor la idea. (explicar)
6. A él no le gusta que yo siempre _____ razón. (tener)
7. Rosa insiste en que su jefe le _____ más dinero. (dar)
8. No creo que Alicia _____ la fecha. (saber)
9. Ellas dudan que _____ mucho tráfico hoy. (haber)
10. Les sugiero a sus padres que _____ de vacaciones. (ir)
11. Me alegro de que no _____ nada grave. (ser)
12. Los expertos nos aconsejan que _____ ejercicio. (hacer)
13. Paula espera que su hermana _____ bien. (estar)
14. Yo dudo que Uds. me _____ en la reunión. (ver)

 Exercise 13.3

Rewrite the following indicative sentences so that the subjunctive is required. Choose any appropriate verb that causes the subjunctive to be needed in the dependent clause.

EXAMPLE   A mis padres les gusta viajar. *Quiero que ellos viajen.*

1. Mi amigo tiene malos sueños. _____
2. Ella no se divierte mucho. _____
3. Nosotros somos buenos estudiantes.

   _____
4. No vamos a volver a los Estados Unidos.

   _____
5. Sara me trae flores a mi casa. _____

6. ¿Conoce Ud. a mi tío? [Write a response.]

   _____

7. Mi hermano y yo no nos vemos mucho.

   _____

8. ¿Hay clase los lunes? _____

9. Carla es de Polonia. _____

Exercise 13.4

Indicative or subjunctive? *Complete the following sentences with the correct form of the verb in parentheses.*

EXAMPLES   Espero que Uds. __*tengan*__ un buen fin de semana. (tener)

Yo sé que Uds. __*tienen*__ muchos amigos. (tener)

1. Ricardo prefiere que yo lo _____ en febrero. (visitar)

2. Él quiere que nosotros le _____ recuerdos. (traer)

3. Nos gusta que él nos _____. (amar)

4. Es importante que nos _____ cada año. (ver)

5. ¿Sabe Ud. que ellos _____ aquí? (estar)

6. Yo pienso que Rosario _____ poco. (quejarse)

7. Dudo que ella _____. (entender)

8. Lo sentimos que tú no _____ acompañarnos. (poder)

9. Espero que ella _____ de las instrucciones. (acordarse)

10. ¿No crees que aquellas tortas _____ deliciosas? (estar)

Exercise 13.5

Complete the story with the correct form (subjunctive, indicative, or infinitive) of each verb in parentheses.

Mariana _____ (1. levantarse) temprano porque hoy

sus nietos quieren _____ (2. ir) al circo. Ella insiste

en que ellos _____ (3. desayunarse) bien antes

de _____ (4. salir). Ella espera que

_____ (5. divertirse) mucho porque el circo

_____ (6. venir) raras veces a su pueblo. Hace frío y ella

les aconseja que _____ (7. ponerse) la chaqueta para

el invierno. Ellos están contentos de que su abuela _____

(8. ser) tan simpática.

After Certain Conjunctions

A subjunctive form follows directly after one of the following conjunctions if the main clause has a different subject than the dependent clause.

a pesar de que	*in spite of*
antes de que	*before*
después de que	*after*
en caso de que	*in case*
hasta que	*until*
para que	*in order that, so that*
sin que	*without*

Here is a sentence in which there is only one subject.

Ella practica el piano **antes de cantar**.	*She practices the piano before singing.*

In the following sentence, there are two subjects connected by the conjunction **que**.

Ella practica el piano **antes de que** él **cante**.	*She practices the piano before he sings.*

The English equivalent does not show the distinction in moods the way Spanish does. However, there are clearly two subjects in the example above: *she* and *he*.

Él enseña **para que** los estudiantes **aprendan**.	*He teaches so that the students learn.*
Voy a esperar **hasta que** tú **llegues**.	*I am going to wait until you arrive.*
Lo voy a hacer **sin que** Ud. me **ayude**.	*I'm going to do it without your helping me.*

If there is only one subject in the sentence, an infinitive will follow the preposition.

Ella estudia para aprender.	*She studies in order to learn.*
Después de trabajar, ella descansa.	*After working, she rests.*
Él habla sin pensar.	*He speaks without thinking.*

Some conjunctions of time always cause a subjunctive, whether there are two subjects or only one in the sentence. Such conjunctions are the following.

a menos que	*unless*
luego que	*as soon as*
tan pronto como	*as soon as*

Vamos a bailar **a menos que** no **haya** música.	*We are going to dance unless there is no music.*
Voy a llegar **tan pronto como** yo **pueda**.	*I am going to arrive as soon as I can.*

After *cuando*

The subjunctive form directly follows **cuando** if the future is implied.

Vamos a viajar **cuando tengamos** tiempo y dinero.	*We are going to travel when we have time and money.*
¿Me puedes llamar **cuando llegues** a casa?	*Can you call me when you arrive home?*
El niño quiere ser bombero **cuando sea** grande.	*The child wants to be a fireman when he grows up.*

When **cuando** introduces a question, the indicative form is used.

¿Cuándo vas a estar en casa?	*When are you going to be home?*
¿Cuándo quieren Uds. viajar?	*When do you want to travel?*

When **cuando** introduces a sentence that involves either a repeated action or a general statement in the present, the indicative mood is used.

Cuando hace frío, los niños juegan en la nieve.	*When it is cold, the children play in the snow.*
Ella se siente alegre cuando baila.	*She feels happy when she dances.*
Cuando voy a la playa, siempre me divierto.	*When I go to the beach, I always have a good time.*

Exercise 13.6

Complete the following sentences, using the verbs and conjunctions in parentheses.

EXAMPLE   Él va a limpiar su apartamento ___antes de que___ *(before)* su

familia lo __visite__. *(to visit)*

1. _____ *(after)* yo _____ *(to bathe myself)*, voy a vestirme.

2. No voy _____ *(unless)* Uds. _____ *(to go)* también.

3. Él va a invitar a su amiga a la fiesta _____ *(as soon as)*

   él _____ *(to have)* confianza.

4. Les doy las instrucciones _____ *(so that)* ellos

   _____ *(to know how)* llegar.

5. Uds. pueden jugar al baloncesto _____ *(as soon as)*

   Uds. _____ *(to finish)* su tarea.

6. _____ *(before)* su novio _____ *(to come)* a verla, Rosa va a arreglarse.

7. Te presto el dinero _____ *(so that)* tú

   _____ *(to be able to)* comprar un carro usado.

8. Vamos a estar aquí _____ *(until)* ellos

   _____. *(to arrive)*

9. _____ *(in case)* Uds. no _____ *(to have)* nada que hacer mañana, ¿podemos ir al cine?

10. A Ricardo no le gusta estudiar. Pero va a estudiar _____

    (so that) sus padres _____ *(to be)* contentos.

11. _____ *(in spite of)* ellos _____ *(to be)* frío, ellos quieren dar una vuelta.

12. Tú puedes venir a mi casa _____ *(without)* yo te

    _____. *(to invite)*

13. Graciela va a descansar _____ *(after)* sus nietos

    _____. *(to go away)*

14. Cuando Ud. _____ (*to be able*), ¿me puede acompañar al tren?

15. Elena me va a ver cuando nosotros _____ (*to meet*) en México.

16. Cuando ellos _____ (*to return*) a los Estados Unidos, van a comprar una casa pequeña.

17. El hombre va a estar contento cuando _____ (*to learn*) a manejar.

In Certain Dependent Adjective Clauses

The subjunctive mood is used in the dependent clause if the object or person described in the main clause is indefinite or nonexistent. In the following examples, the objects and persons described in the main clause are not known.

Busco **un apartamento** que **sea** grande y barato.	*I am looking for an apartment that is big and cheap.*
¿Conoce Ud. a **alguien** que **sepa** hablar alemán?	*Do you know anyone who knows how to speak German?*
¿Hay **alguien** aquí que **baile** bien?	*Is there anyone here who dances well?*
No hay **nadie** que siempre **tenga** razón.	*There is no one who is always right.*

After the Expressions *por más que* and *por mucho que*

Por más que ella **limpie**, su casa está siempre desordenada.	*No matter how much she cleans, her house is always a mess.*
Por mucho que él **coma**, no se engorda.	*No matter how much he eats, he doesn't get fat.*

After *ojalá*

An interjection of Arabic origin, **ojalá** means *would to God that* or *may God grant* and expresses great desire. It can also be translated as *I hope.*

Ojalá que ella **tenga** suerte.	*Would to God that she has luck.*
Ojalá que Uds. **reciban** el cheque.	*I hope you receive the check.*
Ojalá que él **se quede**.	*Would to God that he stays.*

After *acaso, quizás,* and *tal vez*

Acaso él me **visite** mañana.   *Perhaps he will visit me tomorrow.*
Quizás ellos me **digan** la verdad.   *Perhaps they will tell me the truth.*
Tal vez me **digan** mentiras.   *Perhaps they will tell me lies.*

After *aunque*

The subjunctive mood is used if the action has not yet occurred.

Voy al cine **aunque** no **vayan**   *I am going to the movies although*
mis amigos.   *my friends may not go.*
Aunque Pedro **se quede** esta   *Although Peter may stay tonight,*
noche, yo voy a salir.   *I am going to leave.*
Aunque sea difícil, él lo puede   *Although it may be difficult,*
hacer.   *he can do it.*

After Compounds of -*quiera*

Quienquiera que **esté** aquí,   *Whoever is here can leave with us.*
puede salir con nosotros.
Cualquiera que **sea** sincero,   *Whichever (one) is sincere can be*
puede ser un buen amigo.   *a good friend.*
Adondequiera que **vayas**,   *Wherever you go, I wish you the*
te deseo lo mejor.   *best.*
Dondequiera que **estén ellos**,   *Wherever they are, I am going to*
los voy a buscar.   *look for them.*

After *como*

The subjunctive mood is used after **como** if the meaning is *however.*

Ellas van a preparar la comida   *They are going to prepare the meal*
como tú **quieras**.   *however you want.*

 ## Exercise 13.7

Complete the following sentences with the correct form of the verb in parentheses.

1. Tal vez ellos _____ por la comida. (enfermarse)

2. Ojalá que nosotros _____ hoy. (descansar)

3. Aunque él _____ mañana, no quiero lavar el baño. (llegar)

4. Por mucho que ellas _____, no van a hacer nada. (quejarse)

5. Quienquiera que _____ bien, puede ser experto. (cocinar)

6. Ojalá que tú _____ bien esta noche. (dormir)

7. Aunque _____ mucho tráfico, queremos viajar. (haber)

8. Mi amiga busca un apartamento que _____ tres cuartos. (tener)

9. Carlos necesita una casa que _____ en el campo. (estar)

10. El hombre quiere hacer el proyecto como Ud. lo _____. (querer)

11. No conozco a nadie que me _____ a la playa. (acompañar)

12. Ella busca un novio que _____ inteligente. (ser)

13. Quizás él _____ la semana que viene. (venir)

14. Por más que Tomás _____, no sabe nada. (hablar)

Exercise 13.8

Subjunctive or indicative? *Complete the following sentences with the correct form of the verb in parentheses.*

1. Es importante que yo _____ temprano. (acostarse)

2. Esperamos que ella _____. (mejorarse)

3. Yo sé que las lecciones _____ difíciles. (ser)

4. ¿Quiere Ud. que Leopoldo _____ la historia? (estudiar)

5. No pienso que Loreta _____ bien el violín. (tocar)

6. Sabemos que a ella no le _____ practicar. (gustar)

7. Lo sentimos que Uds. no _____ a la conferencia mañana. (ir)

8. Es posible que _____ mucha gente interesante. (haber)

9. Espero que ellos _____ en su casa cuando yo

   _____. (estar/llegar)

10. Cuando Linda _____ de vacaciones, ella se relaja siempre. (ir)

11. María quiere que Pedro _____ a sus padres. (conocer)

12. Por mucho que yo _____, no pierdo peso. (nadar)

13. Ojalá que Uds. _____ pronto. (volver)

14. Ella quiere que tú la _____ el primero de mayo. (visitar)

15. ¿Conoce Ud. a alguien que _____ hacer todo lo que
    quiere hacer? (poder)

16. La madre quiere que los niños _____ la mesa. (poner)

17. Ella insiste en que ellos _____ la tarea antes de jugar.
    (hacer)

18. Se alegran de que Uds. _____ mejor. Esperan que Uds.

    _____ bien y contentos. (sentirse/estar)

19. ¿Por qué dudas que Rosa y Reinaldo _____
    en noviembre? (casarse)

20. Te aconsejo que _____ al dentista tres veces por año. (ir)

21. Pensamos que tú _____ despertarte más temprano para
    llegar a tiempo. (deber)

22. Carmen piensa que su amigo _____ un buen carro.
    (necesitar)

Exercise 13.9

Subjunctive, indicative, or infinitive? *Complete the following sentences with the correct form of the verb in parentheses.*

1. José y Susana están enamorados y _____ casarse. (querer)

2. Es difícil que yo te _____ la respuesta correcta. (dar)

3. ¿Es importante _____ honesto en este mundo? (ser)

4. Después de _____ ocho horas, me siento bien. (dormir)

5. Hablo despacio para que mis estudiantes me _____.
   (entender)

6. A Francisco le gusta _____ mucho. (leer)

7. A los amigos de Julia les gusta que ella _____ mucho. (reírse)

8. Te pido que _____ tu oficio. (hacer)

9. Yo sé que el restaurante que nos gusta _____ lejos de tu oficina. ¿Quieres que yo _____ otro? (estar/escoger)

10. ¿Es posible que nosotros _____ cenar juntos? (poder)

11. Es importante que Uds. _____ del edificio rápida y tranquilamente. (salir)

12. ¿Es importante _____ bien para _____ bien? (comer/vivir)

13. Carla tiene la bolsa que me _____. (gustar)

14. Ella me dice que los guantes _____ de cuero. (ser)

15. ¿Quieren ellos que nosotros _____ los artículos sobre la contaminación de las ciudades grandes? (buscar)

16. ¿Sabe Ud. por qué Irene no _____ nunca la chaqueta cuando _____ frío? (ponerse/hacer)

17. Me alegro de _____ aquí. Me alegro de que Uds. _____ aquí también. (estar/estar)

18. ¿Es necesario _____ para _____ otro idioma? (viajar/aprender)

19. Les muestro a Uds. las fotos luego que _____. (llegar)

20. Él se alegra de que su esposa _____ abogada. (ser)

21. Ella prefiere _____ hasta las nueve, pero su jefe prefiere que ella _____ más temprano. (dormir/despertarse)

22. Es preciso que Uds. no le _____ que su hermana está en la ciudad. Es una sorpresa y ella quiere _____ sin que él lo _____. (decir/llegar/saber)

23. Nos gusta _____ todo. (compartir)

24. Los padres le prohíben a Guillermo que _____ chocolates. (comer)

25. Quiero que Uds. _____ éxito en todo que hagan. (tener)

26. Ojalá que tú _____. (quedarse)

27. Te espero hasta que tú _____. (regresar)

Exercise 13.10

Change the following sentences to the subjunctive mood if necessary.

EXAMPLE   Ricardo no cocina. (Es una lástima)

Es una lástima que no cocine.

1. Enrique se va. (No me gusta)

_____

2. Ella le da flores a su esposo. (Él se alegra)

_____

3. Ella sabe la fecha. (Es importante)

_____

4. Mis amigos están bien. (Me alegro)

_____

5. Paula conoce a Raúl. (Es dudoso)

_____

6. Yo soy una buena estudiante. (Es posible)

_____

7. La película empieza a las dos. (Esperamos)

_____

8. Hace buen tiempo hoy. (Ojalá)

_____

9. El tren llega a tiempo. (Tal vez)

_____

10. Rosa tiene mucha suerte. (Quiero)

_____

11. Nos vemos mucho. (Me alegro)

_____

Exercise 13.11

Translate the following sentences into Spanish.

1. *Peter doesn't think that the trip will be good.*

   _____

2. *I am glad to know you.*

   _____

3. *We hope that you are feeling better.*

   _____

4. *Can you call me when you arrive home?*

   _____

5. *Laura insists that the children put on their jackets.*

   _____

6. *Roberto hopes that Julia will dance with him tonight.*

   _____

Exercise 13.12

On a separate sheet of paper, write the English translation of the following infinitives from Part II.

1. abrazar	12. animarse	23. burlarse	34. contar
2. acompañar	13. apresurarse	24. buscar	35. convenir
3. aconsejar	14. aprovecharse	25. caerse	36. conversar
4. acordarse	15. arreglarse	26. callarse	37. cuidar
5. acostarse	16. asistir	27. calmarse	38. dar
6. afeitarse	17. asustarse	28. cargar	39. darse cuenta
7. agradar	18. atreverse	29. cepillarse	40. decir
8. agradecer	19. ayudar	30. charlar	41. dedicarse
9. alegrarse	20. bajarse	31. cobrar	42. defenderse
10. amar	21. bañarse	32. comenzar	43. dejar
11. andar	22. besar	33. conocer	44. demorarse

45. desayunarse
46. desear
47. despedirse
48. despertarse
49. divertirse
50. doler
51. dormirse
52. ducharse
53. dudar
54. enamorarse
55. encantar
56. encontrarse
57. enfadarse
58. enfermarse
59. enojarse
60. enseñar
61. enviar
62. equivocarse
63. escoger
64. esperar
65. expresarse

66. extrañar
67. faltar
68. fascinar
69. fiarse
70. fijarse
71. gritar
72. haber
73. hacerse
74. hallar
75. importar
76. insistir
77. interesar
78. invitar
79. irse
80. lastimarse
81. lavarse
82. levantarse
83. llamar
84. llamarse
85. mandar
86. maquillarse

87. matar
88. mejorarse
89. meterse
90. molestar
91. morirse
92. moverse
93. mudarse
94. pararse
95. parecer
96. parecerse
97. pedir
98. peinarse
99. permitir
100. pintarse
101. ponerse
102. portarse
103. preguntar
104. preguntarse
105. preocuparse
106. prestar
107. prohibir

108. quedarse
109. quejarse
110. quemarse
111. quitarse
112. recoger
113. reírse
114. reunirse
115. saltar
116. saludar
117. sentarse
118. sentirse
119. sugerir
120. tardar
121. traer
122. tranquilizarse
123. ver
124. vestirse
125. visitar
126. volverse

Reading Comprehension

La despedida

Esta noche, cuando me acueste, va a ser mi última noche en Italia. Es una lástima que ya no pueda pasar las mañanas en pura tranquilidad en ese restaurante acogedor donde tomo mi café.

La soledad es diferente aquí que allí, quizás por el calor humano de los italianos. Mi amiga Beatriz quiere que me quede. Nos llevamos bien. A ella le gusta mostrarme lo histórico de las ciudades y la verdad es que me fascina lo antiguo. Realmente, no me importa mucho adonde vamos, si vamos a un sitio u otro, porque siempre nos divertimos juntas.

Cuando yo esté en los Estados Unidos (no lo puedo imaginar) quiero que ella me escriba desde Italia. La voy a extrañar. Pero es el fin de mi viaje.

A todas las personas con quienes me reúno, les deseo lo mejor y les agradezco por todo. Voy a despedirme de ellos con un abrazo y mucho cariño cuando les diga "adiós".

Verbos

agradecer	*to thank*
despedirse	*to take one's leave*

Nombres

el abrazo	*the embrace*	la despedida	*the farewell*
el calor humano	*human warmth*	el fin	*the end*
el cariño	*affection*	la soledad	*the solitude*

Adverbio

realmente	*actually*

The Spanish word **actualmente** means *nowadays* or *at the present time.*

Expresiones

The neuter article **lo** is used before masculine adjectives to make them into nouns.

lo antiguo	*the ancient*
lo histórico	*the historic*
lo mejor	*the best*

Conjunción

u   *or*

For reasons of pronunciation, **o** is replaced by **u** before words beginning with **o** or **ho**.

Preguntas

After you have read the selection, answer the following questions in Spanish.

1. ¿Piensa Ud. que Isabel debe quedarse en Italia o es mejor que regrese a los Estados Unidos?

    _____

2. ¿Se da cuenta ella que es la primera vez que menciona el nombre de una amiga o un amigo?

    _____

3. ¿Que parte de su viaje le gusta más a Isabel?

    _____

4. ¿Piensa Ud. que hay un cambio en Isabel desde el primer cuento hasta el último?

    _____

III

Preterit Tense, Imperfect Tense, and Double Object Pronouns

14

The Preterit Tense

The preterit expresses an action or actions completed in the past. The English translation is usually the simple past (for example, *I sang*). The preterit is used to express the following.

- Actions completed in the past
- A series of completed actions in the past
- Conditions no longer in effect

Formation of the Preterit

Verbs are considered regular if there is no change in the stem. Most verbs are regular in the preterit. This tense is formed by adding the preterit endings to the stem of the infinitive of **-ar**, **-er**, and **-ir** verbs.

There are only 17 basic irregular verbs in the preterit. Compound forms of these verbs are conjugated in the same way as the main verb.

Some **-ir** verbs have a stem change in the third person of the preterit, but these verbs are not considered irregular.

Regular *-ar* Verbs

In order to conjugate a regular **-ar** verb in the preterit tense, drop the ending and add **-é**, **-aste**, **-ó**, **-amos**, **-asteis**, **-aron** to the stem. All **-ar** verbs except **andar**, **dar**, and **estar** are regular in the preterit.

ayudar	
yo ayudé	nosotros ayudamos
tú ayudaste	vosotros ayudasteis
Ud. ayudó	Uds. ayudaron

cantar	
yo canté	nosotros cantamos
tú cantaste	vosotros cantasteis
él cantó	ellos cantaron

pensar		recordar	
yo pensé	nosotros pensamos	yo recordé	nosotros recordamos
tú pensaste	vosotros pensasteis	tú recordaste	vosotros recordasteis
ella pensó	ellas pensaron	ella recordó	ellas recordaron

trabajar		viajar	
yo trabajé	nosotros trabajamos	yo viajé	nosotros viajamos
tú trabajaste	vosotros trabajasteis	tú viajaste	vosotros viajasteis
Ud. trabajó	Uds. trabajaron	Ud. viajó	Uds. viajaron

In **-ar** verbs, the first-person plural preterit **nosotros** form is identical to the present indicative **nosotros** form. Whether a particular verb is in the present or the past becomes clear in context.

A Word About Pronunciation

Notice that the first- and third-person singular forms carry written accents. It is very important to practice the pronunciation and to stress the accented syllable. Pronounce the verbs in this way: **yo canté, tú cantaste, el cantó, nosotros cantamos, vosotros cantasteis, ellos cantaron.** Review the basic pronunciation rules: All words that end in **n**, **s**, or any vowel have the stress on the second to last, or penultimate, syllable.

Regular -er and -ir Verbs

In order to conjugate regular **-er** and **-ir** verbs, drop the ending and add **-í**, **-iste**, **-ió**, **-imos**, **-isteis**, **-ieron** to the stem. The endings are the same for both **-er** and **-ir** verbs.

-Er Verbs

comer		entender	
yo comí	nosotros comimos	yo entendí	nosotros entendimos
tú comiste	vosotros comisteis	tú entendiste	vosotros entendisteis
él comió	ellos comieron	ella entendió	ellas entendieron

ver	
yo vi	nosotros vimos
tú viste	vosotros visteis
Ud. vio	Uds. vieron

Notice that the verb **ver** is regular. It does not carry an accent mark on the third-person singular, **vio**, because the form has only one syllable.

-Ir Verbs

compartir

yo compartí	nosotros compartimos
tú compartiste	vosotros compartisteis
él compartió	ellos compartieron

descubrir

yo descubrí	nosotros descubrimos
tú descubriste	vosotros descubristeis
Ud. descubrió	Uds. descubrieron

salir

yo salí	nosotros salimos
tú saliste	vosotros salisteis
ella salió	ellas salieron

In **-ir** verbs, the **nosotros** form of the preterit is identical to the present in-dicative **nosotros** form. Its meaning becomes clear in context.

Key Vocabulary

These words will help enhance your ability to communicate. As you learn them, remember to practice them aloud.

anoche	*last night*
ayer	*yesterday*
anteayer	*the day before yesterday*
hace	*ago* (when it is used before a period of time in the past)
hace (dos días)	*(two days) ago*
pasado	*past, last*
la semana pasada	*last week*
el mes pasado	*last month*
el año pasado	*last year*

Exercise 14.1

Complete the following sentences with the correct preterit form of the verb in paren-theses.

1. Ella _____ la puerta. (abrir)

2. Yo _____ la ventana. (cerrar)

3. Nosotros _____ a México hace ocho meses. (viajar)

4. Anoche, el niño _____ televisión por dos horas. (mirar)

5. Ayer, yo _____ a mi amigo, y lo _____
   a tomar unas cervezas conmigo. (visitar/invitar)

6. Anteayer, _____ a llover y _____ hasta
   las nueve de la noche. (empezar/llover)

7. Ellas _____ a casa y _____ las canciones
   de Celia Cruz. (regresar/escuchar)

8. A ellos les _____ la película. (gustar)

9. ¿A qué hora _____ Ud. anoche? (acostarse)

10. Esta mañana a las once _____ el teléfono. (sonar)

11. Anoche, ella _____ con un hombre elegante. (soñar)

12. Yo _____ un elefante en la calle. (ver)

13. Nosotros _____ mucho en la fiesta anoche. (divertirse)

14. Ella le _____ al hombre un vaso de agua. (ofrecer)

15. Ellos me _____ con la pronunciación. (ayudar)

Uses of the Preterit

Always keep in mind that the action or actions expressed by the preterit are over. It doesn't make any difference how long the action went on before; the action has a definite end.

To Express an Action Completed in the Past

Anoche, ella cantó una canción triste.	*Last night, she sang a sad song.*
Ayer, yo estudié por dos horas.	*Yesterday, I studied for two hours.*
Anteayer, escribimos dos cartas.	*The day before yesterday, we wrote two letters.*
La semana pasada, él me llamó por teléfono.	*Last week, he called me on the phone.*
El año pasado, ¿compró Ud. una casa nueva?	*Last year, did you buy a new house?*
¿Perdiste tus llaves esta mañana?	*Did you lose your keys this morning?*
¿Por qué no cocinaron Uds. anoche?	*Why didn't you cook last night?*
Ellos salieron hace tres horas.	*They left three hours ago.*

No vimos a nadie.	*We didn't see anyone.*
No me prestaron dinero.	*They didn't lend me money.*
Yo no les enseñé a los estudiantes a nadar.	*I didn't teach the students to swim.*
Samuel jugó al tenis.	*Samuel played tennis.*
Ella lo amó mucho, ¿verdad?	*She loved him a lot, right?*

To Express a Series of Completed Actions in the Past

Anoche en la fiesta, bailamos, cantamos y hablamos.	*Last night at the party, we danced, we sang, and we talked.*
El domingo pasado, ellos corrieron en el maratón, descansaron y comieron.	*Last Sunday, they ran in the marathon, rested, and ate.*
Él se despertó, se lavó y se afeitó.	*He got up, washed, and shaved.*
Caminé a la tienda, compré lechuga y tomates, saludé a los dueños y salí.	*I walked to the store, bought lettuce and tomatoes, greeted the owners, and left.*

To Express a Condition That Is No Longer in Effect

¿Te sentiste mal la semana pasada?	*Did you feel ill last week?*
Me sentí bien la semana pasada, pero me siento mal hoy.	*I felt well last week, but I feel bad today.*
A Miguel le dolió todo el cuerpo ayer, pero hoy está bien.	*Yesterday, Michael had pain in his whole body, but today he is fine.*

Exercise 14.2

Rewrite each of the following sentences in the preterit.

1. Me gusta viajar. _____

2. Cada mañana, leo un periódico. Ayer, yo _____

3. Ellos cierran la puerta del apartamento. Anoche, ellos _____
   _____

4. Les ofrezco ayuda. _____

5. ¿Por qué vuelves tú tarde? ¿Por qué _____

6. Los niños no se callan. Anoche, ellos _____

7. Leonora no se acuerda de la idea. La semana pasada _____

_____

8. La película empieza a las ocho. Anoche, _____

_____

Irregular Verbs

It is important to memorize all the irregular verbs. Once you do, you will be able to use any verb you wish in the preterit.

Irregular verbs in the preterit have an irregular stem and a special set of endings. Note that the endings do not carry accent marks. In order to conjugate an irregular verb in the preterit, add the endings **-e**, **-iste**, **-o**, **-imos**, **-isteis**, **-ieron** to the irregular stems.

andar

yo anduve	nosotros anduvimos
tú anduviste	vosotros anduvisteis
él anduvo	ellos anduvieron

caber

yo cupe	nosotros cupimos
tú cupiste	vosotros cupisteis
ella cupo	ellas cupieron

estar

yo estuve	nosotros estuvimos
tú estuviste	vosotros estuvisteis
Ud. estuvo	Uds. estuvieron

hacer

yo hice	nosotros hicimos
tú hiciste	vosotros hicisteis
él hizo	ellos hicieron

poder

yo pude	nosotros pudimos
tú pudiste	vosotros pudisteis
Ud. pudo	Uds. pudieron

poner

yo puse	nosotros pusimos
tú pusiste	vosotros pusisteis
él puso	ellos pusieron

querer

yo quise	nosotros quisimos
tú quisiste	vosotros quisisteis
ella quiso	ellas quisieron

saber

yo supe	nosotros supimos
tú supiste	vosotros supisteis
Ud. supo	Uds. supieron

tener

yo tuve	nosotros tuvimos
tú tuviste	vosotros tuvisteis
él tuvo	ellos tuvieron

venir

yo vine	nosotros vinimos
tú viniste	vosotros vinisteis
él vino	ellos vinieron

decir	
yo dije	nosotros dijimos
tú dijiste	vosotros dijisteis
ella dijo	ellas dijeron

producir	
yo produje	nosotros produjimos
tú produjiste	vosotros produjisteis
Ud. produjo	Uds. produjeron

traer	
yo traje	nosotros trajimos
tú trajiste	vosotros trajisteis
él trajo	ellos trajeron

Dar, **ir**, and **ser** have slightly different endings.

dar	
yo di	nosotros dimos
tú diste	vosotros disteis
ella dio	ellas dieron

ir	
yo fui	nosotros fuimos
tú fuiste	vosotros fuisteis
Ud. fue	Uds. fueron

ser	
yo fui	nosotros fuimos
tú fuiste	vosotros fuisteis
él fue	ellos fueron

The conjugations for **ir** and **ser** are identical in the preterit. The meaning is clarified in context, as in the following examples.

Ella fue doctora.	*She was a doctor.*
Ella fue a la tienda.	*She went to the store.*

Haber is used to express English *there was, there were, was there?, were there?* The third-person singular preterit form **hubo** is used with both singular and plural subjects.

Note the following about the irregular preterit verbs above.

- **Hizo** (the third-person singular of **hacer**) shows the spelling change **c** > **z** to maintain the sound of /s/.

- Irregular preterits whose stem ends in **j** have **-eron**, not **-ieron**, in the third-person plural, for example, **dijeron**, **trajeron**.

Compound forms of verbs are conjugated in the same way as the main verb.

decir
contradecir   *to contradict*   contradije, *etc.*

hacer
deshacer   *to undo*   deshice, *etc.*

poner
componer   *to compose*   compuse, *etc.*
proponer   *to propose*   propuse, *etc.*

tener
contener   *to contain*   contuve, *etc.*
detener   *to detain*   detuve, *etc.*
mantener   *to maintain*   mantuve, *etc.*

producir
conducir   *to drive*   conduje, *etc.*
traducir   *to translate*   traduje, *etc.*

traer
atraer   *to attract*   atraje, *etc.*
distraer   *to distract*   distraje, *etc.*

venir
prevenir   *to prevent*   previne, *etc.*

Here are some examples of irregular verbs in the preterit.

Pedro y Jorge anduvieron en las montañas por dos días.
Peter and George walked in the mountains for two days.

¿Hicieron Ud. su tarea para hoy?
Did you do your homework for today?

Tuve una cita con el dentista, pero no fui.
I had an appointment with the dentist, but I didn't go.

¿Por qué no vino Ud. a mi fiesta anoche?
Why didn't you come to my party last night?

¿Quién le dijo a Sofía la verdad?
Who told Sophie the truth?

Los estudiantes produjeron su propia obra de teatro.
The students produced their own play.

Le trajimos una bicicleta al niño.
We brought the child a bicycle.

Miguel le dio a su novia un anillo.
Michael gave a ring to his girlfriend.

En mil novecientos ochenta, Nestor fue músico. Ahora él es maestro.	*In 1980, Nestor was a musician. Now he is a teacher.*

Exercise 14.3

Complete the following sentences with the preterit form of the verb. Try to memorize the irregular verbs as you do the exercise.

1. ¿Qué me _____ Ud. anoche? No le _____ nada. (decir/decir)

2. Nosotros no _____ nada ayer. ¿Qué _____ Uds.? (hacer/hacer)

3. ¿Por qué me _____ tú tantos regalos. No tengo nada para _____ a ti. (dar/dar)

4. _____ una fiesta ayer. (haber)

5. Yo _____ vino a la fiesta. Mis amigos no _____ nada. (traer/traer)

6. Los niños _____ los platos sucios en el horno. Su mamá los sacó del horno y los _____ en el lavaplatos. (poner/poner)

7. Yo _____ en el banco a las nueve esta mañana. ¿Dónde _____ Uds.? (estar/estar)

8. Él _____ un accidente en carro ayer. Yo no _____ nunca un accidente. (tener/tener)

9. ¿A qué hora _____ Uds. a la biblioteca? Nosotros _____ a las cuatro. (ir/ir)

10. Él _____ pintor; ahora es abogado. Yo _____ camarera; ahora soy actriz. (ser/ser)

11. ¿Por qué _____ Uds. a mi casa en tren? ¿Cómo _____ Beatriz? (venir/venir)

12. Nosotros _____ lentamente a la escuela. Nuestros maestros _____ rápidamente. (andar/andar)

13. Yo _____ una obra de teatro hace un año. (producir)

14. Once payasos _____ en el carro del circo esta mañana. (caber)

Exercise 14.4

Review the conjugations for the irregular verbs, and complete the following sentences with the correct form of the appropriate verb. Use each irregular verb only one time.

> andar, caber, dar, decir, estar, haber, hacer, ir, poder,
> poner, producir, querer, saber, ser, tener, traer, venir

1. El hombre trató de meter todos sus libros en su carro, pero no

   _____ en el carro pequeño.

2. Empezó a llover y la hija le _____ a su madre un paraguas.

3. Ayer _____ un día de mucha lluvia; hace buen tiempo
   hoy.

4. Los viajeros no _____ salir del país sin su pasaporte;
   se quedaron en los Estados Unidos.

5. Ella no _____ subir la pirámide. Sus amigos subieron
   sin ella.

6. Nosotros _____ a ver una película popular pero no nos
   gustó.

7. Nosotros _____ hacia el parque. Miramos la puesta del sol
   y salimos.

8. El paciente _____ en la oficina del doctor precisamente
   a las siete y media de la mañana.

9. Yo _____ mis llaves en el carro en vez de ponerlas en
   mi bolsillo.

10. La muchacha se despertó y le _____ a su hermana,

    "_____ un mal sueño."

11. ¿Por qué no _____ tú una cita con tu dentista la semana
    pasada?

12. Hubo un ataque terrorista ayer. Nosotros lo _____ hoy.

13. El papá les _____ muchos regalos a sus hijos porque
    los quiere mucho.

14. ¿Quién _____ aquella obra de arte? Es horrible.

15. Mis primos y mis sobrinos _____ a verme hace dos días.

16. El sábado pasado, _____ una fiesta en el club.

Exercise 14.5

Complete the following sentences, using only **ser**, **ir**, **irse**, *and* **estar** *in the preterit, according to the context of the sentence.*

1. Ella es profesora hoy, pero antes _____ azafata.

2. Yo _____ gerente por dos años.

3. Nosotros _____ muy contentos ayer porque nos ganamos la lotería.

4. ¿Por qué _____ tan rápido sin despedirte de nosotros?

5. Ellos _____ al supermercado hoy a comprar alimentos.

6. La semana pasada, Raúl _____ en México. Regresó a casa ayer.

7. Los muchachos _____ enfermos anteayer, pero están bien hoy.

8. _____ una buena idea.

9. ¿Dónde _____ la familia de Federico esta tarde?

10. ¿Quién _____ a la librería a las nueve y media esta mañana?

Exercise 14.6

Answer the following questions orally in Spanish.

1. Yo no hice nada anoche. ¿Qué hicieron Uds.?

2. ¿Le gusta comer? ¿Cocinó anoche?

3. ¿A qué hora te acostaste anoche? ¿A qué hora te despertaste esta mañana?

4. ¿Quién fue el presidente en el año mil novecientos noventa y seis?

5. ¿Vio Ud. a sus amigos ayer?

6. ¿Piensa Ud. que Cristóbal Colón descubrió América?

7. ¿Hizo sol ayer?

8. ¿Por qué decidieron Uds. asistir a clases de español?

9. ¿Dónde nació Ud.?

10. ¿Quién bailó contigo la semana pasada?

-Ir Verbs with Stem Changes in the Third Person

-Ir verbs that are irregular in the present indicative have a stem change in the preterit. This stem change occurs only in the third-person singular and plural forms of the preterit.

e > **ie** in the present indicative
e > **i** in the preterit

Infinitive	Present Indicative	Preterit	
divertirse	me divierto	me divertí	nos divertimos
		te divertiste	os divertisteis
		se divirtió	se divirtieron
mentir	yo miento	yo mentí	nosotros mentimos
		tú mentiste	vosotros mentisteis
		él mintió	ellos mintieron
preferir	yo prefiero	yo preferí	nosotros preferimos
		tú preferiste	vosotros preferisteis
		Ud. prefirió	Uds. prefirieron
sentirse	me siento	me sentí	nos sentimos
		te sentiste	os sentisteis
		se sintió	se sintieron
sugerir	yo sugiero	yo sugerí	nosotros sugerimos
		tú sugeriste	vosotros sugeristeis
		ella sugirió	ellas sugirieron

e > **i** in the present indicative
e > **i** in the preterit

Infinitive	Present Indicative	Preterit	
corregir	yo corrijo	yo corregí	nosotros corregimos
		tú corregiste	vosotros corregisteis
		ella corrigió	ellas corrigieron
despedirse	me despido	me despedí	nos despedimos
		te despediste	os despedisteis
		se despidió	se despidieron
pedir	yo pido	yo pedí	nosotros pedimos
		tú pediste	vosotros pedisteis
		Ud. pidió	Uds. pidieron

Infinitive	Present Indicative	Preterit	
reírse	me río	me reí	nos reímos
		te reíste	os reísteis
		se rió	se rieron
repetir	yo repito	yo repetí	nosotros repetimos
		tú repetiste	vosotros repetisteis
		Ud. repitió	Uds. repitieron
seguir	yo sigo	yo seguí	nosotros seguimos
		tú seguiste	vosotros seguisteis
		él siguió	ellos siguieron
servir	yo sirvo	yo serví	nosotros servimos
		tú serviste	vosotros servisteis
		Ud. sirvió	Uds. sirvieron
sonreír	yo sonrío	yo sonreí	nosotros sonreímos
		tú sonreíste	vosotros sonreísteis
		él sonrió	ellos sonrieron
vestirse	me visto	me vestí	nos vestimos
		te vestiste	os vestisteis
		se vistió	se vistieron

o > ue in the present indicative
o > u in the preterit

Infinitive	Present Indicative	Preterit	
dormir	yo duermo	yo dormí	nosotros dormimos
		tú dormiste	vosotros dormisteis
		ella durmió	ellas durmieron
morir	yo muero	yo morí	nosotros morimos
		tú moriste	vosotros moristeis
		él murió	ellos murieron

 ## Exercise 14.7

Complete the following sentences with the correct form of the preterit.

1. Anoche, el niño _____ nueve horas. (dormir)

2. ¿Por qué no _____ Uds. las instrucciones? (seguir)

3. Yo _____ quedarme en un hotel de lujo; ella

   _____ quedarse también; él _____ irse.

   (preferir/preferir/preferir)

4. Anoche, su novio _____ de ella por última vez. (despedirse)

5. Nosotros _____ mucho en la fiesta. Nuestros amigos no

   _____ nada y se fueron. (divertirse/divertirse)

6. Siempre la mujer elegante se viste bien, pero ayer ella no

   _____ bien y _____ mal. (sentirse/vestirse)

7. Su sobrino _____ ayer. Él lo supo hoy. (morirse)

8. Anoche fuimos a un buen restaurante. Nos _____
   una mariscada en salsa verde. (servir)

9. Casi nunca miento. Pero ayer, _____. Estuve con unas

   amigas y ellas _____ también. (mentir/mentir)

10. La niña _____; con su sonrisa el mundo se alegró. (sonreír)

11. No sé porque el hombre _____. Yo no vi nada cómico.
    (reírse)

12. La estudiante aplicada _____ la lección para entenderla bien.
    (repetir)

13. Sus maestros les _____ la gramática. (corregir)

14. Yo _____ bien ayer. ¿Cómo _____ Uds.?
    (sentirse/sentirse)

Verbs with Orthographic Changes

-Ar Verbs

Verbs with orthographic changes are not irregular. The spelling changes simply maintain the necessary sound. Only verbs in the **yo** form are affected by the spelling changes in the preterit of **-ar** verbs.

- Verbs that end in **-gar** change **g** to **gu**.
- Verbs that end in **-car** change **c** to **qu**.
- Verbs that end in **-zar** change **z** to **c**.

apagar	yo apa**gué**	nosotros apagamos
	tú apagaste	vosotros apagasteis
	él apagó	ellos apagaron

buscar	yo bus**qué**	nosotros buscamos
	tú buscaste	vosotros buscasteis
	ella buscó	ellas buscaron
comenzar	yo comen**cé**	nosotros comenzamos
	tú comenzaste	vosotros comenzasteis
	Ud. comenzó	Uds. comenzaron
explicar	yo expli**qué**	nosotros explicamos
	tú explicaste	vosotros explicasteis
	él explicó	ellos explicaron
llegar	yo lle**gué**	nosotros llegamos
	tú llegaste	vosotros llegasteis
	ella llegó	ellas llegaron
tocar	yo to**qué**	nosotros tocamos
	tú tocaste	vosotros tocasteis
	Ud. tocó	Uds. tocaron

Note that the spelling change **z** > **c** occurs before the vowel **e** without affecting the sound, as in **comenzar**, **comencé**.

A Word About Pronunciation

Make sure to stress the final sound of the first-person singular (**yo** form) and the third-person singular (**él**, **ella**, **Ud.** form). Spanish pronunciation is precise, and the tense you use depends on the correct pronunciation. So continue to practice in this way: **yo apagué, tú apagaste, él apagó, nosotros apagamos, vosotros apagasteis, ellos apagaron.**

Here are more **-ar** verbs with spelling changes.

-gar

ahogarse	*to drown*
cargar	*to carry, to load*
castigar	*to punish*
colgar	*to hang*
entregar	*to hand in, to deliver*
madrugar	*to get up early*
pegar	*to hit, to glue*
tragar	*to swallow*
vagar	*to wander*

-car

acercarse	*to approach*
arrancar	*to pull out, to root out*
colocar	*to put, to place*
destacar	*to stick out*
justificar	*to justify*
mascar	*to chew*
pescar	*to fish*
publicar	*to publish*
sacar	*to take out*
suplicar	*to beg*

-zar

alcanzar	*to reach, to overtake*
amenazar	*to threaten*
lanzar	*to throw, to shoot*
realizar	*to fulfill*
rezar	*to pray*
tropezarse (con)	*to bump into*

 Exercise 14.8

Complete the following sentences with the correct form of the preterit.

1. Me desperté con vértigo y _____ con la pared. (tropezarse)

2. Hace una semana, Laura pagó la cuenta, pero ayer yo la

   _____. (pagar)

3. El estudiante orgulloso le _____ su tarea a la profesora. (entregar)

4. Nosotros _____ de un lado a otro el año pasado. (vagar)

5. Anoche, yo _____ una pintura en la pared. (colgar)

6. Su papá se enojó anteayer y _____ a sus hijos. (castigar)

-Er and *-ir* Verbs

Verbs with spelling changes are not irregular. The spelling changes shown for **-er** and **-ir** verbs with stems ending in a vowel avoid the use of three vowels in a row.

Verbs with a vowel immediately preceding the infinitive ending change **i** to **y** in the third-person singular and plural. In these verbs, there is a written accent over the letter **i** on the **yo**, **tú**, **nosotros**, and **vosotros** endings.

caer	yo caí	nosotros caímos
	tú caíste	vosotros caísteis
	él ca**yó**	ellos ca**yeron**
leer	yo leí	nosotros leímos
	tú leíste	vosotros leísteis
	ella le**yó**	ellas le**yeron**
oír	yo oí	nosotros oímos
	tú oíste	vosotros oísteis
	Ud. o**yó**	Uds. o**yeron**

Note, for example, that the third-person singular of **caer** is **cayó** rather than **caió**.

Verbs that end in **-uir** change **i** to **y**; the accent over the **i** appears only over the first-person singular.

construir	yo construí	nosotros construimos
	tú construiste	vosotros construisteis
	él constru**yó**	ellos constru**yeron**
destruir	yo destruí	nosotros destruimos
	tú destruiste	vosotros destruisteis
	ella destru**yó**	ellas destru**yeron**

Here are more **-er** and **-ir** verbs with spelling changes.

creer	*to believe*	huir	*to flee*
concluir	*to conclude*	incluir	*to include*
contribuir	*to contribute*	influir	*to influence*
distribuir	*to distribute*	poseer	*to possess*
fluir	*to flow*		

Exercise 14.9

Complete the following sentences with the correct preterit form of the verb in parentheses.

1. El hombre tacaño se puso feliz la primera vez que él _____ con dinero. (contribuir)

2. El niño _____ del árbol pero no se lesionó. (caerse)

3. Mi maestro de la escuela secundaria _____ mucho en mi educación. (influir)

4. Hubo un incendio y todas las personas en la ciudad _____. (huir)

5. Los carpinteros _____ dos casas el año pasado. (construir)

6. ¿Por qué _____ tú la bicicleta de Susana? (destruir)

Exercise 14.10

Translate the following sentences into Spanish.

1. *I worked a lot yesterday. Last night, I rested.*

   _____

2. *Last night, we watched television instead of studying.*

   _____

3. *I gave him my dog; he gave me nothing.*

   _____

4. *She read her friend's letter a month ago.*

   _____

5. *We received the package a week ago.*

   _____

6. *What did you say to her? I told you that he died last year.*

   _____

7. *The children went to bed at nine o'clock last night.*

   _____

8. *I saw your sister yesterday.*

   _____

Verbs with Special Meanings in the Preterit

Meaning in the Preterit

conocer *to know, to be acquainted with*

¿Dónde conociste a tu novio?   *Where did you **meet** your boyfriend?*

Lo conocí en España.   *I **met** him in Spain.*

¿Cuándo conocieron Uds. a Paulina?   *When did you **meet** Pauline?*

La conocimos hace tres años.   *We **met** her three years ago.*

saber *to know a fact, to know how to do something*

Ella tuvo un accidente ayer. Lo supe hoy.   *She had an accident yesterday. I **found out** today.*

No nos dijeron nada pero supimos la verdad.   *They didn't tell us anything but we **found out** the truth.*

no querer *not to want*

Ella no quiso bajar en el ascensor.   *She **refused** to go down in the elevator.*

El niño no quiso comer.   *The child **refused** to eat.*

no poder *not to be able*

Hubo un incendio y la gente no pudo salir.   *There was a fire and the people **failed** to leave.*

A Word About Translations

The preterit expresses an action completed in the past. These translations are as close as possible to transmitting the idea of the sentence. **No querer** means *not to want.* But in the preterit, the action is over, so the concept is stronger than she didn't want to go down in the elevator. She didn't want to, and she didn't; therefore, she refused. Similarly, **no poder** means *not to be able.* But in the preterit, the people were not able to leave, and the action is completed; therefore, they didn't manage to leave, or failed to leave.

Exercise 14.11

Complete the following sentences with the correct form of the preterit.

1. Yo _____ en el apartamento a las ocho anoche. (entrar)

2. Nosotros _____ un chocolate caliente. (tomar)

3. Ellos _____ a las once. Yo _____ a la una. (dormirse/dormirse)

4. ¿Me _____ Uds. ayer? Yo no los _____. (ver/ver)

5. _____ a nevar a las siete esta mañana. (empezar)

6. _____ mucho sol ayer. (hacer)

7. El taxista le _____ a mi primo veinte pesos. ¿Cuánto te _____ a ti? (cobrar/cobrar)

8. Nosotros les _____ a nuestros parientes dos tarjetas, pero ellos no las _____. (escribir/recibir)

9. El trabajador _____ temprano esta mañana. (despertarse)

10. ¿_____ tú las llaves? (encontrar)

11. Yo no _____ bajar en el ascensor. (querer)

12. Cuando él _____ joven, él _____ un buen deportista. (ser/ser)

13. ¿Por qué no me _____ Ud. la verdad? (decir)

14. La tarea fue difícil, pero los estudiantes la _____ hacer. (poder)

A Word About the Preterit

Practice and study. Learn the irregular verbs and the regular verbs. Pronounce all regular **-ar**, **-er**, and **-ir** verbs aloud as much as you can. Use the verb lists in this chapter as reference, and use the verbs as you need them. Spend at least a week on the preterit to learn the form and the concept.

Reading Comprehension

Estimados lectores,

Espero que a Uds. les guste la siguiente historia. Está en forma de diálogo y basada en acontecimientos de la vida real. Intenten adivinar quien es el personaje principal según las claves que aparecen en esta escena. Para que gocen de lo lindo y para que aprendan de la historia, es necesario que Uds. lean con cuidado.

En la corte (primera escena)

La escena tiene lugar en 399 B.C. en la corte griega ante una asamblea de 501 ciudadanos. El acusado entra y empieza a hablar.

ACUSADO   Tengo setenta años y es la primera vez que me ven en la corte. ¿Cuál es la primera acusación contra mí?

ACUSADOR   Ud. es culpable de investigar bajo la tierra y en el cielo y de enseñarles a otros las mismas cosas.

ACUSADO   No tengo nada que ver con estas acusaciones y nada de esto es verdad.

ACUSADOR   Pero, ¿cuál es el problema, entonces? ¿Por qué hay tantos prejuicios contra Ud. si dice que no hace nada diferente de los demás? Nos puede decir Ud. lo que es, para que le demos un veredicto justo.

ACUSADO   Bueno. Voy a decirles toda la verdad. Me dan esta reputación por cierta sabiduría que tengo. Menciono el dios de Delfos para que él sea mi testigo. ¿Se acuerdan Uds. de Querefón? Él fue al dios de Delfos y le preguntó si hay una persona más sabia que yo. El dios contestó que no hay nadie. Pero, ¿qué significa la idea de que yo soy el hombre más sagaz de todos? Me tocó investigar la cuestión. Yo fui a ver a un hombre que tiene la reputación de ser sagaz. Lo examiné. No es necesario que les diga su nombre, él es un político, y esto es el resultado.

Verbos

adivinar	*to guess*
intentar	*to intend, to try*

Nombres

los acontecimientos	*the events*
el ciudadano	*the citizen*
la clave	*the key, the code*

la corte	*the court*
la cuestión	*the issue*
los demás	*the rest*
el diálogo	*the dialogue*
el dios de Delfos	*the god of Delphi*
la escena	*the scene*
el personaje	*the character*
el político	*the politician*
el prejuicio	*the prejudice*
la sabiduría	*the knowledge*
el veredicto	*the verdict*

Adjetivos

justo	*fair, just*
principal	*main, principal*
sabio	*wise*
sagaz	*wise, clever*
siguiente	*following*

Preguntas

After you have read the selection, answer the following questions in Spanish.

1. ¿En que sitio empieza la acción?

   _____

2. ¿Cuántos años tiene el acusado?

   _____

3. ¿Cuál es la acusación contra él?

   _____

4. ¿Qué hizo el acusado después de escuchar que él es el más sabio de todos?

   _____

15

The Imperfect Tense

The imperfect tense expresses an action or actions in the past that are not seen as completed. The imperfect is used in the following ways.

- To "set the stage" in the past; to express a narration, situation, or background in the past
- To express habitual, customary, or repeated actions in the past
- To express continuous actions or actions in progress in the past
- To express a description in the past
- To express point of origin in the past
- To express time in the past
- To express one's age in the past

Formation of the Imperfect

Almost all verbs are regular in the imperfect tense. The tense is formed by adding the imperfect endings to the stem of the **-ar**, **-er**, and **-ir** verbs. There are only three irregular verbs in the imperfect.

Regular *-ar* Verbs

To conjugate an **-ar** verb in the imperfect tense, drop the ending and add **-aba**, **-abas**, **-aba**, **-ábamos**, **-abais**, **-aban** to the stem. Note that the first- and third-person singular forms (**yo**, **él/ella/Ud.**) are identical in the imperfect. There are no irregular **-ar** verbs.

acompañar

yo acompañaba	nosotros acompañábamos
tú acompañabas	vosotros acompañabais
él acompañaba	ellos acompañaban

dar

yo daba	nosotros dábamos
tú dabas	vosotros dabais
ella daba	ellas daban

estar

yo estaba	nosotros estábamos
tú estabas	vosotros estabais
Ud. estaba	Uds. estaban

hablar

yo hablaba	nosotros hablábamos
tú hablabas	vosotros hablabais
él hablaba	ellos hablaban

recordar

yo recordaba	nosotros recordábamos
tú recordabas	vosotros recordabais
ella recordaba	ellas recordaban

trabajar

yo trabajaba	nosotros trabajábamos
tú trabajabas	vosotros trabajabais
Ud. trabajaba	Uds. trabajaban

A Word About the Imperfect
Practice the pronunciation of the imperfect **-ar** verbs. There are one-syllable, two-syllable, three-syllable, and four-syllable verbs. Be sure to pronounce the imperfect in this way: **yo trabajaba, tú trabajabas, él trabajaba, nosotros tra-bajábamos, vosotros trabajabais, ellos trabajaban**.

Regular *-er* and *-ir* Verbs

To conjugate regular **-er** and **-ir** verbs in the imperfect, drop the ending and add **-ía, -ías, -ía, -íamos, -íais, -ían** to the stem. The endings are the same for both **-er** and **-ir** verbs.

-*Er* Verbs

entender

yo entendía	nosotros entendíamos
tú entendías	vosotros entendíais
él entendía	ellos entendían

hacer

yo hacía	nosotros hacíamos
tú hacías	vosotros hacíais
ella hacía	ellas hacían

poder

yo podía	nosotros podíamos
tú podías	vosotros podíais
Ud. podía	Uds. podían

querer

yo quería	nosotros queríamos
tú querías	vosotros queríais
él quería	ellos querían

saber

yo sabía	nosotros sabíamos
tú sabías	vosotros sabíais
ella sabía	ellas sabían

tener

yo tenía	nosotros teníamos
tú tenías	vosotros teníais
Ud. tenía	Uds. tenían

Haber is used to express English *there was, there were, was there?, were there?* The third-person singular imperfect form **había** is used with both singular and plural subjects.

-*Ir* Verbs

decir

yo decía	nosotros decíamos
tú decías	vosotros decíais
él decía	ellos decían

divertirse

me divertía	nos divertíamos
te divertías	os divertíais
ella se divertía	ellas se divertían

sentirse

me sentía	nos sentíamos
te sentías	os sentíais
Ud. se sentía	Uds. se sentían

venir

yo venía	nosotros veníamos
tú venías	vosotros veníais
él venía	ellos venían

Irregular Verbs

ir

yo iba	nosotros íbamos
tú ibas	vosotros ibais
él iba	ellos iban

ser

yo era	nosotros éramos
tú eras	vosotros erais
ella era	ellas eran

ver

yo veía	nosotros veíamos
tú veías	vosotros veíais
Ud. veía	Uds. veían

The translation of **ir** in the imperfect is *was going, were going.*

Yo iba a hablar.	*I was going to speak.*
Nosotros íbamos a comprar un carro nuevo.	*We were going to buy a new car.*

Uses of the Imperfect

The imperfect tense expresses actions in the past that are not seen as completed. It is used to indicate situations or actions in the past with no specific reference to their beginning or end.

To "Set the Stage" in the Past; to Express a Narration, Situation, or Background

El sol brillaba y los pájaros cantaban.	*The sun was shining and the birds were singing.*
La luna alumbraba el río y los pescadores lanzaban sus redes.	*The moon lit up the river and the fishermen were throwing out their nets.*
Había un silencio profundo en el bosque; ya caía la noche.	*There was a profound silence in the forest; night was already falling.*
No había nadie en la casa. Los ladrones esperaban afuera.	*There was no one in the house. The thieves were waiting outside.*

To Express Habitual, Customary, or Repeated Actions in the Past

Todos los veranos, yo jugaba al tenis con mis amigos.	*Every summer, I used to play tennis with my friends.*
Todos los días, Paulina y yo almorzábamos a la una de la tarde.	*Every day, Pauline and I used to have lunch at one o'clock in the afternoon.*
Cada noche, antes de dormirse, el viejo ponía sus dientes en un vaso de agua.	*Each night, before going to sleep, the old man put his teeth in a glass of water.*

A Word About the Translations
Read the example sentences again, and try to understand the concepts without the translations. Try to imagine these examples as scenes: they are situations, narrations in the past; they are backgrounds; they "set the stage." The English translations are not precise or consistent in the imperfect. Make sure you understand this important concept and choose whichever translation or idea is clearest for you.

To Express Continuous Actions in the Past

Marisol cuidaba su jardín mientras sus nietos jugaban.	*Marisol was taking care of her garden while her grandchildren were playing.*
Eduardo bailaba y su novia cantaba.	*Ed was dancing and his girlfriend was singing.*
Ella buscaba sus llaves cuando el teléfono sonó.	*She was looking for her keys when the telephone rang.*
Ella iba a contestar pero escuchó un sonido en la puerta.	*She was going to answer but she heard a sound at the door.*
Yo hablaba cuando mi profesor me interrumpió.	*I was speaking when my professor interrupted me.*

Note that in the last three example sentences above, both the imperfect and the preterit tenses are used. The first part of the sentence is the ongoing action, the action in progress. The second part of the sentence, which requires the preterit, is a completed action. Here, the imperfect is used as a continuous action that is interrupted by another action.

To Express a Description in the Past

La casa era blanca.	*The house was white.*
La comida estaba buena.	*The meal was good.*
Nuestro vecino era viejo, pero tenía el pelo negro.	*Our neighbor was old, but he had black hair.*

To Express Point of Origin in the Past

El hombre era de Perú.	*The man was from Peru.*
Sus amigos eran de Chile.	*His friends were from Chile.*
Las flores rojas eran de Bolivia.	*The red flowers were from Bolivia.*

To Express Time in the Past

Eran las cinco y Federico iba
a la tienda por última vez.

*It was five o'clock and Fred was
going to the store for the last time.*

¿Qué hora era? Eran las dos de
la tarde.

*What time was it? It was two in
the afternoon.*

Eran las nueve de la noche y los
niños dormían.

*It was nine at night and the
children were sleeping.*

To Express One's Age in the Past

Ella tenía veinte años cuando
se graduó de la universidad.

*She was 20 years old when she
graduated from the university.*

Mi abuelo tenía noventa y cinco
años cuando se murió.

*My grandfather was 95 years old
when he died.*

El presidente tenía cincuenta y
cinco años cuando lo elegimos.

*The president was 55 years old
when we elected him.*

Exercise 15.1

*Complete the following sentences with the correct form of the imperfect. In the
parentheses, write your reason for choosing the imperfect.*

EXAMPLES   Todas las noches, Teodoro ___*llamaba*___ a Elena. (llamar)

(___*repeated action*___)

Su hijo ___*tenía*___ dos años cuando empezó a correr. (tener)

(___*age*___)

1. De niña, Loreta _____ pasta cada noche. (comer)

(_____)

2. Ella _____ alta y bonita como su madre. (ser)

(_____)

3. ¿Por qué _____ los niños a la escuela los sábados? (ir)

(_____)

4. La mujer y su esposo _____ de España. (ser)

(_____)

5. Nosotros _____ todos los días. (verse) (_____)

6. ¿De dónde _____ sus abuelos? (ser) (_____)

7. El tren _____ todos los días precisamente a las nueve.
   (llegar) (_____)

8. Nosotros siempre _____ a casa a las seis de la tarde. (volver)
   (_____)

9. _____ una fiesta en la casa de un conocido. (haber)
   (_____)

10. Ella _____ el piano cuando su hermano gritó. (practicar)
    (_____)

11. ¿Por qué _____ a vender tu casa? (ir) (_____)

12. Me di cuenta que yo _____ a tener éxito. (ir)
    (_____)

13. La estudiante _____ veintiún años al graduarse. (tener)
    (_____)

14. Los niños _____ pollo y sus padres _____
    pescado en el restaurante. (comer/comer) (_____,
    _____)

15. Los amigos de Pedro lo _____ en Hawai cada año. (visitar)
    (_____)

16. En el pasado, ellos _____ vino todos los fines de semana;
    ahora beben mucha agua. (beber) (_____)

17. La gente _____ muy valiente. (ser) (_____)

18. El adolescente _____ el pelo largo; yo _____
    el pelo corto. (tener/tener) (_____, _____)

19. _____ las doce y el sol _____. (ser/brillar)
    (_____, _____)

20. Él _____ su libro cuando su amigo lo llamó. (leer)
    (_____)

21. Ana _____ su tarea cuando sonó el teléfono. (hacer)
    (_____)

22. Nosotros _____ cansadas de trabajar. (estar)
    (_____)

23. La película _____ cómica; todo el mundo

    _____. (ser/reírse) (_____, _____)

24. ¿Qué me _____ cuando él me distrajo? (decir)

    (_____)

25. ¿Qué _____ Uds. cuando empezó a nevar? (hacer)

    (_____)

26. Mi amigo me dijo que _____ a verme. (venir)

    (_____)

27. _____ buen tiempo. _____ viento y sol.

    Los pájaros _____ en los árboles y todo el mundo

    _____ feliz. (hacer/hacer/estar/estar) (_____,

    _____, _____, _____)

28. Antes, yo _____ mucho. Ahora prefiero comer

    en restaurantes. (cocinar) (_____)

Exercise 15.2

*Review **ser** and **estar** in the imperfect, and then rewrite the following sentences in the imperfect.*

EXAMPLE   Yo soy de Venezuela. *Yo era de Venezuela.*

1. Ellos son de España. _____

2. ¿Qué hora es? _____

3. Nosotros estamos bien. _____

4. Mi jardín es el más hermoso de la ciudad.

    _____

5. Los tres amigos están aquí. _____

6. No estoy cansada. _____

7. Somos cantantes. _____

8. ¿Dónde estás? _____

9. Yo estoy en la casa con mi perro.

    _____

Preterit and Imperfect Compared

Compare the differences in meaning between the following sentence pairs (preterit followed by imperfect).

Ella llegó ayer.	*She arrived yesterday.*
Ella llegaba a la cinco todos los días.	*She arrived at five o'clock every day.*
La semana pasada, leí un buen libro.	*Last week, I read a good book.*
Antes, yo leía mucho.	*Before, I used to read a lot.*
Beatriz vino a verme.	*Beatriz came to see me.*
Él me dijo que Beatriz venía a verme.	*He told me that Beatriz was coming to see me.*
Me levanté a las seis esta mañana.	*I got up at six o'clock this morning.*
Me levantaba tarde.	*I used to get up late.*
Fui a la tienda.	*I went to the store.*
Yo iba a la tienda cuando vi a José.	*I was going to the store when I saw Joe.*
Fuimos a la playa hoy.	*We went to the beach today.*
Íbamos a la playa todos los veranos.	*We used to go the beach every summer.*
¿Qué me dijiste hace dos minutos?	*What did you tell me two minutes ago?*
¿Qué me decías cuando el perro ladró?	*What were you saying to me when the dog barked?*
Marta comió temprano esta mañana.	*Martha ate early this morning.*
Marta siempre comía temprano.	*Martha always ate early.*
Mi papá pagó la cuenta ayer.	*My father paid the bill yesterday.*
Mi papá siempre pagaba la cuenta.	*My father always paid the bill.*
Eduardo hizo su tarea.	*Edward did his homework.*
Eduardo hacía su tarea todos los lunes.	*Edward did his homework every Monday.*
¿Qué compró Ud. ayer?	*What did you buy yesterday?*
¿Qué compraba Ud. cuando le llamé?	*What were you buying when I called you?*

Caminamos al parque hoy.	*We walked to the park today.*
Caminábamos al parque todos los días.	*We used to walk to the park every day.*
Recibimos un cheque esta tarde.	*We received a check this afternoon.*
Recibíamos cheques cada semana.	*We used to receive checks every week.*
Ella tuvo una operación anoche.	*She had an operation last night.*
Él no tenía tiempo para verla.	*He didn't have time to see her.*
Anoche, ella durmió hasta las ocho.	*Last night, she slept until eight o'clock.*
Todos los días, ella dormía hasta tarde.	*Every day, she slept until late.*
Conocimos a Silvia en Colombia.	*We met Sylvia in Colombia.*
No la conocíamos por mucho tiempo.	*We didn't know her for very long.*

Querer, poder, saber

Affirmative

Yo quise ir al circo.	*I wanted to go to the circus.*
Yo quería ir al circo.	*I wanted to go to the circus.*
Pudimos entender la lección.	*We were able to understand the lesson.*
Podíamos entender la lección.	*We were able to understand the lesson.*
Ella supo que él tuvo un accidente.	*She found out that he had an accident.*
Ella sabía que él iba a estar bien.	*She knew that he was going to be well.*

For the verbs **querer** and **poder**, the English translations of the example sentences above showing the preterit and the imperfect are the same. However, the preterit **pudimos** from **poder** indicates that the action is over. The idea is that we were able to understand the lesson; the action is completed, so we succeeded in understanding the lesson.

Negative

¿Por qué no quiso Ud. ir conmigo?	*Why did you refuse to go with me?*
¿Por qué no quería Ud. ir conmigo?	*Why didn't you want to go with me?*
No pude hacer mi tarea.	*I failed to do my homework.*
Yo no podía hacer mi tarea ayer.	*I wasn't able to (couldn't) do my homework yesterday.*
No lo supe hoy.	*I didn't find it out today.*
Yo no sabía que él estaba enfermo.	*I didn't know that he was sick.*

 ## Exercise 15.3

Preterit and imperfect. *Translate the following sentences into Spanish.*

1. *It was one o'clock and it was raining.*

   _____

2. *I knew it.* _____

3. *He was able to do it well.* _____

4. *The children wanted to eat hamburgers.*

   _____

5. *We were studying when the teacher entered.*

   _____

6. *The man was fleeing when the police caught him.*

   _____

7. *Every night for many years, she had the same dream.*

   _____

8. *What were you saying to me?* _____

9. *What was I going to say to you?*

   _____

10. *Why did he call her?* _____

11. What time was it when you fell asleep last night?

_____

12. Who got sick yesterday? _____

13. We were going to travel to Cuba, but we had no money.

_____

14. I met your friend in Mexico. _____

15. He left without saying anything to us.

_____

16. Who gave him the good news today?

_____

17. The man was in the bank when the thief entered. Everyone was afraid.

_____

18. Last year, we went to Spain. We had a good time.

_____

Exercise 15.4

Complete the following sentences with **ir** *in either the preterit or the imperfect.*

1. ¿Por qué _____ Ud. al museo ayer?

2. En julio, Graciela _____ a California a ver a sus nietos.

3. Yo _____ a llamarla, pero no tenía su número de teléfono.

4. Nosotros _____ al circo todos los veranos en el pasado.

5. Nosotros _____ al cine anoche; nos gustó la película.

6. Mis amigos _____ a vender su carro antes de ganarse la lotería.

7. Carmen _____ al banco los viernes e _____
   a la playa los sábados.

8. ¿_____ tú al campo los fines de semana?

9. Isabel _____ a Italia y no regresó.

10. Marisol y su esposo _____ a Portugal.

Exercise 15.5

Translate the following sentences into English.

1. La madre del hijo le dijo que todo iba a estar bien.

   _____

2. ¿Te dolían los pies durante tu viaje?

   _____

3. Hubo un tiempo cuando yo visitaba museos.

   _____

4. Vine, vi y vencí. _____

5. Entre el primero y segundo piso, me di cuenta de que iba a caerme.

   _____

6. Nos divertíamos mucho cada día hace mucho tiempo.

   _____

7. Yo no sabía qué hacer. _____

8. Tenían una buena relación. Él siempre cocinaba y ella siempre lavaba los platos.

   _____

Exercise 15.6

Preterit or imperfect. *Complete the sentences with the correct form of the verb in parentheses.*

1. ¿Por que no _____ tú la comida ayer? (comprar)

2. Anoche, yo _____ el vino a la fiesta. (traer)

3. _____ mediodía y el niño _____ hambre. (ser/tener)

4. _____ a llover y yo _____ la ventana. (empezar/cerrar)

5. La muchacha _____ la calle cuando su mamá la _____. (cruzar/llamar)

6. ¿Dónde _____ Uds. esta mañana precisamente a las nueve? (estar)

7. Nosotros _____ en el parque cuando _____ el animal exótico. (andar/ver)

8. El taxista nos _____ veinte dólares. ¿Cuánto te _____ a ti? (cobrar/cobrar)

9. Nosotros les _____ cartas a nuestros parientes desde Bolivia, pero ellos no las _____. (escribir/recibir)

10. Yo _____ por la calle equivocada cuando _____ que no _____ donde _____. (caminar/darse cuenta de/saber/estar).

11. Me agrada su amigo. ¿Dónde lo _____ Ud.? (conocer)

12. Pedro y sus amigos _____ todas las noches antes de acostarse. (divertirse)

13. Melisa _____ al cine cada domingo durante su juventud. (ir)

14. Los viajeros de Inglaterra _____ a mi casa la semana pasada y _____ conmigo hasta hoy. (llegar/quedarse)

Double Object Pronouns

In Spanish, two object pronouns can appear together with a verb.

- Double object pronouns cannot be separated from each other.

- In a negative sentence, the word **no** (or any other word of negation) comes directly before the first pronoun.

- Positions of the double object pronouns are the same as single object pronouns: The pronouns are placed directly before the first verb *or* they are attached to the infinitive.

Indirect Object Pronoun with Direct Object Pronoun

An indirect object pronoun precedes a direct object pronoun when they occur together. In the first position, the object pronouns are placed directly before the first verb.

Me lo / me la / me los / me las

Necesito tu carro esta noche.	*I need your car tonight.*
¿**Me lo** prestas?	*Will you lend it to me?*
Él tiene una revista interesante.	*He has an interesting magazine.*
Él **me la** va a dar.	*He is going to give it to me.*
Ella tiene dos secretos.	*She has two secrets.*
Ella no **me los** quería decir.	*She didn't want to tell them to me.*
El maestro explicó las nuevas lecciones.	*The teacher explained the new lessons.*
Él **me las** explicó.	*He explained them to me.*

In the second position, the object pronouns are attached to the infinitive and become one word. A written accent is added to maintain the natural stress of the infinitive. Whether the object pronouns are placed in front of the first verb or attached to the infinitive, the meaning of the sentence is the same.

Necesito tu carro esta noche.	*I need your car tonight.*
¿Puedes prestár**melo?**	*Can you lend it to me?*
Él tiene una revista interesante.	*He has an interesting magazine.*
Él va a dár**mela**.	*He is going to give it to me.*
Ella tiene dos secretos.	*She has two secrets.*
Ella no quería decír**melos**.	*She didn't want to tell them to me.*
Él trató de explicar las nuevas lecciones.	*He tried to explain the new lessons.*
Él trató de explicár**melas**.	*He tried to explain them to me.*

 ## Exercise 15.7

Translate the following sentences into English. Practice the use of the double object pronouns along with the tenses you have learned: present indicative, present subjunctive, preterit, and imperfect.

1. Yo quería tomar un café esta mañana. Mi colega me lo trajo.

   _____

2. Los niños tienen muchos regalos. Sus abuelos quieren que me los den.

   _____

3. Ella me compró una chaqueta. Después de comprármela, se puso feliz.

_____

4. Mi papá no quiso darme su carro. En vez de dármelo, me lo vendió.

_____

5. Aprendí bien las direcciones porque mis parientes me las dieron con mucho cuidado.

_____

6. Ella quiere darme tres maletas para mi viaje. Prefiero que ella me las preste.

_____

7. Cada mañana, los vendedores me vendían vegetales. Hoy no me vendieron nada.

_____

8. Necesito dos buenos libros. Tengo que comprarlos porque mi amiga no quiere prestármelos.

_____

A Word About Pronunciation
Practice all these examples aloud. The more you get used to the sound, the easier it becomes.

Te lo / te la / te los / te las

Te doy mi abrigo porque hace frío.	*I'll give you my coat because it is cold.*
Te lo doy esta noche.	*I'll give it to you tonight.*
¿Por qué no me dijiste la verdad?	*Why didn't you tell me the truth?*
Te la dije, pero no me escuchaste.	*I told it to you, but you didn't listen to me.*
José tuvo que leer dos cuentos anoche.	*Joe had to read two stories last night.*
Él tuvo que leér**telos** antes de las nueve.	*He had to read them to you before nine.*
Queremos mandar cartas desde Madrid.	*We want to send letters from Madrid.*
Queremos mandár**telas** esta noche.	*We want to send them to you tonight.*

Exercise 15.8

Translate the following sentences into English.

1. Ella no te da agua; ella te la vende.

   _____

2. Debemos regalarte el anillo que quieres este año. Debemos regalártelo.

   _____

3. Anoche, mi hermano mayor me trajo una manzana. Me la trajo porque yo tenía hambre.

   _____

4. Todavía tienes mis discos compactos. Quiero que me los devuelvas.

   _____

5. Me gusta la langosta en este restaurante. Espero que el camarero me la sirva rápidamente.

   _____

6. Te di el dinero porque eres un buen amigo. Te lo di porque tengo confianza en ti.

   _____

7. No sé por qué ella no quiso mostrarte sus lámparas. A mí me las mostró ayer.

   _____

8. Al principio, no queríamos darte una bicicleta, pero por fin te la dimos.

   _____

Se lo / se la / se los / se las

For reasons of pronunciation, **se** replaces the indirect object pronouns **le** and **les** when they are followed by a direct object pronoun.

le lo → **se lo**	les lo → **se lo**
le la → **se la**	les la → **se la**
le los → **se los**	les los → **se los**
le las → **se las**	les las → **se las**

Se lo traigo.

- *I bring it to him.*
- *I bring it to her.*
- *I bring it to you.* (sing.)
- *I bring it to them.*
- *I bring it to you.* (pl.)

Out of context, there is no way to know what the meaning of the indirect object pronoun is. To clarify the ambiguity, a prepositional phrase is added.

Se lo traigo **a Ud.**	*I bring it to you.*
Se lo traigo **a ellas**.	*I bring it to them.*

In context, however, the meaning is clear without an additional prepositional phrase.

Le doy a Enrique el periódico.	*I give the newspaper to Henry.*
Se lo doy.	*I give it to him.*
Ella quiere comprar una camisa.	*She wants to buy a shirt.*
Nosotros **se la** vendemos.	*We'll sell it to her.*
Les enviamos dinero a los estudiantes.	*We send money to the students.*
Se lo enviamos.	*We send it to them.*
Ana les trae dos pasteles a sus amigas.	*Ana brings two pastries to her friends.*
Ana **se los** trae.	*Ana brings them to them.*
Yo les quiero escribir a Uds. tres cartas.	*I want to write you three letters.*
Yo quiero escribír**selas**.	*I want to write them to you.*
Él les muestra las fotos a Juan y a Ana.	*He shows the photos to John and Ana.*
Él trata de mostrár**selas**.	*He tries to show them to them.*

A Word About Double Object Pronouns

Try to practice the **se lo / se la / se los / se las** combination without going through two steps. Every time you think of *to her, to him, to you, to them* followed by a direct object pronoun, use **se**. Note also that the intransitive verbs you learned in Chapter 10 are used over and over. These are the most frequently used verbs that take indirect objects.

Exercise 15.9

Complete the following sentences with the correct double object pronoun, according to the context of the sentence.

EXAMPLE   Les trajimos las flores. ___*Se las*___ trajimos.

1. Yo quería comprarte el carro, pero no tenía bastante dinero. Al fin

   y al cabo, no _____ pude comprar.

2. Él no me dio el libro. No sé dónde está. ¿Él _____ dio
   a Ud.?

3. Necesito tu lápiz. ¿_____ prestas?

4. ¿Por qué no les dijeron Uds. a los muchachos la verdad? ¿Por qué

   no _____ dijeron?

5. Los hombres querían leer los periódicos de hoy. El vendedor

   _____ vendió.

6. Yo les traje una torta a Uds. Yo _____ traje anoche.

7. Tratamos de hacerles muchas preguntas. Tratamos de [hacer]

   _____ porque no sabemos nada.

8. Loreta y Roberto me mandaron dos paquetes. _____
   mandaron ayer.

9. Te dimos la respuesta ya. _____ dimos hace dos horas.

10. ¿Por qué les prestaste dinero? ¿_____ prestaste porque
    necesitan ayuda?

11. Vamos a enseñarle la lección. _____ vamos a enseñar.

12. ¿Tienen Uds. frío? ¿Necesitan otra chaqueta? _____ puedo
    traer.

13. Ella no sabe que decirte. ¿Por qué no le cuentas el cuento? Es mejor

    [contar] _____.

14. Nadie quería decirle los resultados de las elecciones. Nadie

    _____ quería decir.

Nos lo / nos la / nos los / nos las

Él va a devolvernos el suéter.	He is going to return the sweater to us.
Él va a devolvér**noslo**.	He is going to return it to us.
La mujer nos trajo una flor.	The woman brought us a flower.
Ella **nos la** trajo.	She brought it to us.
Nuestros amigos nos dan regalos cada año.	Our friends give us gifts every year.
Nuestros amigos **nos los** dan.	Our friends give them to us.
Ud. nos traía tortas los domingos.	You used to bring us cakes on Sundays.
Ahora Ud. nunca **nos las** trae.	Now you never bring them to us.

Os lo / os la / os los / os las

Vuestra tía os lee un libro en la noche.	Your aunt reads a book to you at night.
Ella **os lo** lee.	She reads it to you.
Él no quiere escribiros una carta.	He doesn't want to write a letter to you.
Él no quiere escribír**osla**.	He doesn't want to write it to you.
Ana no os mandó recuerdos.	Ana didn't send you souvenirs.
Ella debe mandár**oslos**.	She should send them to you.
El doctor no os dio las pastillas.	The doctor didn't give you the pills.
El farmacista **os las** vendió.	The pharmacist sold them to you.

Note that **os** means *to you* in the plural familiar **vosotros** form. It is used only in Spain.

 Exercise 15.10

Translate the following sentences into Spanish. Practice indirect objects, direct objects, and double object pronouns, as well as the tenses.

1. *I told you everything. You said nothing to me.*

_____

2. We were going to give two notebooks to the students.

_____

3. Lisa doesn't have anything to write with. I have two pens and decide to give them to her.

_____

4. I gave a violin to my nephew. I gave it to him.

_____

5. He was going to give the guitar to Hector. He decided to give it to me.

_____

6. Who can show us the new coats? Who wants to show them to us?

_____

7. The birds were singing and the children were playing.

_____

8. Carmen read a good book two weeks ago. She gave it to me yesterday.

_____

9. I returned the book to her today. I returned it to her at ten o'clock in the morning.

_____

10. Elena had bad dreams last night. She told them to me this morning.

_____

11. We like to share everything.

_____

12. Your grandmother wants you to read the article to her.

_____

13. We hope that he knows how to swim so that he can teach us.

_____

14. Joe lent Michael the money. He lent it to him yesterday.

_____

15. Your cousin did you a favor. He did it for you because he is a good friend.

_____

16. *After bringing her coffee, I went to my office. She called me later.*

_____

17. *She was buying a guitar when her friend offered her a piano.*

_____

18. *We saw the sofa that she had in her house. She gave it to us.*

_____

Reflexive Pronoun with Direct Object Pronoun

This combination does not occur with many verbs. It is most common with the action of putting on or taking off clothes (**ponerse la ropa**, **quitarse la ropa**), with verbs that are used with parts of the body (**lavarse**, **cepillarse**, **lesionarse**, **peinarse**, **secarse**), and with some idiomatic verbs (**comerse**). A reflexive object pronoun precedes a direct object pronoun when they occur together.

The objects are either placed directly before the first verb or attached to the infinitive.

Me pongo un abrigo en el invierno.	*I put on a coat in the winter.*
Me lo quito en el apartamento.	*I take it off in the apartment.*
¿Te lavaste la cara hoy?	*Did you wash your face today?*
¿**Te la** lavaste hoy?	*Did you wash it today?*
Nos cepillamos los dientes cada noche.	*We brush our teeth every night.*
Nos los cepillamos en la mañana también.	*We brush them in the morning, too.*
Ellos se peinaron el pelo.	*They combed their hair.*
Ellos **se lo** peinaron.	*They combed it.*
Me comí todo el pescado.	*I ate up all the fish.*
Me lo comí.	*I ate it all up.*
Él se puso los zapatos.	*He put on his shoes.*
Él **se los** puso.	*He put them on.*
Ella se quitó la gorra.	*She took off her hat.*
Ella **se la** quitó.	*She took it off.*
¿Por qué se quitó Ud. la chaqueta?	*Why did you take off your jacket?*
¿Por qué **se la** quitó Ud.?	*Why did you take it off?*

Yo no quería cortarme el pelo.	*I didn't want to cut my hair.*
No quería cortár**melo**.	*I didn't want to cut it.*
Ella no pudo lavarse las manos anoche.	*She couldn't wash her hands last night.*
Ella no pudo lavár**selas**.	*She couldn't wash them.*
El niño trató de ponerse los calcetines.	*The child tried to put on his socks.*
Él trató de ponér**selos**.	*He tried to put them on.*

A Reminder

When reflexive verbs are used with clothes and parts of the body, the possessive adjective is not used.

Se Plus the Indirect Object Pronoun and Unplanned Occurrences

Se + the indirect object pronoun + the verb express the concept of an action that just seemed to happen—an unplanned occurrence. The indirect object pronoun indicates the person or persons *responsible for* or *affected by* the action.

This construction occurs only in the third person because the subject is a thing or things. It usually occurs in the preterit because the action has already happened.

Yo rompí el vaso.	*I broke the glass. (It was not an accident; I broke the glass on purpose.)*
Se rompió el vaso.	*The glass broke. (It was an accident, and no one is responsible.)*
Se **me** rompió el vaso.	*I broke the glass by accident. (The glass broke by accident, but I am responsible.)*
El gato se murió.	*The cat died. (No one is responsible.)*
El gato se **me** murió.	*The cat died. (The cat died because I did not take care of it properly and I am responsible.)*
	The cat died. (I took care of the cat, but it died anyway, and I am affected.)

El niño se cayó.   *The child fell. (No one is responsible or*
                                   affected.)

                                   The child fell. (The child fell because we were
                                   inattentive, and we are responsible.)

El niño se **nos** cayó.   *The child fell. (We took care of the child, but*
                                   he fell anyway. It is not our fault, but we
                                   are affected.)

Here are other verbs that often express this concept.

acabarse	*to run out of*
irse	*to go away, to leave quickly*
ocurrirse	*to get the idea of, to occur to*
olvidarse	*to forget*
perderse	*to lose*

No pudiste hacer los sándwiches;   *You couldn't make the sandwiches;*
se **te** acabó el pan.   *you ran out of bread. (It wasn't*
                                          your fault.)

No se **me** ocurrió trabajar ayer.   *It didn't occur to me to work*
                                          yesterday.

Se **le** olvidó la fecha de tu   *He forgot the date of your*
cumpleaños.   *birthday by accident.*

Se **me** perdieron mis gafas.   *I lost my glasses by accident.*

Exercise 15.11

Complete the following sentences with the correct verb form and object pronouns.

EXAMPLE   Me lastimé el tobillo. Yo ___me lo lastimé___.

1. ¿Por qué no te secas el pelo? ¿Por qué no _____?

2. Vamos a quitarnos el vestido. Vamos a _____.

3. Ellos se cepillaron los dientes. Ellos _____.

4. Él se puso las medias. Él _____.

5. Me corté el dedo. Yo _____.

6. Los niños se van a lavar las manos. Ellos _____.

7. Ella se peina el pelo bonito cada día. Ella _____.

Exercise 15.12

Translate the following sentences into English.

1. A él le gustó el pollo y se lo comió.

   _____

2. Miguel no pudo entrar en su casa porque se le perdieron las llaves.

   _____

3. Se me cayó la cuchara en la mesa y me puse furiosa.

   _____

4. Ellos se dieron cuenta de que sus amigos no venían a verlos.

   _____

5. ¿Cómo se les ocurrió escribir un libro juntos?

   _____

6. Se me olvidó hacer mi tarea. Se me acabó la paciencia.

   _____

7. ¡Cuidado! Se les van a caer los vasos. Ya se nos rompieron dos.

   _____

8. Después de ponerse las medias, ellos se pusieron los zapatos y se fueron.

   _____

Exercise 15.13

On a separate sheet of paper, write the English translation of the following infinitives from Part III.

1. acercarse	8. castigar	15. contener	22. destruir
2. ahogarse	9. colgar	16. contradecir	23. detener
3. alcanzar	10. colocar	17. contribuir	24. distraer
4. amenazar	11. componer	18. corregir	25. distribuir
5. arrancar	12. concluir	19. creer	26. entregar
6. atraer	13. conducir	20. deshacer	27. fluir
7. caber	14. construir	21. destacar	28. huir

29. incluir	35. mascar	41. proponer	47. traducir
30. influir	36. pegar	42. publicar	48. tragar
31. justificar	37. pescar	43. realizar	49. tropezarse
32. lanzar	38. poseer	44. rezar	50. vagar
33. madrugar	39. prevenir	45. sacar	
34. mantener	40. producir	46. suplicar	

 # Reading Comprehension

El juicio (segunda escena)

ACUSADO   Cuando yo hablé con él, me di cuenta de que él no era sabio.
Cuando me fui, pensaba, "Yo soy más sabio que este hombre; ninguno
de nosotros no sabe nada que valga la pena saber, pero él piensa que
él tiene sabiduría cuando él no la tiene, y yo, sin saber nada, no pienso
que yo sea sagaz. No pienso que sé lo que no sé." Después, fui a ver
a los poetas, pensando que ellos iban a ser más sagaces que yo.

　　Pero averigüé que no es por la sabiduría que los poetas crean sus
poemas sino por una inspiración divina. Por fin, fui a ver a los artesanos.
Ellos sabían lo que yo no sabía y por eso eran más sabios que yo. Pero
me pareció que cada uno se creía extremadamente sagaz en cuestiones
importantes porque eran hábiles en su propio arte.

　　Mucho prejuicio contra mi resultó de mi investigación. Y yo sigo
con mi tarea de investigar y examinar a cada persona que pienso que
es sagaz y si él no es sagaz yo se lo digo. Estoy tan ocupado en mi
investigación que no he tenido tiempo ni para servir en posiciones del
estado ni de ganar dinero. Como resultado, yo soy pobre. Es verdad
lo que les dije. Y yo sé que por esta investigación de la gente hay mucha
rabia contra mí. Pero lo que Uds. escuchan es mi defensa contra estas
primeras acusaciones.

Verbos

averiguar	*to check out, to verify*
darse cuenta (de)	*to realize*
he tenido	*I have had* (present perfect tense)
valer	*to value*

Nombre

el arte   *the art*

NOTE: **El arte** is masculine in the singular but feminine in the plural.

el arte español   *Spanish art*
las bellas artes   *fine arts*

Adjetivos

hábil   *skillful, capable*
propio   *own*

Preguntas

After you have finished reading the selection, answer the following questions in Spanish.

1. ¿Con quiénes habló?

_____

2. ¿Qué es lo que el acusado siempre busca?

_____

3. ¿Se defendió bien el acusado?

_____

4. ¿Quién es el acusado?

_____

Answer Key

Chapter 1
Nouns, Articles, and Adjectives

1.1   1. el   2. el   3. la   4. la   5. el   6. el   7. la   8. el   9. el   10. la   11. la   12. la
    13. el   14. el   15. la   16. la   17. el   18. el   19. la   20. la

1.2   1. los animales   2. las amistades   3. los teléfonos   4. los trenes   5. las ventanas
    6. los doctores   7. las ciudades   8. las bolsas   9. las mesas   10. los idiomas
    11. las plantas   12. las flores   13. los perros   14. las ilusiones   15. las clases
    16. las lecciones   17. los taxistas   18. las lámparas   19. las sillas   20. las luces

1.3   1. the book   2. the page   3. the house   4. the flowers   5. the bathroom
    6. the wine   7. the boy   8. the brother   9. the library   10. the coffee   11. the train
    12. the planet   13. the (male) dentist   14. the garden   15. the flower   16. the beer
    17. the plant   18. the friendship   19. the truth   20. the luck   21. the (male)
manager   22. the store   23. the window   24. a museum   25. a mirror
    26. a bookstore   27. a pen   28. a lesson   29. an idea   30. a suitcase
    31. the armchair   32. the friends

1.4   1. viejo   2. difícil   3. maravilloso   4. simpática   5. amarilla   6. hermoso
    7. delgada OR flaca   8. blanco   9. caro   10. barato   11. pequeño   12. fantástico
    13. inteligente   14. interesante   15. grande   16. rico   17. joven   18. roja
    19. azul   20. verde

1.5   1. las lámparas azules   2. los amigos fantásticos   3. los perros grises   4. las cervezas
negras   5. los vinos rosados   6. las personas fuertes   7. los días maravillosos
    8. las luces verdes   9. las ciudades pequeñas   10. los muchachos jóvenes

1.6   1. los tomates rojos   2. los hombres fuertes   3. las mujeres delgadas   4. las blusas
amarillas   5. las canciones interesantes   6. los planetas verdes   7. las ventanas azules
    8. los hoteles viejos

Chapter 2

Estar, Ser, and Subject Pronouns

2.1   1. está (changing condition)   2. están (location)   3. está, está (health)
4. están (health)   5. están (location)   6. está (location)   7. está, está (changing mood)
8. están (changing mood)   9. estoy (changing mood)   10. está (location)

2.2   1. Yo estoy en la casa amarilla. ¿Dónde está Ud.? OR ¿Dónde estás tú? OR ¿Dónde
están Uds.?   2. Las blusas rojas están en la tienda grande.   3. La flor blanca está
en la ventana.   4. Estamos en el tren.   5. ¿Cómo está Ud.? Estoy bien, gracias. OR
¿Cómo están Uds.? OR ¿Cómo estás tú?   6. Estamos cansados y estamos contentos.

2.3   1. es (point of origin)   2. son, es (profession)   3. son (point of origin)
4. son (description)   5. es (description)   6. somos (identification)   7. son (material)
8. son (point of origin)   9. soy, es (point of origin)   10. es (possession)
11. Eres (identification)   12. son (description)   13. es (profession)

2.4 *A*   1. es (point of origin)   2. es (identification)   3. son (profession)   4. son (description)
5. somos (profession)

    B   1. está (location)   2. está, estoy (health)   3. está (health)   4. estamos (location)
5. Estás (changing mood)   6. están (location)

    C   1. están (health)   2. eres (profession)   3. es (description)   4. están (location)
5. están (health), estamos (health)   6. son (description)   7. están (location)
8. está (changing mood)   9. son (description)   10. están (location), es (description)
11. está (health), está (changing mood)   12. son (description)   13. están (location),
son (point of origin), son (point of origin)   14. es (point of origin)
15. están (location), están (changing mood), son (identification)   16. está (location)
17. está (location)   18. estamos (changing mood), somos (identification)
19. Es (point of origin), son (point of origin)   20. está (changing mood),
es (description)

2.5   *Answers will vary.*   1. Estoy bien, gracias.   2. Ella está en la casa.
3. Soy de Nueva York.   4. El hombre está en el carro.   5. El concierto es en el
parque.   6. Estoy alegre.   7. La lección es difícil.   8. Las flores están en el piso.
Son de Florida.   9. El apartamento de Tomás es pequeño.   10. Sí, estoy muy
cansado.   11. No, los periódicos no están en la casa de Alicia.   12. Está en la calle
once.   13. No, soy de Chicago.   14. Yo soy profesor.

2.6   1. están   2. estoy   3. es   4. está   5. es   6. es   7. es

Chapter 3

Hay, Interrogative Words, Days, and Months

3.1 *A*   1. Is there an easy lesson in the book?   2. There are no cockroaches in the restaurant.
3. Are there red blouses in the store?   4. There are flowers on the balcony of the
apartment.   5. Is there class today?   6. Are there more questions from the students?

    B   1. Hay muchas plumas en la mesa del maestro.   2. ¿Hay un doctor en el hospital?
3. Hay dos mujeres en la clase.   4. No hay cerveza en la casa de Lisa.

3.2   1. Cuál   2. Qué   3. Cómo OR Dónde   4. Por qué   5. Quién   6. Por qué
7. Cuántos   8. Cómo OR Dónde

3.3   1. En   2. De   3. De   4. Con   5. En   6. De

3.4 A   1. the beautiful room   2. the pleasant person   3. the sweet friendship
4. the exciting play   5. the beautiful day   6. the low building   7. the strange dream
8. the long war   9. the wide avenue   10. the new year

B   1. el niño cariñoso   2. la tarea fácil   3. la ciudad peligrosa   4. la persona baja
5. el mes corto   6. la playa hermosa   7. la mujer amistosa   8. el hombre amable
9. la avenida estrecha   10. las personas orgullosas

3.5   *Answers will vary.*

3.6   1. es   2. está   3. es   4. es   5. Hay   6. está, está, está   7. Hay   8. están, hay
9. Hay, Es   10. hay   11. son, son   12. somos, son   13. Es, está   14. estoy, está
15. Es   16. Hay   17. es, es   18. son, están   19. están, está   20. es   21. es, son

3.7   1. Where are the students on Sundays?   2. Saturday and Sunday are holidays.
3. In the spring, there are beautiful flowers in the parks.   4. In the autumn, there are
yellow and red leaves on the trees.   5. What day is today? Today is Wednesday. What
month is it? It is September.   6. How many days are there in June? How many days
are there in a year?   7. The streets of Mexico are narrow. The houses are low and
pretty.   8. Why are the newspapers and the magazines on the floor?   9. There is
class, but the students are at the beach where there is a swimming pool also.
The professor is angry but the students are happy.   10. The buildings of the big cities
are tall.   11. The children are at the beach because it is summer.   12. A lot of people
are in the restaurants because it is winter.

Chapter 4
Numbers, Dates, and Time

4.1   1. veintiocho, cuatro, veintinueve   2. treinta y un   3. siete, cincuenta y dos
4. setenta y seis, sesenta y siete   5. veintiuna, un   6. ciento treinta y cinco
7. dos mil cuatrocientos cincuenta y seis   8. Noventa y uno, quinientos cuarenta
y dos, seiscientos treinta y tres   9. Ochocientos sesenta, cincuenta, ochocientos diez
10. cien, cien   11. quince, doscientas cincuenta y cuatro   12. doscientos treinta
y cinco

4.2   1. la calle setenta y dos   2. el piso cuarenta   3. la calle ciento treinta y cinco
4. El tercer capítulo   5. La cuarta lección   6. el quinto mes

4.3   1. jueves, once   2. los sábados   3. cien   4. el dieciocho de octubre mil novecientos
setenta y tres   5. catorce, dos mil seis   6. primer, primera

4.4 A   1. a las seis de la tarde   2. A las ocho de la mañana   3. A la una de la tarde
4. A las siete y quince de la noche   5. Son las diez de la noche.

B   1. Son las dos y veinte de la tarde.   2. Son las cuatro y media de la mañana.
3. Son las nueve y cuarto de la noche.   4. Son las seis en punto.   5. Son las cuatro
menos veinticinco de la tarde.   6. Son las siete y diez de la mañana.   7. A eso de las
dos de la tarde.   8. A las nueve de la mañana exactamente.

4.5   1. It is two o'clock in the afternoon and the students are in class.   2. The kitchen is dirty, but the bathroom is clean.   3. Where are the restaurant's 13 waiters? 4. There is class on Mondays and Thursdays.   5. At eight thirty, the soup is cold and the dishes are dirty.   6. How many glasses are there on the table at seven in the morning in Richard's house?

4.6   *Answers will vary.*   1. Hay cincuenta y dos semanas en un año.   2. Hay trescientos sesenta y cinco días en un año.   3. Son cincuenta y seis.   4. Son ciento noventa y siete.   5. Es grande.   6. Porque hay muchas flores.   7. Sí, es deliciosa. 8. El desayuno es a las siete de la mañana.

Chapter 5
Regular Verbs

5.1   1. nada   2. estudia   3. descansamos   4. llega   5. cantan, bailan   6. hablan 7. compra   8. trabaja, cocina   9. entran   10. escucho   11. mira   12. practican 13. limpian   14. viajo, bajo   15. contesta

5.2   *Answers will vary.*

5.3   1. corre   2. bebe   3. comemos   4. aprenden   5. leo, leen   6. comprendemos 7. venden   8. rompen

5.4   1. comparte   2. abre   3. vive   4. discutimos   5. Escribes   6. deciden   7. recibe 8. suben

5.5   1. toman   2. lleva   3. debe   4. toca   5. debemos   6. llevo   7. pasa   8. toca 9. gana   10. Toma

Chapter 6
Irregular Verbs

6.1   1. cierro   2. piensa   3. juegan   4. almorzamos   5. Recuerdas   6. empieza

6.2   1. sabe, saben   2. perdemos   3. hace   4. tengo, tiene, tenemos   5. vuelve 6. entienden   7. puedo   8. vemos   9. devuelve   10. pongo   11. quiere

6.3   1. Yo sé donde hay un restaurante barato en la quinta avenida.   2. Carlos no quiere hacer una cita con el dentista.   3. No queremos limpiar el apartamento hoy. 4. Veo un gato gris y un pájaro azul.   5. Ella entiende las ideas pero no quiere hablar. 6. ¿Quién puede cantar y bailar en la fiesta?   7. Hago la tarea a las ocho los lunes. 8. Queremos volver al trabajo el martes.

6.4   1. repite   2. miente   3. salir   4. dormimos   5. seguir   6. vienen   7. oír 8. prefiere   9. sirven

6.5   *Answers will vary.*

6.6   1. cierran, salen   2. juegan   3. almorzamos   4. empieza   5. sabe   6. entiende, recuerda   7. prefiero   8. tengo   9. ser   10. seguimos   11. duermen   12. encontrar 13. viene   14. estamos   15. Puede   16. veo, veo   17. hay   18. volver   19. pongo, sirve   20. hacer, hago

6.7   1. What floor do Pablo's friends live on? Are they from Peru? Do they speak English?
2. What are you talking about? With whom are you speaking?   3. Sebastián leaves
Carla's house at eight o'clock in the morning. He arrives at the office at nine o'clock.
He works eight hours. At what hour can he arrive at Carla's house?   4. Why is there
a tree in the house?   5. To be or not to be.   6. At noon, we enter the building and
go up to the third floor; at three o'clock in the afternoon, we go down to the first floor
and we leave.

Chapter 7
Ir and the Future

7.1   1. van   2. vamos   3. ir   4. va   5. ir   6. voy   7. Vas   8. ir, ir

7.2   1. van a estar   2. va a firmar   3. voy a terminar   4. va a comprar   5. vamos
a celebrar   6. va a aceptar   7. vamos a disfrutar, vamos   8. voy a cocinar, ir
9. va a apagar   10. van a pasar

7.3   *Answers will vary.*

7.4   1. tienen hambre   2. tiene sed   3. tengo suerte   4. tienen sueño   5. tenemos frío,
tenemos calor   6. tiene la palabra   7. Tienes (tú) miedo   8. tengo prisa   9. tiene
éxito   10. tiene dolor   11. tener cuidado   12. tiene razón   13. tiene lugar
14. tenemos ganas   15. años tiene   16. tiene que ver con

7.5   1. acabo de   2. tengo que   3. tratar de   4. dejar de

7.6   1. para aprender   2. que ella está aquí   3. que vive aquí   4. que yo debo ir
5. para tocar   6. Para quién   7. que necesito   8. para dos personas

7.7   1. ser   2. correr   3. cocinar   4. está   5. cerramos   6. abro, salen   7. trata
8. tienen   9. hace, Bebe   10. ir, vive   11. empieza, debemos   12. trabajo
13. duerme, come, nada, juega   14. sabe   15. pierde

7.8   1. ir, va   2. vas   3. vamos   4. van   5. voy, voy

7.9   1. tiene sueño, tiene hambre   2. venir   3. hacer, tiene miedo   4. salen, vuelven OR
regresan   5. lee, saber   6. hay   7. toma, prefiere   8. ganar   9. llegar   10. son, está
11. subo, bajo   12. regresa OR vuelve, cocinar   13. tengo frío   14. tiene calor
15. tiene sed   16. perdemos   17. tiene razón

7.10   1. el pelo, los ojos   2. la cara   3. pie OR tobillo   4. la boca, los dientes   5. el oído
6. el hígado   7. los pulmones   8. rodilla   9. estómago   10. los labios

7.11   1. está   2. son   3. estar   4. es   5. Ser, ser   6. está   7. estar   8. somos   9. es
10. es   11. es, es   12. soy, son

7.12   1. hijos   2. hermanos   3. esposa   4. esposo   5. nietos   6. abuela   7. tío   8. tía
9. cuñado   10. cuñada   11. suegro   12. suegra   13. abuelo   14. parientes

Chapter 8
Adjectives and Adverbs

8.1 1. mis 2. sus 3. sus 4. nuestros 5. su 6. su 7. sus 8. sus 9. nuestra 10. nuestra 11. su 12. su

8.2 1. Esta, ese 2. estas, esas 3. aquel, aquella 4. Esta, esos 5. Aquellas 6. esos 7. Este

8.3 1. francesa 2. japonesa 3. los guatemaltecos 4. canadiense 5. Los nicaragüenses 6. Los costarricenses 7. hindú, hindú 8. portugués

8.4 1. todos 2. única 3. mucha 4. bastante, ambos 5. último 6. cada 7. buen 8. mala 9. algunas, algunos 10. pocos 11. próximo 12. otro 13. varias

8.5 1. misma clase 2. ciudades antiguas 3. hombre pobre 4. pobre niña 5. gran mujer 6. viejas amigas

8.6 1. la mejor 2. tan caro 3. el más grande 4. más interesante 5. tantos 6. más pequeña 7. más alta, más alto 8. más emocionantes 9. menor, más contenta, mayor 10. menos anchas 11. tan inteligentes 12. más vieja 13. más que 14. menos que 15. más bello 16. la mejor 17. mayor 18. la menor 19. más picante 20. más limpio 21. más cariñosos 22. el mejor, el peor 23. más importante, más importante 24. más triste 25. más cansados 26. tanta 27. tantos 28. mejor 29. menos 30. más

8.7 1. sinceramente 2. locamente 3. totalmente 4. verdaderamente 5. inocentemente 6. cariñosamente 7. completamente 8. normalmente

8.8 1. siempre, temprano 2. bien, claramente 3. lentamente 4. felizmente 5. frecuentemente 6. Todavía no 7. Ya no 8. arriba, abajo 9. rápida, alegremente 10. siempre, cariñosamente 11. mucho 12. Derecho 13. allá 14. honesta, sinceramente

8.9 1. Mi hermano menor tiene diez años. 2. Él entiende este capítulo, pero no quiere aprender todas las palabras. 3. Yo sé porque su hermana quiere ir a España. Sus parientes están allí. 4. Cada año, el día de acción de gracias, cocinamos demasiado. 5. Juan siempre pierde sus guantes. 6. Su abuela es mayor que su abuelo. 7. El último mes del año es diciembre; el primer mes es enero. 8. Tenemos una buena clase; aprendemos mucho. 9. Su libro acaba de llegar. 10. Yo sé que mi gato es más inteligente que su perro. 11. Estos árboles son más viejos que aquellos árboles. 12. Escuchamos las mismas canciones tristes todos los días. 13. Piensas que el presidente de los Estados Unidos es un gran hombre? 14. ¿Viene Ud. a nuestra fiesta el viernes? Empieza a las nueve de la noche. 15. Carolina es tan alta como Enrique; su hermana es la más alta de todos. 16. Este libro es el libro más interesante de la biblioteca. 17. ¿Cuál es el animal más peligroso del mundo? 18. Soy la única persona de la familia que sabe jugar al tenis. A veces, yo gano; a veces, pierdo.

8.10 1. Mr. Gomez does his work with difficulty. 2. She speaks sincerely and her friend answers humbly (with humility). 3. This woman always explains everything clearly. 4. Frankly, I don't want to go out tonight. I prefer to read and to write calmly. 5. Bernard always goes to the same restaurant. He thinks that it is the best restaurant in the city.

Chapter 9

Negatives and Prepositions

9.1 1. no aprendemos nada.   2. Nadie va a la fiesta. / Ninguna persona va a la fiesta.
3. no escucho nunca (jamás).   4. no tienen ningún enemigo.   5. no hay ningún
hospital por aquí.   6. nunca viajo.   7. no es nada cómica.   8. no bailo nunca.

9.2 1. No tengo más que treinta dólares en mi cartera.   2. Nunca estamos contentos.
3. No hago nada hoy.   4. No quiero ir tampoco.   5. Este programa no es nada
interesante.   6. ¿No quieres tomar nada?   7. No hay ninguna farmacia por aquí.
8. Ella no tiene ninguna amiga.   9. El novio nunca limpia el apartamento.
10. Ella no estudia jamás.   11. Ninguna mujer quiere bailar con él.
12. Nadie vive en la casa blanca.

9.3 *Answers will vary.*   1. No quiero ir tampoco.   2. Nadie cocina para mí.
3. No es nada interesante.   4. Yo nunca voy de vacaciones.   5. No hablo con nadie
tan temprano a las seis de la mañana.   6. No corro nunca al tren.

9.4 1. conmigo   2. sin ti   3. en él   4. consigo   5. para ellos   6. Entre él y ella
7. Entre tú y yo   8. hacia nosotros   9. conmigo, con él   10. cerca de él
11. delante de ellos / ante ellos   12. delante de nosotros / ante nosotros
13. detrás de ella   14. lejos de él, cerca de mí

9.5 1. Antes del almuerzo   2. Después de la cena   3. Después de comer   4. Antes de ir
5. A pesar de salir   6. sin escuchar   7. para aprender   8. debajo de, encima de
9. cerca de   10. hacia   11. para   12. detrás de   13. sobre   14. por
15. delante de / ante   16. por   17. por, por   18. lejos de   19. por   20. para

9.6 1. She never speaks against her friends.   2. Sara's shoes are underneath her bed.
3. Australia is far from the United States.   4. The school is between the church and
the bank.   5. I can see the river from my window.   6. She sleeps eight hours every
night. She sleeps from 11:00 until 7:00.   7. Under the law, who has protection?
8. I put one book on top of the other.   9. Anthony never sings without us.
10. The witness has to appear before the judge.   11. The children talk a lot about the
film.   12. The author writes about history and human rights.   13. The movie theater
is far from the market.

9.7 1. Entro en la tienda por la puerta.   2. Todo el mundo quiere ir, excepto Samuel.
3. Todos los hombres bailan salvo Pablo.   4. Mi jardín está pegado al jardín de mi
vecino.   5. Caminamos hacia el parque.   6. Hay una parada de buses enfrente
de la casa de Laura.   7. Según las noticias, mucha gente no va a votar.   8. Hay sillas
cómodas alrededor de la piscina.   9. Día tras día, ellos trabajan mucho.
10. La casa de Jaime está detrás de la escuela.   11. ¿Vas a estudiar para el examen?
12. Ella no quiere viajar por miedo.

9.8 *Answers will vary.*

9.9 1. bebe, toma/bebe   2. toca, practica   3. hay   4. Van   5. sé, ser   6. quiere ir, viven
7. limpio, tengo que   8. dejar   9. es   10. sabemos, está   11. empieza, salimos
12. entendemos   13. están   14. puede   15. trata de cocinar, tiene éxito   16. hace
17. viaja   18. toca, toca, juegan   19. va a pagar   20. volver/regresar   21. tiene,
debe ir   22. comprar   23. Vienes, tomar   24. nadar   25. corren

9.10   1. Antes de cantar   2. Después de descansar   3. Para llegar   4. Después de comer   5. después de estar   6. sin escuchar   7. A pesar de trabajar   8. antes de ir   9. Antes de tomar   10. En vez de hacer   11. por   12. por   13. para, por   14. para, por

9.11   1. sexta, séptima   2. rápidamente, a la izquierda   3. octavo   4. A las once menos quince, tercer   5. treinta y cuatro, tercera   6. A veces, debajo de, Frecuentemente, en   7. mayor   8. menor   9. séptima, a la derecha, a la izquierda, recto/derecho   10. hasta las once de la mañana   11. a las ocho de la mañana   12. a las ocho menos cuarto/quince   13. la primera   14. más estrechas   15. más alta que, mayor que   16. mejor   17. más triste que   18. menores   19. más fuerte que, mejor   20. peor

9.12   1. Mi sobrina va a tener trece años la próxima semana.   2. Las muchachas tienen hambre y sed y nadie sabe cocinar.   3. Ningún niño quiere ir al dentista. No sé porque todo el mundo tiene miedo de ir.   4. La película empieza a las ocho. Tenemos que llegar a las siete y media.   5. Ella piensa que él debe tratar de correr todos los días para ser más fuerte.   6. Ella va siempre a Las Vegas en el invierno. Pierde frecuentemente. Pero hoy tiene suerte y gana cien dólares.   7. Esa iglesia es vieja. Es mucho más vieja que este templo.   8. Trato de hablar con mis amigos en español. Tengo mucho que aprender. Debo estudiar cada mañana.   9. Carla pasa mucho tiempo en la tienda. Mira la ropa, pero sale sin comprar nada.   10. ¿Cuántos terremotos hay en California cada año?   11. ¿Quién está aquí? Soy yo.   12. Jorge es un buen hombre.   13. Elena y sus amigos son inteligentes.   14. Su abuela y su abuelo están contentos porque sus nietos están bien.

9.13   1. to open   2. to have just   3. to accept   4. to save (money)   5. to have lunch   6. to turn off   7. to appear   8. to learn   9. to arrange, to fix   10. to dance   11. to go down, to descend   12. to drink   13. to change   14. to walk   15. to sing   16. to celebrate   17. to close   18. to cook   19. to eat   20. to share   21. to buy   22. to understand   23. to answer   24. to run   25. to cross   26. to owe, should, must, ought to   27. to decide   28. to stop (doing something)   29. to rest   30. to describe   31. to return (an object)   32. to draw   33. to enjoy   34. to turn, to fold   35. to sleep   36. to begin   37. to find   38. to understand   39. to enter   40. to write   41. to listen to   42. to be   43. to study   44. to explain   45. to sign   46. to smoke   47. to win   48. to enjoy   49. to speak   50. to do, to make   51. to go   52. to play   53. to read   54. to clean   55. to arrive   56. to fill   57. to wear, to carry   58. to cry   59. to drive   60. to dial, to mark   61. to lie   62. to put in   63. to look at, to watch   64. to swim   65. to need   66. to hear   67. to stop   68. to pass, to spend (time)   69. to think   70. to lose   71. to paint   72. to be able   73. to put   74. to practice   75. to prefer   76. to turn on   77. to prepare   78. to want   79. to receive   80. to remember   81. to return   82. to review   83. to repeat   84. to break   85. to know, to know how   86. to leave, to exit   87. to follow, to continue   88. to be   89. to serve   90. to smile   91. to go up, to ascend   92. to have   93. to have to (do something)   94. to finish   95. to throw   96. to touch, to play (an instrument)   97. to take   98. to work   99. to try to (do something)   100. to use   101. to sell   102. to come   103. to see   104. to travel   105. to live   106. to return   107. to vote

Chapter 10
The Indirect Object

10.1   *Pronunciation exercise only.*

10.2   1. me gusta   2. le gusta   3. le gusta   4. me gusta   5. les gusta   6. les gusta
7. les gusta   8. me gusta   9. te gusta   10. nos gusta   11. le gustan   12. le gustan
13. les gustan   14. me gustan   15. te gustan   16. le gusta   17. le gusta
18. nos gusta   19. les gusta   20. les gusta   21. les gusta   22. les gusta

10.3   1. A ella   2. A Ud.   3. A mí   4. a ti, a ellos   5. a nadie   6. A quién

10.4   1. Les encantan esos carros rojos.   2. Te agradan los programas.   3. Me gustan las
sillas.   4. Nos importan nuestros amigos.   5. Le fascinan esas computadoras.

10.5   1. Susan's head hurts.   2. I lack a pencil with which to write.   3. Why isn't dancing
pleasing to you?   4. Exotic trips enchant us.   5. News of the day is interesting to her.
6. Does her perfume bother you?   7. Are the lessons important to you?   8. Is it
convenient for you to continue your studies this year?   9. To drive in the rain is not
pleasing to him.   10. Hot weather is not pleasing to her.

10.6   *Answers will vary.*

10.7   1. me escribe   2. nos escriben   3. me da   4. te pregunto   5. me dice   6. le presta
a él   7. les enseñamos a Ana y José   8. nos traen   9. le digo a él   10. le pregunto
al taxista, me cobra

10.8   1. me quiere dar   2. les quiere enseñar a sus estudiantes   3. me van a comprar
4. le quiero vender/te quiero vender   5. te puedo traer   6. le debe decir
7. nos puede enseñar   8. Me puede hacer   9. le quiero dar   10. me preguntan

10.9   1. quiere contarme   2. va a prestarle   3. va a escribirle   4. vamos a venderles
5. quiero prestarles

10.10   1. te doy   2. le trae   3. nos quiere enseñar/quiere enseñarnos   4. les vamos
a escribir/vamos a escribirles   5. me prestas

10.11   1. Can you tell me, why doesn't Sandra like to play the guitar?   2. Elena's friend
lends her books to you.   3. Elena gives her brother the pens that he needs.
4. The music lessons are not expensive. The teacher charges his students $15 per hour.
5. Playing tennis is fascinating to me, but it suits me more to swim.   6. The doctor is
not in his office. I don't know if he wants to speak with me.   7. Between you and me,
we have to decide who is going to tell the children a story.   8. Why does the lawyer
ask the witnesses questions, if he already knows the answers?   9. Can you sell me
two suitcases quickly? I am going to travel tomorrow.   10. She wants to call us
on Thanksgiving Day.   11. Celebrating St. Valentine's Day is pleasing to her.
12. Does it suit you to have chicken soup when you are sick?   13. I tell her that her
idea is good.   14. Coffee is not pleasing to her; her colleague always brings her tea.
15. The waiter brings a glass of water to the man. He brings a glass of milk to the
youngsters.

10.12 1. Do you want to travel with me next year? Do you have a vacation? Where do you want to go? 2. Where do you like to eat? Do you prefer to eat in a restaurant or at home? 3. Does the pollution of the big cities bother you? 4. Is dancing pleasing to you? Who likes to dance with you? 5. The restaurant on 42nd Street and Ninth Avenue is not pleasing to them. Do you know the reason? 6. It is Susan's birthday. Should I bring her flowers? 7. We tell the children that it is important to study. Why don't they pay attention to us? 8. I lend money to Mary because she is a good friend and she always returns the money to me. Do you lend money to your friends? 9. What do you answer the child if he tells you that he is afraid to swim? 10. They want to give you a car in order to celebrate the New Year, but they only have $500. What should they do? 11. We are hungry. Who is going to teach us to cook? 12. Where am I? Can you give me good directions? 13. Your best friend wants to give you a good gift. He wants to do you the favor of cleaning your apartment. How many rooms do you have? 14. The child asks you, "Why are there clouds in the sky?" Do you know the reason?

10.13 1. Cada año él le da un regalo a su novia. 2. Carla nunca me dice sus secretos. 3. Enrique no nos quiere prestar dinero. / Enrique no quiere prestarnos dinero. 4. ¿Quién les va a comprar libros a los niños? / ¿Quién va a comprarles libros a los niños? 5. Después de escribirles a sus amigos, él va al cine. 6. Ellos nos cobran demasiado. Les cobramos poco. 7. ¿Por qué no les contesta Ud. a los estudiantes? Le hacen muchas preguntas. 8. Les vamos a dar un perro a Pedro y a Rosa. / Vamos a darles un perro a Pedro y a Rosa. 9. Te traigo café si me traes té. 10. Le digo a Ud. que el tren viene. 11. ¿Por qué nos enseña Ud. el alemán si queremos aprender el francés? 12. Ella escucha todo, pero no te dice nada. 13. La tía de Susana le dice que quiere ir a México para sus vacaciones. Ella me dice a mí que quiere ir a París. 14. Después de estudiar mucho, ¿le duelen los ojos? 15. Todo el mundo quiere ir al partido de fútbol, salvo yo.

Chapter 11
The Direct Object

11.1 1. besa a su esposo 2. llamar a sus amigos 3. acompaño a mi abuela 4. hallar a mi hermano menor 5. extraña a su familia 6. miramos a la maestra 7. ayudar a los pacientes 8. conozco a Pedro 9. ven a sus estudiantes 10. cuidan a sus hijos 11. lleva a los turistas 12. escucha al maestro 13. encontrar a su hermana 14. grita a su jefe 15. invitar a Ramona 16. esperar a su amiga

11.2 1. me espera 2. te conoce 3. van a ayudarnos / nos van a ayudar 4. extrañarlas 5. lo busco, lo encuentro 6. lo ama 7. visitarla 8. Las ven 9. los saludamos 10. lo va a dejar / va a dejarlo 11. los cuida 12. Después de llamarlo 13. la conocemos 14. la escucha 15. Antes de invitarla

11.3 1. If a man accompanies a beautiful woman to the reunion, is he going to kiss her? 2. It seems to us that the boy is sick and cannot do his homework. We decide to help him. 3. Sara always arrives late and we don't want to wait for her any longer. 4. Do you miss your family who lives far away? Do you want to visit them? 5. The English people are going to arrive in the United States this afternoon. We are going to take them from the airport to a good hotel.

11.4   1. Veo a José pero no me ve.   2. No sabemos donde están los turistas que nos visitan de España.   3. Ellos van a visitar a sus amigos en el Canadá después de vender su barco.

11.5   1. lo tengo, quiero leerlo   2. la quiere limpiar / quiere limpiarla   3. los tenemos, los vemos   4. no los puede usar, los quiere vender   5. comprarlos   6. los encuentra / los halla   7. estudiarla   8. encontrarlas/hallarlas   9. los aman   10. tenerlo

11.6   1. la   2. Lo   3. la   4. le   5. me, te   6. les   7. Los   8. nos   9. Les   10. les   11. me   12. les   13. la   14. los   15. lo   16. la   17. las   18. las   19. las, las   20. Me, me

11.7   *Answers will vary.*

11.8   1. Veo a mis amigos todos los sábados. Nos gusta ir al cine.   2. Ella mira a la profesora, escucha bien, pero todavía no entiende nada.   3. Lisa espera a su hermana que siempre llega tarde.   4. Viajamos a Ecuador para estar con nuestros parientes. 5. La lección es difícil y él la quiere estudiar para el examen.   6. ¿Puede Ud. ir al correo por mí? Tengo una carta para mi amiga y la quiere mandar hoy. 7. ¿Quieres acompañarlo a la fiesta? Él es tímido y no quiere ir solo.   8. ¿De dónde la conoce Ud.? ¿La ve todo el tiempo?   9. Ella tiene zapatos nuevos pero no los lleva nunca.   10. Casi nunca te veo.

Chapter 12
Reflexive Verbs

12.1   1. despertarme   2. me levanto   3. me baño, me ducho   4. me siento   5. se llaman 6. se dedican   7. nos divertimos   8. expresarnos   9. acostarse   10. Me duermo

12.2   1. caerse   2. se afeita, se pinta   3. te enojas   4. nos quitamos   5. se ponen 6. quedarme   7. se preocupa   8. mudarme   9. tranquilizarse   10. nos alegramos 11. me cepillo   12. se peinan

12.3   1. se desayunan   2. se encuentran con   3. se ponen   4. se ríe   5. se equivoca 6. me acuerdo   7. Se aprovecha   8. se queja de   9. se fija en   10. burlarse de 11. Se parecen   12. meterme en   13. se demoran   14. se enamora   15. nos callamos 16. se atreve a   17. se portan   18. se fía en

12.4   1. se despierta   2. se ducha   3. vestirse   4. desayunarse   5. se encuentra con / se reúne con   6. se dedican   7. Se ayudan   8. Se dice   9. se atreven 10. preocuparse   11. tranquilizarse/calmarse   12. sentirse   13. se demoran 14. se quema   15. se queda   16. se baña   17. se acuesta   18. se duerme

Chapter 13

The Present Subjunctive

13.1   1. diga   2. haga   3. conozcan   4. durmamos   5. sepa   6. tomemos   7. se levanten   8. llegue   9. me quede   10. esté   11. dé   12. vayas   13. sean   14. lean   15. tenga   16. traigamos   17. se sientan

13.2   1. diga   2. pague   3. se sientan   4. deje de llorar   5. expliquemos   6. tenga   7. dé   8. sepa   9. haya   10. vayan   11. sea   12. hagamos   13. esté   14. vean

13.3   *Answers will vary.*   1. Lo siento que mi amigo tenga malos sueños.   2. Es posible que ella no se divierta mucho.   3. Él duda que seamos buenos estudiantes.   4. Ella teme que no volvamos a los Estados Unidos.   5. Yo le pido que Sara me traiga flores a mi casa.   6. Dudo que Ud. conozca a mi tío.   7. Es una lástima que no nos veamos mucho.   8. ¿Es posible que no haya clase los lunes?   9. No creo que Carla sea de Polonia.

13.4   1. visite   2. traigamos   3. ame   4. vea/veamos   5. están   6. se queja   7. entienda   8. puedas   9. se acuerde   10. estén

13.5   1. se levanta   2. ir   3. se desayunen   4. salir   5. se diviertan   6. viene   7. se pongan   8. sea

13.6   1. Después de que, me bañe   2. a menos que, vayan   3. luego que, tenga   4. para que, sepan   5. luego que, terminen   6. Antes de que, venga   7. para que, puedas   8. hasta que, lleguen   9. En caso de que, tengan   10. para que, estén   11. A pesar de que, tengan   12. sin que, invite   13. después de que, se vayan   14. pueda   15. nos reunamos / nos encontremos   16. vuelvan/regresen   17. aprenda

13.7   1. se enfermen   2. descansemos   3. llegue   4. se quejen   5. cocine   6. duermas   7. haya   8. tenga   9. esté   10. quiera   11. acompañe   12. sea   13. venga   14. hable

13.8   1. me acueste   2. se mejore   3. son   4. estudie   5. toque   6. gusta   7. vayan   8. haya   9. estén, llegue   10. va   11. conozca   12. nade   13. vuelvan   14. visites   15. pueda   16. pongan   17. hagan   18. se sientan, estén   19. se casen   20. vayas   21. debes   22. necesita

13.9   1. quieren   2. dé   3. ser   4. dormir   5. entiendan   6. leer   7. se ríe   8. hagas   9. está, escoja   10. podamos   11. salgan   12. comer, vivir   13. gusta   14. son   15. busquemos   16. se pone, hace   17. estar, estén   18. viajar, aprender   19. lleguen   20. sea   21. dormir, se despierte   22. digan, llegar, sepa   23. compartir   24. coma   25. tengan   26. te quedes   27. regreses

13.10   1. No me gusta que se vaya.   2. Él se alegra de que ella le dé flores a su esposo.   3. Es importante que ella sepa la fecha.   4. Me alegro de que mis amigos estén bien.   5. Es dudoso que Paula conozca a Raúl.   6. Es posible que yo sea una buena estudiante.   7. Esperamos que la película empiece a las dos.   8. Ojalá que haga buen tiempo hoy.   9. Tal vez el tren llegue a tiempo.   10. Quiero que Rosa tenga mucha suerte.   11. Me alegro de que nos veamos mucho.

13.11   1. Pedro no piensa que el viaje sea bueno.   2. Me alegro de conocerle.
3. Esperamos que te sientas mejor.   4. ¿Me puede llamar cuando llegue a casa?
5. Laura insiste en que los niños se pongan la chaqueta.   6. Roberto espera que Julia
baile con él esta noche.

13.12   1. to embrace   2. to accompany   3. to advise   4. to remember   5. to go to bed
6. to shave   7. to be agreeable   8. to thank   9. to become happy   10. to love
11. to walk   12. to cheer up   13. to rush   14. to take advantage of
15. to fix oneself up   16. to attend (an event)   17. to get frightened   18. to dare
19. to help   20. to get off   21. to bathe oneself   22. to kiss   23. to make fun of
24. to look for   25. to fall down   26. to become quiet   27. to calm down
28. to carry   29. to brush (one's hair/teeth)   30. to chat   31. to charge   32. to begin
33. to be acquainted with, to know   34. to tell a story   35. to be convenient to
36. to converse   37. to take care of   38. to give   39. to realize   40. to say, to tell
41. to dedicate oneself   42. to defend oneself   43. to leave (something or someone)
44. to delay   45. to have breakfast   46. to desire, to want   47. to take one's leave
48. to wake up   49. to have a good time   50. to be painful, to hurt   51. to fall asleep
52. to take a shower   53. to doubt   54. to fall in love   55. to be enchanting
56. to meet   57. to get angry   58. to get sick   59. to get angry   60. to teach
61. to send   62. to make a mistake   63. to choose   64. to wait for
65. to express oneself   66. to miss (a person or place)   67. to lack
68. to be fascinating   69. to trust   70. to notice   71. to yell at   72. to have (helping
verb)   73. to become (a profession)   74. to find   75. to be important   76. to insist
77. to interest   78. to invite   79. to go away, to leave quickly   80. to hurt oneself
81. to wash oneself   82. to get up   83. to call   84. to call oneself   85. to send
86. to put makeup on   87. to kill   88. to get better   89. to meddle, to get involved in
90. to be annoying, to bother   91. to die   92. to move   93. to move (from one place
to another)   94. to stand up   95. to seem   96. to resemble   97. to ask for, to request
98. to comb (one's hair)   99. to permit   100. to put makeup on, to put nail polish on
101. to put on (clothing), to become (an emotion)   102. to behave oneself
103. to ask, to question   104. to wonder   105. to worry   106. to lend
107. to prohibit   108. to remain   109. to complain   110. to burn oneself
111. to take off (clothing)   112. to pick up   113. to laugh   114. to meet
115. to jump   116. to greet   117. to sit down   118. to feel (health or emotion)
119. to suggest   120. to delay   121. to bring   122. to calm down   123. to see
124. to get dressed   125. to visit   126. to become (an emotion)

Chapter 14

The Preterit Tense

14.1   1. abrió   2. cerré   3. viajamos   4. miró   5. visité, invité   6. empezó, llovió
7. regresaron, escucharon   8. gustó   9. se acostó   10. sonó   11. soñó
12. vi   13. nos divertimos   14. ofreció   15. ayudaron

14.2   1. Me gustó viajar.   2. leí un periódico.   3. cerraron la puerta.   4. Les ofrecí ayuda.
5. volviste tarde?   6. no se callaron.   7. se acordó de la idea.   8. empezó a las ocho.

14.3   1. dijo, dije 2. hicimos, hicieron 3. diste, darte 4. Hubo 5. traje, trajeron
6. pusieron, puso 7. estuve, estuvieron 8. tuvo, tuve 9. fueron, fuimos
10. fue, fui 11. vinieron, vino 12. anduvimos, anduvieron 13. produje
14. cupieron

14.4   1. cupieron 2. trajo/dio 3. fue 4. pudieron 5. quiso 6. fuimos 7. anduvimos
8. estuvo 9. puse 10. dijo, tuve 11. hiciste 12. supimos 13. dio/trajo
14. produjo 15. vinieron 16. hubo

14.5   1. fue 2. fui 3. estuvimos 4. te fuiste 5. fueron 6. estuvo 7. estuvieron
8. Fue 9. estuvo 10. fue

14.6   *Answers will vary.*

14.7   1. durmió 2. siguieron 3. preferí, prefirió, prefirió 4. se despidió
5. nos divertimos, se divirtieron 6. se sintió, se vistió 7. se murió 8. sirvieron
9. mentí, mintieron 10. sonrió 11. se rió 12. repitió 13. corrigieron
14. me sentí, se sintieron

14.8   1. me tropecé 2. pagué 3. entregó 4. vagamos 5. colgué 6. castigó

14.9   1. contribuyó 2. se cayó 3. influyó 4. huyeron 5. construyeron 6. destruiste

14.10   1. Trabajé mucho ayer. Anoche, descansé. 2. Anoche, miramos televisión en vez de estudiar. 3. Yo le di a él mi perro; él no me dio nada. 4. Ella leyó la carta de su amigo hace un mes. 5. Recibimos el paquete hace una semana. 6. ¿Qué le dijiste a ella? Te dije que él se murió el año pasado. / ¿Qué le dijo Ud. a ella? Le dije que él se murió. 7. Los niños se acostaron a las nueve anoche. 8. Vi a su hermana ayer.

14.11   1. entré 2. tomamos 3. se durmieron, me dormí 4. vieron, vi 5. Empezó
6. Hizo 7. cobró, cobró 8. escribimos, recibieron 9. se despertó 10. Encontraste
11. quise 12. fue, fue 13. dijo 14. pudieron

Chapter 15
The Imperfect Tense

15.1   1. comía (repeated action) 2. era (description) 3. iban (repeated action)
4. eran (point of origin) 5. nos veíamos (repeated action) 6. eran (point of origin)
7. llegaba (repeated action) 8. volvíamos (repeated action) 9. Había (situation)
10. practicaba (continuous action) 11. ibas (continuous action) 12. iba (continuous action) 13. tenía (age) 14. comían, comían (continuous action, continuous action)
15. visitaban (repeated action) 16. bebían (repeated action) 17. era (description)
18. tenía, tenía (description, description) 19. Eran, brillaba (time, situation)
20. leía (continuous action) 21. hacía (continuous action) 22. estábamos (condition)
23. era, se reía (description, continuous action) 24. decía/decías/decían (continuous action) 25. hacían (continuous action) 26. venía (continuous action)
27. Hacía, Hacía, estaban, estaba (narration, narration, narration, narration)
28. cocinaba (repeated action)

15.2 1. Ellos eran de España. 2. ¿Qué hora era? 3. Nosotros estábamos bien.
4. Mi jardín era el más hermoso de la ciudad. 5. Los tres amigos estaban aquí.
6. No estaba cansada. 7. Éramos cantantes. 8. ¿Dónde estabas?
9. Yo estaba en la casa con mi perro.

15.3 1. Era la una y llovía. 2. Yo lo sabía. 3. Él lo podía hacer bien. 4. Los niños
querían comer hamburguesas. 5. Estudiábamos cuando el maestro entró.
6. El hombre huía cuando el policía lo cogió. 7. Todas las noches por muchos años,
ella tenía el mismo sueño. 8. ¿Qué me decía/decías? 9. ¿Qué te iba a decir?/
¿Qué le iba a decir? 10. ¿Por qué la llamó él? 11. ¿Qué hora era cuando te
dormiste (se durmió) anoche? 12. ¿Quién se enfermó ayer? 13. Íbamos a viajar a
Cuba, pero no teníamos dinero. 14. Conocí a tu/su amigo en México. 15. Se fue sin
decirnos nada. 16. ¿Quién le dio las buenas noticias hoy? 17. El hombre estaba en
el banco cuando el ladrón entró. Todo el mundo tenía miedo. 18. El año pasado,
fuimos a España. Nos divertimos.

15.4 1. fue 2. fue 3. iba 4. íbamos 5. fuimos 6. iban 7. iba, iba 8. Ibas 9. fue
10. fueron

15.5 1. The child's mother told him that everything was going to be fine. 2. Did your
feet hurt you during your trip? 3. There was a time when I visited museums.
4. I came, I saw, I conquered. 5. Between the second and third floor, I realized
that I was going to fall down. 6. A long time ago, we used to have a very good time.
7. I didn't know what to do. 8. They had a good relationship. He always cooked
and she always washed the dishes.

15.6 1. compraste 2. traje 3. Era, tenía 4. Empezó, cerré 5. cruzaba, llamó
6. estuvieron 7. andábamos, vimos 8. cobró, cobró 9. escribimos, recibieron
10. caminaba, me di cuenta de, sabía, estaba 11. conoció 12. se divertían
13. iba 14. llegaron, se quedaron

15.7 1. I wanted to have coffee this morning. My colleague brought it to me.
2. The children have a lot of gifts. Their grandparents want them to give them to me.
3. She bought me a jacket. After buying it for me, she became happy.
4. My father refused to give me his car. Instead of giving it to me, he sold it to me.
5. I learned the directions well because my relatives gave them to me carefully.
6. She wants to give me three suitcases for my trip. I prefer that she lend them to me.
7. Each morning, the vendors used to sell me vegetables. Today they didn't sell me
anything. 8. I need two good books. I have to buy them because my friend doesn't
want to lend them to me.

15.8 1. She doesn't give you water; she sells it to you. 2. We ought to give you the ring that
you want this year. We ought to give it to you. 3. Last night my older brother brought
me an apple. He brought it to me because I was hungry. 4. You still have my compact
discs. I want you to return them to me. 5. I like the lobster in this restaurant. I hope
that the waiter serves it to me quickly. 6. I gave you the money because you are a
good friend. I gave it to you because I have confidence in you. 7. I don't know why
she didn't want (refused) to show you her lamps. She showed them to me yesterday.
8. At the beginning, we didn't want to give you a bicycle, but finally we gave it to you.

15.9 1. te lo 2. se lo 3. Me lo 4. se la 5. se los 6. se la 7. hacérselas 8. Me los
9. Te la 10. Se lo 11. Se la 12. Se la 13. contárselo 14. se los

15.10 1. Yo le dije todo. Ud. no me dijo nada./Yo te dije todo. Tú no me dijiste nada.
2. Íbamos a darles dos cuadernos a los estudiantes.   3. Lisa no tiene nada con que
escribir. Tengo dos bolígrafos y decido dárselos.   4. Le di a mi sobrino un violín.
Se lo di.   5. Él le iba a dar la guitarra a Héctor. Decidió dármela.   6. ¿Quién nos
puede mostrar los abrigos nuevos? ¿Quién nos los quiere mostrar?   7. Los pájaros
cantaban y los niños jugaban.   8. Carmen leyó un buen libro hace dos semanas.
Ella me lo dio ayer.   9. Le devolví el libro hoy. Se lo devolví a las diez de la mañana.
10. Elena tuvo malos sueños anoche. Me los contó esta mañana.   11. Nos gusta
compartir todo.   12. Su abuela quiere que Ud. le lea el artículo./Tu abuela quiere
que le leas el artículo.   13. Esperamos que él sepa nadar para que nos pueda enseñar.
14. José le prestó a Miguel el dinero. Se lo prestó ayer.   15. Tu primo te hizo un favor.
Él te lo hizo porque es un buen amigo./Su primo le hizo un favor. Él se lo hizo porque
es un buen amigo.   16. Después de traerle café, fui a mi oficina. Ella me llamó más
tarde.   17. Ella compraba una guitarra cuando su amigo le ofreció un piano.
18. Vimos el sofá que ella tenía en su casa. Nos lo dio.

15.11 1. te lo secas   2. quitárnoslo   3. se los cepillaron   4. se las puso   5. me lo corté
6. se las van a lavar   7. se lo peina

15.12 1. He liked the chicken and ate it up.   2. Michael couldn't enter his house because
he lost his keys.   3. The spoon fell (I dropped the spoon) on the table and I
became furious.   4. They realized that their friends were not coming to see them.
5. How did it occur to you to write a book together?   6. I forgot to do my homework.
My patience ran out.   7. Watch out! You are going to drop the glasses. We broke
two already.   8. After putting on their socks, they put on their shoes and left.

15.13 1. to approach   2. to drown   3. to reach, to overtake   4. to threaten   5. to pull out,
to root out   6. to attract   7. to fit   8. to punish   9. to hang   10. to put in place,
to place   11. to compose   12. to conclude   13. to drive   14. to build, to construct
15. to contain   16. to contradict   17. to contribute   18. to correct   19. to believe
20. to undo   21. to stick out   22. to destroy   23. to detain   24. to distract
25. to distribute   26. to hand in, to deliver   27. to flow   28. to flee   29. to include
30. to influence   31. to justify   32. to throw, to shoot   33. to get up early
34. to maintain   35. to chew   36. to hit, to glue   37. to fish   38. to possess
39. to prevent   40. to produce   41. to propose   42. to publish   43. to fulfill
44. to pray   45. to take out   46. to beg   47. to translate   48. to swallow
49. to bump into   50. to wander

Index